# THE WORLD'S
# MOST DIFFICULT QUIZ
## 2

# THE WORLD'S MOST DIFFICULT QUIZ
## 2

More King William's College
General Knowledge Papers

Edited by Pat Cullen

LIVERPOOL UNIVERSITY PRESS

First published 2012 by
Liverpool University Press
4 Cambridge Street
Liverpool
L69 7ZU

British Library Cataloguing-in-Publication data
A British Library CIP record is available

ISBN 978-1-84631-837-5 limp

Typeset by Carnegie Book Production, Lancaster
Printed in the UK by Bell and Bain Ltd, Glasgow

# Contents

# Introduction

As *The World's Most Difficult Quiz* was well received, I have now been asked to put together this second compilation of King William's College General Knowledge Papers, which of necessity is a prequel. This collection again contains thirty sets of 180 questions, but whereas the first volume contained all the papers from 1981 to 2010 in their entirety, this time, in order to justify the rather large claim of the title, I have had to be more selective.

Many of the early papers (the first was produced in 1905) contained relatively simple questions, asked in a very direct and obvious manner. After 1920 the questions became more demanding, but little attempt was made to conceal the theme of each set of ten. Perusing papers from the 1920s, I found that only two or three sets in each of the early years might merit inclusion, whereas this proportion increased notably after 1927 and more especially from the mid-thirties. Denis Thompson, whose idiosyncrasies are described in the first volume, was the sole author from 1932 and developed the style which has continued to this day. He wrote of his own efforts: '[The GKP] has tried to be topical, it has tried to be interesting, it has tried to avoid ponderousness'. As a result, the papers have justified reproduction, initially in *The Times* and, since 1951, publication just before Christmas in the *Guardian*. One of the more deceitful, and dare one say appealing, features of the GKP is the concealment of the theme of many of the sets of questions, so that 'cracking the code' can be quite a challenge. Denis Thompson did not indulge in such subterfuge, and it was during the reign of Dick Boyns, long-serving history master and champion of Lady Margaret Beaufort, that this mischievous behaviour started to appear.

In assessing every one of almost 11,000 questions and answers, many of which I had never seen before, I found that a number of subjects recur with remarkable frequency, especially in the earlier papers. Leading the way are, not surprisingly, Dickens and Shakespeare. *The Pickwick Papers* accounted for more than a quarter of all the Dickensian questions, with *Martin Chuzzlewit* a comfortable second, and good contributions from *Nicholas Nickleby* and *Barnaby Rudge*. *Macbeth* easily leads the way for Shakespeare, after which there is a fairly even spread over many of his plays. Of the poets, Tennyson is very much the favourite, with nearly twice as many questions as the next most popular – Longfellow and Lewis Carroll. Gilbert and Sullivan have become increasingly popular, roughly equalling the latter two poets.

I have attempted to check all the answers for accuracy – not entirely straightforward when dealing with questions set as long as ninety years ago. Tony Glover, my predecessor as quizmaster, would never include two questions from the same source within the same section, but this discipline was not observed by earlier quizmasters. I felt that to exclude questions of this nature, or to create substitutes, would disrupt the style of those earlier sages. Nowadays the answers are often justified by giving names of authors, titles or other explanations in brackets, and where possible I have added such details in this collection.

It should be remembered that the entire contents of this compilation preceded the internet search engines, so that the majority of answers will be fairly easily accessed electronically, should the reader stoop to such perfidy. Nevertheless, a significant number of the early sets of questions were either far too easy or too directly related to then current events, and so in some cases I have had to make up a set of eighteen from several years, while in others the paper is reproduced in its entirety. I have been particularly intrigued by the topics chosen during the war years and in years of significant royal events, and have been less critical in my choices there because of the historical relevance of the questions. All the questions (with the exception of a few sections from the 1960s) have previously been published, either in *General Knowledge Papers. 1905–1953. Prepared for King William's College, Isle of Man* (Cresset Press, 1954) or *The King William's College Tests* (Hutchinson/Guardian, 1982).

The worldwide appeal of the quiz has been mentioned previously, but I was recently intrigued to find a cutting from *The Rangoon Gazette*, written in 1934, which runs as follows:

The General Knowledge Paper of a certain Public School reached me by last mail. This paper is set on the last day of the Christmas term in order that the boys shall have something to do other than breaking the house room windows or driving sheep into rival dormitories. [Neither was the school St Custards, nor the writer Geoffrey Willans!] At the end of the examination each boy takes a copy of the paper away with him and upon being received into the bosom of his family produces same, and hands it to his father with the words – 'Look here, old man, you might see what you can do with this, I've got to mug it up for next term.' The father, much pleased to be noticed, surrounds himself with dictionaries and sets to work, the while his offspring goes out on the beat-up in the family motor car. It is an excellent system, as the father is so busy during the vac, trying to remember what he learnt since he left school, that he quite forgets to make awkward enquiries as to what his son has *failed* to learn during the previous term. There are in all eighteen sections in the paper, each section having ten questions, and most of them are very puzzling.

He goes on to give some examples of the questions, and then writes, 'Having the answers before me of course gives me a nice feeling of superiority and erudition, although I feel that some of them are rather arbitrary.' My own view is that this is an unfair criticism. The problem is one that also concerned Boyns in his introduction to the 1982 book: 'The particular hazard in editing lies in avoiding questions which have more than one valid answer. Nothing can be more infuriating for the reader than to see the official answer and to find that his own undoubtedly correct one is not given.' Like Boyns, I have endeavoured to exclude ambiguous questions, which can, unfortunately, like a contagious disease, necessitate the exclusion of an entire section. If appropriate, I have occasionally added a second answer to the original. Very occasionally I have created an alternative, when for example a 1935 question had no fewer than 14 correct answers!

When I was a pupil at King William's, it was usual for the quizmaster to include one give-away question in most of the sets, and this generous approach is, I hope, apparent in this book.

# Questions

# 1920–1928

**• 1 •** (1920, 12) *What poets perpetrated the following:*

1   A Mr Wilkinson, a clergyman.
2   The dead of night? How, Henry, how?
3   There is not such a treat among them all.
4   His prominent feature like an eagle's beak.
5   Where is my wife? Where is my Wogg?
    I am alone and life's a bog.
6   Across the wires, the electric message came:
    He is no better, he is much the same.
7   Stand off, or else my skipping rope
    Will hit you in the eye.
8   So to amend it, I was told to go
    And seek the firm of Clutterbuck & Co.
9   Arms ...
    Seem most at variance with all moral good
    And incompatible with serious thought.
10  At duty's call, I left my legs
    In Badajos's breaches.

**• 2 •**   (1920, 17) *What:*

1   is 'the beginning of wisdom'?
2   are 'an abomination to the Lord'?
3   is 'mightiest in the mighty'?
4   is 'the homage that vice pays to virtue'?
5   is 'the last refuge of a scoundrel'?
6   'oft loses both itself and friend'?
7   'mixed with something else makes something worse'?
8   is 'a lively sense of benefits to come'?
9   are 'the counters of wise men and the money of fools'?
10   is 'the last thing that will be civilised by man'?

**• 3 •**   (1922, 12) *Distinguish between the following:*

1   Gresham's Law.
2   Lydford Law.
3   Mitre Law.
4   Common Law.
5   Volstead Law.
6   Lynch Law.
7   Grimm's Law.
8   Salic Law.
9   Levirate Law.
10   Berwick Law.

**• 4 •**   (1923, 8) *With whom do you associate the following:*

1   'Wait and see.'
2   'Searching their pockets.'
3   'Tranquility.'
4   'Digging rats out of holes.'
5   'Spiritual home.'
6   'Baby's bun.'
7   'I am not a clever man.'
8   'A moral gesture.'
9   'The Dartmoor Shepherd.'
10   'Halving the income tax by doubling it.'

**• 5 •** (1924, 7) *In what famous dramas do we find:*

1    a king entangled in a carpet?

2    a hero in a clothes-basket?

3    a sewing machine aboard a ship?

4    a king and a monk at chess?

5    a fountain running blood?

6    a picture that came to life?

7    a heroine married blindfolded?

8    a screen scene?

9    a sleep-walking scene?

10    a hero in galoshes?

**• 6 •** (1924, 9)

1    who lost an orchard by tasting an apple?

2    who lost a race and won a husband through an apple?

3    who made an enemy of two ladies through an apple?

4    who wondered how the apple got inside the dumpling?

5    who told a story about an apple?

6    what apple do you owe to curiosity?

7    who was poisoned by an apple?

8    what scientific law do we owe to an apple?

9    what apple had a monument to its memory?

10    what Duke appears to live on apples?

**• 7 •**  (1925, 16) *Fill in the appropriate creature or creatures in the following:*

1   As I was walking all alane I heard twa – – – – making a mane.
2   Instead of the Cross the – – – –
    About my neck was hung.
3   The friendly – – – – all red and white
    I love with all my heart.
4   There is eloquent outpouring
    When the – – – – is a-roaring
    And the – – – – is a-lashing of his tail.
5   Hush! The Naked – – – – will hear thee.
6   His spots are the joy of the – – – –: his horns are the – – – –'s pride.
7   I run before my – – – – to market.
8   Against the Capitol I met a – – – –
    Who glar'd upon me and went surly by.
9   But Solomon talked to a – – – –
    As you would talk to a man.
10  The – – – –'s on the wing
    The – – – –'s on the thorn.

**• 8 •**  (1926, 8)

1   who laughs on canvas?
2   when is the price of a laugh too great?
3   where was laughter threatened with excommunication?
4   what did the loud laugh speak?
5   who laugh like parrots at a bagpiper?
6   who was the laughing philosopher?
7   who was the laughing executioner?
8   who laughs longest?
9   who went behind the pantry door to hide her joy?
10  what contortion are you invited to practise when you laugh at unseemly times?

**· 9 ·** (1927, 6) *Answer, naming the books in which the incidents occur:*

1 how did William get his silk handkerchief for the party?
2 what was the advice given by his father to Sam Weller?
3 why did not Lady Derby obey the orders of Charles II's Government?
4 why did Tar Baby keep on sayin' nothin'?
5 why did the White Queen scream before she pricked her finger?
6 why was Gruffamuff made into a door-knocker?
7 what embarrassment would occur when Soames, Fleur and Michael reached America?
8 how did Moses become the possessor of a gross of green spectacles, with silver rims and shagreen cases?
9 how did Mrs Forrester recover the lace?
10 what was the defence of 'Tulkissimus' when accused of kissing Mary Yeo?

**· 10 ·** (1927, 8)

1 who refused to go either to Rome or Tennessee?
2 whose spiritual home was Germany?
3 who 'came to the Beauteous Isle, where the heavens lean low on the land'?
4 who came to the Dark Tower?
5 who when they came, answered sadly, 'we bring only ourselves'?
6 who came with dyed garments from Bozrah?
7 who 'came last and last did go'?
8 who came with 'all her silken flanks with garlands drest'?
9 who would not have been great, if he had come from Seriphos?
10 who 'came from Knebworth in a chaise
and uttered anything but praise
about the author of my days'?

• 11 • (1927, 9) *Who said he preferred:*

1    honour to his mistress?

2    his wife's ring to a wilderness of monkeys?

3    to reign in hell than to serve in heaven?

4    one crowded hour of glorious life to an age without a name?

5    to have written a certain poem than to take a certain city?

6    to be damned with Plato and Lord Bacon than to go to heaven with Paley and Malthus?

7    to live above ground as another's hireling than lord it over all the dead that ever died?

8    a dinner of herbs where love is to a stalled ox and hatred therewith?

9    fifty years of Europe to a cycle with Cathay?

10    to 'dwell in the midst of alarms

than reign in this horrible place'?


• 12 • (1928, 1) *Who lived:*

1    on a pillar?

2    under a gourd?

3    under the blossom?

4    in a bee-loud glade?

5    in a tub?

6    in a shoe?

7    in a kennel?

8    in a cromlech?

9    in a treacle-well?

10    in his breaches?

• 13 • (1928, 3) *What ship:*

1   found herself?

2   stopped a smile?

3   solved a riddle?

4   sailed to Lily Lock?

5   had cylindrical sails?

6   was a pack o' rotten plates puttied up wi' tar?

7   was a victim of the first recorded shipwreck?

8   should have avoided railway shares?

9   disguised herself as a tropical forest?

10  after ship wreck was tight and yare and bravely rigged?

• 14 • (1928, 4) *Give the occasion of the following excuses:*

1   'I thought it was spinach.'

2   'Am I my brother's keeper?'

3   'I have a subsequent engagement.'

4   'Ah! But remember how early I go.'

5   'My heart told me that in killing you I should do great service to Germany and to Europe.'

6   'If I throw this rich sword into the water, thereof shall never come good but harm and loss.'

7   'My words are my own, and my acts are my ministers'.'

8   'I have only one eye – I have a right to be blind sometimes.'

9   'I thought the Archbishop was inside.'

10  'I must have shaved the wrong face, sir.'

• 15 • (1928, 5) *To whom or what are the following epithets applied:*

1    False, fleeting, perjured?
2    Unhousel'd, disappointed, unanel'd?
3    Poor, reckless, rude, lowborn, untaught?
4    The fair, the chaste, the unexpressive?
5    Cabin'd, cribbed, confined?
6    Unwept, unhonour'd, and unsung?
7    Remote, unfriended, melancholy, slow?
8    Wee, sleekit, cow'rin, tim'rous?
9    Greenery-yallery, Grosvenor Gallery?
10   Rat-riddled, bilge bestank,
     Slime-slobbered, horrible?

• 16 • (1928, 6) *Who gave the following advice:*

1    'First think out a really good beginning, then think out a really good ending
     and bring the two as closely together as you can.'?
2    'I charge thee … throw away ambition,
     By that sin fell the angels.'?
3    'Be thou familiar, but by no means vulgar.'?
4    'Take a little wine for thy stomach's sake.'?
5    'Love as brethren, be pitiful be courteous.'?
6    'Fear God, honour the King.'?
7    'Keep your rifle and yourself, jus' so.'?
8    'Doänt thou marry for munny but goä whee-r munny is!'?
9    'Be werry careful o' widders.'?
10   'Don't.'?

• 17 • (1928, 9) *Who wished to rest:*

1   in 'Little Melstock.'?

2   'at Jedburgh.'?

3   on the top of the Matoppo Hills?

4   'under the wide and starry sky.'?

5   'not in the senseless earth
but in the living sea.'?

6   under 'a ninth great peaceful wave.'?

7   'where the sun might shine and the rain might fall and the feet of men trample.'?

8   'in a winding sheet of vineleaf wrapped
… by some sweet garden side.'?

9   'the green grass above me
With showers and dewdrops wet.'?

10            'Oh! Where,
Sad true lover never find my grave,
To weep there.'?


• 18 • (1928, 12)

1   who shall dream dreams?

2   what poem was composed in a dream?

3   who 'in the troubled dreams a slave has … could see her city shining as of old.'?

4   who thought it 'sweet to dream of fatherland, of child and wife and slave.'?

5   who saw Hector in a dream mangled by a chariot?

6   who dreamed that the sheep held a parliament?

7   who dreamed of his parents as heavenly bodies?

8   who in dreams saw 'their wives go in with viscounts and their daughters dance with lords.'?

9   who dreamed that the Prince Consort kissed him?

10   who dreamed that he looked in a Bible to find a text and there were no texts in it?

# 1930–1933

• 1 • (1930, 11) *Indicate briefly the episodes or stories finished or characterised by the following words:*

1  Peccavi!
2  We are not amused.
3  I'm killed, Sir.
4  The half has not been told.
5  I will die in the last ditch.
6  By God, Mr Chairman, at this moment I stand astonished at my own moderation.
7  In parts, my Lord.
8  Wart and all.
9  A dumb laity, I hope.
10  Now only God knows.

• 2 • (1930, 13) *From whose funeral dirges do the following lines come:*
1  Leave now for dogs and apes! Man has forever.
2  Who never spoke against a foe.
3  A favourite has no friend.
4  Lightly they'll talk of the spirit that's gone.
5  How often you and I have tired the sun with talking.
6  He is a portion of the loveliness which once he made more lovely.
7  His virtues walked their narrow road.
8  Still with his soul severe account he kept.
9  There thou, sweet Saint, before the quire shalt go.
10  And oh, the difference to me!

• 3 • (1930, 14) *What prophet or prophetess:*

1   came to curse and stayed to bless?
2   sank in the mire?
3   made horns of iron?
4   was a herdsman?
5   described wizards as men 'who peep and mutter'?
6   was notoriously bald-headed?
7   preferred pulse and water to meat and wine?
8   raced a royal chariot?
9   sang a duet with a victorious general?
10   called his eldest daughter 'Jemima'?

• 4 • (1930, 18) *What places are conjured up by the following lines:*

1   Earth has not anything to show more fair?
2   Sunset ran one glorious blood-red?
3   The lights begin to twinkle from the rocks?
4   Sparkling bright in nature's glee?
5   There midnight's all aglimmer and noon a purple glow?
6   Go visit it in the pale moonlight?
7   What are those blue remembered hills?
8   Land of brown heath and shaggy wood
    Land of the mountain and the flood?
9          … an emerging prow
    Lifting the cool-hair'd creepers stealthily?
10   The gate of the star, a white speck glittering in the sun, and the city a mere mound in a plain – two dark square towers rising out of it, and light and shadow descending on it aslant, like the angels in Jacob's dream?

**• 5 •** (1931, 7) *Who greeted or introduced whom in the following words:*

1  Doctor – – – – I presume?
2  Here is a Prince that hath no English?
3  My Lord of Canterbury, we greet you well?
4  Pudding, – – – –; – – – –, Pudding; Remove the Pudding?
5  Be acquainted with this stranger – 'tis as like you as cherry is to cherry?
6  Morituri te salutamus?
7  Shake, King?
8  – – – – my name and – – – – my nature?
9  Be kind and courteous to this gentleman?
10  No names at all – incog. the thing – Gentlemen from London – distinguished strangers – anything?


**• 6 •** (1931, 8) *Who was:*

1  The Admirable Doctor?
2  The Angelic Doctor?
3  The Dulcifluous Doctor?
4  The Mellifluous Doctor?
5  The Most Enlightened Doctor?
6  The Evangelical Doctor?
7  The Irrefragable Doctor?
8  The Solid Doctor?
9  The Subtle Doctor?
10  The Dop Doctor?

• 7 • (1931, 18) *What famous pairs of lovers are indicated in the following passages:*

1 Bid me discourse, I will enchant thine ear
Or like a fairy trip upon the green.

2 I did not know the dead could have such hair
Hide them. They look like children fast asleep.

3         Die where thou hast lived,
Quicken with kissing: had my lips that power,
Thus would I wear them out.

4         Swear by thy gracious self
Which is the God of my idolatry.

5         and knelt before her there
The perfect Knight before the perfect Queen.

6 In Paradise what have I to win? Therein I ask not to enter, but only to have my sweet lady that I love so well.

7 Not on the Cross my eyes were fixed but you!

8 How do I love thee? Let me count the ways – .

9 Say, is it the day, is it dusk in thy bower,
Thou whom I long for, who longest for me.

10 He calls us back: my pride fell with my fortunes, I'll ask him what he would.

• 8 • (1932, 1)

1 what Olympian reconciliation was effected by the theft of the royal lipstick?

2 whose face surpassed Harland and Wolff's output?

3 who gave a nightly representation of a well known poem by Hood?

4 who, on what occasion, found the Alpheus more efficacious than the Hoover?

5 whose taste for pomegranates cost her four months' exile every year?

6 who found what work less petrifying when performed through the Looking Glass?

7 who wasted his time and himself in gazing into a pool?

8 what pair of lovers caused the mulberry tree to act like a chameleon?

9 whose entertainment frequently resulted in the sign 'Road Up'?

10 whose life would have been saved by total immersion?

**· 9 ·** (1932, 5)

1    what river is reached 'on wings of song'?

2    were not what rivers of Damascus greater than what rivers?

3    of what river shall the torrent flow yet bloodier?

4    what river gives its name to an immortal waltz?

5    what river gives its name to a Chopin nocturne?

6    in what river does a siren lure sailors to destruction?

7    what river 'would have risen before his time and flooded at our nod'?

8    down what river did an armed brig sail to demonstrate its freedom?

9    what river does Merriman compare to modern youth, 'being both fast and shallow'?

10    'At the sight of this river … (they) were much stunned; but the men that went with them said 'You must go through or you cannot come at the gate' – what river?

**· 10 ·** (1932, 7) *Who are or were:*

1    The Thirsty Woman of Tutbury?

2    The Cock Lane Ghost?

3    The Fat Boy of Leicester?

4    The Mad Mullah?

5    La Reine boiteuse?

6    The Man in the Iron Mask?

7    The Old Lady of Threadneedle Street?

8    The Bavarian Baby?

9    The Nun of Kent?

10    The Wandering Jew?

• 11 • (1932, 16) *In what works do the following descriptions of storms appear:*

1   When descends on the Atlantic
      The gigantic
   Storm-wind of the equinox
   Landward in his wrath he scourges
      The toiling surges
   Laden with sea-weed from the rocks.

2   Bells in steeples ... ragged nest of birds ... tilted wagons that came tearing past ... in a trembling vivid flickering instant, everything was clear and plain; then came a flush of red into the yellow light ... a brightness so intense that there was nothing else but light; and then the deepest and profoundest darkness.

3   They looked at the squall and they looked at the shower,
   And the night-wrack came rolling up ragged and brown.

4   The sky would pour down stinking pitch,
   But that the sea, mounting to the welkin's cheek,
   Dashes the fire out.

5   A wailing rushing sound ... then a hoarse roar as if the sea had risen, then such a whirl and tumult that the air seemed mad; and then the waves of wind swept on.

6   Through a jagged aperture in the dome of clouds the light of a few stars fell upon the black sea, rising and falling confusedly.

7   A violent equinoctial gale came storming in from the south-west. The waters of the North Sea were piled in vast masses upon the southern coast of Holland, and then dashed furiously landward ... across the ruined dikes.

8   They hadna sailed a league, a league,
   A league but barely three,
   When the lift grew dark, and the wind blew loud
   And gurly grew the sea.

9   A wind from the the lands they had ruined awoke from sleep,
   And the water began to heave, and the weather to moan
   And or ever that evening ended, a great gale blew.

10   When through the torn sail the wild tempest is streaming,
   When o'er the dark wave the red lightning is gleaming ...

- 12 • (1932, 17) *How old were:*

  1 Antigonus' eldest daughter?
  2 Queen Charlotte when her sedan chair was stopped?
  3 Mr Pickwick's cab horse?
  4 The hero of *Devonshire Cream and Cider*?
  5 Elsie Maynard?
  6 Miss Plunkett?
  7 Maud?
  8 Ida (twenty years ago)?
  9 Salah (at death)?
  10 James James Morrison Morrison Wetherby George Dupree?

- 13 • (1933, 1) *Whose fatness:*

  1 led to the refitting of the Royal Crane?
  2 'Caused her some trouble to look over herself'?
  3 gave him 'a kind of alacrity in sinking'?
  4 caused him to exhibit a bone instead of a finger?
  5 led to his continual damnation?
  6 caused him, in avenging a quip thereon, to make a fatal error in horsemanship?
  7 elicited the treasonable snub 'Who is your fat friend'?
  8 suggested the nickname 'Schwammerl'?
  9 led to the description 'marvellous grosse'?
  10 Proved an exit by window harder in the Isle of Wight than in London?

- 14 • (1933, 7) *Which Elizabeth:*

  1 was 'placed upon the bier
    In happier hour than on a throne'?
  2 agreed with her husband in naming their son?
  3 performed miracles from her tomb?
  4 was named the Queen of Hearts?
  5 was known as Carmen Sylva?
  6 was known as the Ladye Bessee?
  7 had fits of Pope and Byron and Coleridge?
  8 was her authoress's 'darling child'?
  9 had a passion for building?
  10 recalls in name and talent a great composer?

• 15 • (1933, 13) *What Jew in history or fiction:*

1 turned a Queen into an Empress?

2 crossed the North Sea to interview Cromwell?

3 caused a Roman to crash?

4 ruled an empire for a Christian king?

5 was the hero of *Nathan the Wise*?

6 kept a school for pickpockets?

7 wrote on ethics for pleasure and polished lenses for a living?

8 borrowed his gabardine from Reuben of Tadcaster?

9 claimed 'hands, organs, dimensions, senses'?

10 preferred his wife's throat to be cut by Jewish rather than by Christian hands?


• 16 • (1933, 14) *What saint:*

1 floated upstream?

2 carried his head under his arm?

3 purged a neighbouring island of reptiles?

4 had, with her ten thousand companions, an unpleasant termination to her pilgrimage?

5 taught the devil not to poke his nose into the metal shop?

6 was 'twelve cubits of length'?

7 should be the patroness of November the fifth?

8 hid her three daughters in the kitchen?

9 bent a tower to the ground?

10 'Long lived the pride of that countryside
And at last in the odour of sanctity died'?

• 17 • (1933, 15) *What royal residence:*

1    is built on thirteen thousand piles?

2    saw its sovereigns thrown from its windows?

3    is built in the form of a gridiron?

4    was built for a termagant?

5    saw the escape of its mistress by the back door?

6    did a queen refuse to enter 'unless drawn by ropes'?

7    contains a cathedral?

8    was the scene of the 'princely pleasures'?

9    owes its name to a miraculous appearance of the Cross?

10   contained a throne flanked by lions?

• 18 • (1933, 17) *Whose deaths are described by whom in the following lines:*

1    He nothing common did nor mean upon that memorable scene,
     But bowed his comely head.

2    So he passed over and all the trumpets sounded for him on the other side.

3    With slow and steady step there came a lady through the hall,
     And breathless silence chained the lips and touched the hearts of all.

4    And all … looking steadfastly on him, saw his face, as it had been the face
     of an angel.

5    'With a joyful spirit I … die'
     And he fell upon the deck and he died.

6    He died as one that had been studied in his death
     To throw away the dearest thing he ow'd
     As 'twere a careless trifle.

7    Till that her garments, heavy with their drink
     Pulled the poor wretch from her melodious lay
     To muddy death.

8    (He) led me to the shore … I saw him lying with his head upon his arm, as I
     had often seen him lie at school.

9    Sceptre and orb and crown …
     Pass from her, and she fades
     Into the old inviolable peace.

10   The murmuring of many voices, the upturning of many faces, … all flashes
     away. Twenty-three.

# 1934–1935

**• 1 •** (1934, 1)

1    who was boiled for putting 'something' into the episcopal porridge?

2    who hated the idea of a trip to Rome more than poison?

3    whose bower was disturbed by whose ultimatum of steel or strychnine?

4    who was said to have died from an 'overdose of wedlock'?

5    who was strangled with a bridle by her husband for poisoning her step-son?

6    who balked who of his fame 'with a worm'?

7    who saved three cardinals by mixing the drinks?

8    who was more upset by breaking a Fast Day than by poisoning her father, two brothers and a child?

9    what operatic heroine finds the *Datura* leaf an aid to reaching *B* flat?

10    what Prime Minister's suggestion to change the name of the poisoner's town to his own was rejected?

**• 2 •** (1934, 3)

1    who struck the first Noble?

2    in whose reign were gold coins in England introduced?

3    what English King first dated his coins?

4    who issued three-farthing pieces?

5    what coin shows a distant view of spires and ponds?

6    on what English coins was the first attempt at portraiture?

7    what King instituted Maundy pennies?

8    whence did the Angel get its name?

9    what was the Thistle Noble?

10    when was a groat worth a sovereign?

• 3 •  (1934, 4) *What do you understand by the following:*

1   Dutch myrtle?
2   Dutch uncle?
3   Dutch news?
4   Dutch courage?
5   Dutch oil?
6   Dutch rushes?
7   Dutch auction?
8   Dutch bargain?
9   Dutch consort?
10  Dutch nightingale?

• 4 •  (1934, 8)

1   what must you not forget, Best Beloved?
2   who ate Bath Olivers with plenty of salt on 'em to show what kind of man he was?
3   who have hair between every toe?
4   what's that that whimpers overhead?
5   who trust to the stick of the paint?
6   what, according to one masquerading as a squire of low degree, must you buy if you wish to see life?
7   who was advised to poultice his nose?
8   which side of Persimmon looked noblest?
9   what did the doctor find in mummil's bed?
10  what will you be if you can do all this my son?

• 5 • (1934, 14)

1 who wept when the Royal shaving water was muddy?

2 who objected to being shaved by an axe?

3 who persuaded her husband to shave when he had grown a beard in emulation of whose?

4 what was the 'National Razor that shaved close'?

5 who made his army shave to deprive his enemies of a handle?

6 who was the first Roman to shave every day?

7 who dedicated to whom the result of his first shave in a casket of gold?

8 whose chin having 'never known razor' provides what favourite oath?

9 whose tonsorial taxation should have made them the Patrons of barbers?

10 what French word points a connection between beards and boredom?

• 6 • (1934, 16) *What actions were fought on the following festivals:*

1 St Nicomede

2 St Crispin

3 St Ursula

4 St Hippolytus

5 St John the Baptist

6 St George

7 St Ethelreda

8 St Basil

9 Corpus Christi

10 Easter

• 7 • (1934, 17) *What Queens are referred to, and by whom, in the following lines:*

1    A daughter of the gods, divinely tall,
     And most divinely fair.

2    Vénus était blonde, l'on m'a dit:
     L'on voit bien qu'elle est brunette.

3    The Sea-King's daughter, as happy as fair,
     Blissful bride of a blissful heir.

4    And the Imperial votaress passed on,
     In maiden meditation, fancy free.

5    Mère du vain caprice et du léger prestige,
     La fantaisie ailée autour d'elle voltige.

6    Great Gloriana! Bright Gloriana!
     Fair as high heaven is, and fertile as earth!

7    Here thou ... whom three realms obey,
     Dost sometimes counsel take ... and sometimes tea.

8    Before my face me-thought I saw this queen,
     ... all be-wept, in black, and poor estate.

9    Queen of the gourd flower, Queen of the harvest,
     Sweet and omnipotent Mother.

10   Royal and dower-royal, I, the Queen,
     Fronting thy richest sea with richer hands.


• 8 • (1935, 3) *What Bishop:*

1    resigned a strip of his garden to save his Bishopric?

2    was challenged to a fight in his cathedral?

3    foreshadowed the immortal burning of a candle?

4    allowed that the clergy might be Irishmen too?

5    provided trills for Galli-Curci?

6    provided food for rats?

7    was sent to care for 'the barbarous people of the Isle of Man'?

8    is considered the founder of Copenhagen?

9    had a seat but no vote in the House of Lords?

10   is more spirituous than spiritual?

**• 9 •** (1935, 5) *Who 'regardless of grammar' said:*

1   That's him.
2   Curiouser and curiouser.
3   No, nor no-one never.
4   I tank I go home.
5   We come for your goods.
6   I don't believe there's no sich a person.
7   The Navy is us.
8   I want to see the wheels go wound.
9   Dat is one big lie.
10  Specs I growed.

**• 10 •** (1935, 6)

1   where in England was organised football played in AD 217?
2   who decreed that 'Football should be utterlie cryed down'?
3   where is Foot- and Push-ball played in a river?
4   when did England resort to Stoop to conquer?
5   in what game has no goal been scored for many years?
6   who saved the Twickenham record in borrowed boots?
7   in what International match did what Headmaster score a try from the kick-off?
8   of whom was it said 'If you can't collar him, ruffle his hair'?
9   who first ran with the ball?
10  in what French Cathedral is there an annual football match?

• 11 • (1935, 7) *Who were the two other members of the following sisterhoods:*

1  Medusa – – – – – – – – ?
2  Cordelia – – – – – – – – ?
3  Euphrosyne – – – – – – – – ?
4  Charlotte – – – – – – – – ?
5  Alexandra – – – – – – – – ?
6  Hera – – – – – – – – ?
7  Mary Beaton – – – – – – – – ?
8  Norma – – – – – – – – ?
9  Masha – – – – – – – – ?
10  Yum-Yum – – – – – – – – ?

• 12 • (1935, 8) *Who, on first seeing his intended:*

1  said 'Harris, pray get me a glass of brandy'?
2  sighed, 'Alas, whom shall men trust'?
3  was declared by Thackeray to have 'winced'?
4  'Swore a Royal oath'?
5  said 'I should always find the materials for comfort where Mary was'?
6  asked 'Whose damsel is this'?
7  observed 'She is our capital demand'?
8  remarked 'Most sure the goddess on whom these airs attend'?
9  opined 'She is tolerable, but not handsome enough to tempt me'?
10  cried 'Queen of my soul this goblet sip'?

• 13 • (1935, 10)

1  whose cat led his master to the Mansion House?
2  what cat's successor is a mouse?
3  what inn has had half its name supplied by a cat?
4  who were the cat's three supporters in the Bremen orchestra?
5  what cat defied the laws of decapitation?
6  with what dog does Kipling unfavourably compare the cat?
7  what cat paid dearly for angling?
8  with what companion did the cat embark?
9  what cat gilds the chocolates?
10  with what purpose did the cat visit the metropolis?

• 14 • (1935, 11)

1  who writes of those blue remembered hills?
2  where do the mountains sweep down to the sea?
3  what hills are so dear to me?
4  from what mountain did a traveller see a land he was forbidden to reach?
5  on what mountain did Moses store his smuggled liquor?
6  what mountain separates a maiden from an ogre?
7  what is the highest mountain in Switzerland?
8  from what mountain did a brave man acquire an ingredient for gunpowder?
9  what mountain was heaving his huge bulk on high?
10  what mountain announced the sunrise to the fishing fleet?

• 15 • (1935, 12) *Which Anne:*

1  became her husband's 'sister'?
2  'attracted as much admiration at the English Court as formerly in the Swiss chalet'?
3  was carried to the stake in a chair?
4  thought a world of faults 'looked handsome in three hundred pounds a year'?
5  was 'the ugliest woman in England'?
6  married her husband's murderer?
7  'is mostly known for being dead'?
8  may have married a Cardinal?
9  was credited by her sister with long sight?
10  repaid Pavia by Susa?

• 16 • (1935, 14) *Where do the following take place:*

1  Up Helly Aa Festival?
2  Hallaton Bottle kicking?
3  Hobby-horse procession?
4  Furry Dance?
5  Feis Ceoil competition?
6  Penny Hedge planting?
7  Dicing for Bibles?
8  Rush-bearing Festival?
9  Hunt the Wren?
10  Goose Fair?

• 17 • (1935, 15) *To whom do the following refer:*

1    My name's Mary too?
2    His name is John?
3    His intimate friends called him Candle-ends?
4    I am Roland?
5    Her name is Harris?
6    I had intended to call her after her aunt Grissel?
7    Only Brooks of Sheffield?
8    Let her be called after her mother, but the name must come after Alexandrina?
9    I'll have no worse a name than Jove's own page?
10   He pronounced it so as to rhyme with mayor?

• 18 • (1935, 16) *What does a bus-driver mean by:*

1    domino?
2    headways?
3    nobby?
4    tub?
5    scratching?
6    set?
7    spot?
8    sticky nob?
9    output?
10   his holiday?

# 1936–1938

**• 1 •**  (1936, 1)

1  who ate a Saracen?

2  who dragged his bride-to-be through the streets of Bruges by her hair?

3  who ordered a parade of the inhabitants of a French seaside resort in insufficient costume?

4  whose sense of humour was lost in a shipwreck?

5  who skated away from prison?

6  who found an alliance between Crown and gangster profitable?

7  who shook her fist at her grandson from the top of Mirebeau Tower?

8  who extinguished all his worries in drink?

9  who anticipated modern complaints against the Laundry?

10  who claimed to possess an internal gazetteer?

**• 2 •**  (1936, 5)

1  who, seeing snakes late one night on the top of a London bus, thereby evolved an important theory?

2  which ophidian has its caudal vertebrae so modified as to resemble a noisy toy?

3  which molluscan added a splash of colour to an Eastern Court?

4  what bird is employed as a colloquial standard of mortification?

5  which annelid has lent its name to an honourable profession?

6  which of the coleoptera was used to replace the heart of a mummy?

7  which of the fresh-water fishes, tiring of the dull life inland, takes an Atlantic cruise before it dies?

8  which is the only mammal to possess nucleated erythrocytes?

9  what bird has no wings?

10  who proposed to treat diseases of the lower limbs with an embrocation of strong sulphuric acid and water?

**· 3 ·** (1936, 8) *What is or was:*

1   a trebuchet?
2   a pavise?
3   a camail?
4   a solleret?
5   a sear?
6   a falconet?
7   a gonfanon?
8   a voulge?
9   a hagbut?
10  a snaphance?

**· 4 ·** (1936, 9)

1   how far is it from Wimbledon to Wombledon?
2   how many miles to Dublin Town?
3   how far is it from Jerusalem to Bethany?
4   how far is it from Jerusalem to Emmaus?
5   how far is Merrow Down from Guildford?
6   how far from Edinburgh did bonnie Jockie kiss young Jenny?
7   how far was Oliver Twist's walk to London?
8   how far was Captain Bligh's open boat journey to Timor?
9   how far was it from the Maypole to the Standard in Cornhill?
10  how far is there from the deposition of Princes to the grave of Princes?

**· 5 ·** (1936, 14) *What:*

1   feeds you while you sleep?
2   did the Vicar's tutor advise?
3   makes you envy the shirt of your neighbour's little boy?
4   does three jobs in one?
5   fills up in ten minutes?
6   would Red Riding Hood have asked about her grandmother's teeth?
7   please?
8   is that, was that?
9   goodness did the ostrich steal?
10  does the Chairman strongly recommend?

• 6 •  (1936, 17) *Who wrote and in what work the following lines on 'Night':*

1   I heard the trailing garments of the Night
    Sweep through her marble halls?

2   Allah be with us when the last deep night
    Shall wrap us round about?

3   Twilight and evening bell – and after that the dark?

4   Thou makest darkness that it may be night, wherein all the beasts of the
    forest do move?

5   O lovely Night, thou sweet and gentle maiden
    Binding the world with dreams so silently?

6   Come thick night and pall thee
    In the dunnest smoke of hell?

7   Night has spread her pall once more
    And the prisoner still is free?

8   One of those dark nights that hold their breath by the hour together, and
    then heave a long low sigh, and hold their breath again?

9   If thou would view fair Melrose aright,
    Go visit it by pale moonlight ...
    When the broken arches are black in night?

10  Over the city bridge, Night comes majestical
    Borne like a Queen, to a sumptuous festival?

• 7 •  (1937, 1)

1   at what Coronation was there a Royal gate-crasher?

2   who was anointed with oil that was 'grease and smelt ill'?

3   what King 'giggled throughout his Coronation'?

4   at whose Coronation banquet were puddings thrown about?

5   whose Coronation became a massacre?

6   whose Coronation was insufficiently rehearsed?

7   at whose Coronation did the Archbishop collapse?

8   from whose Coronation banquet was the plate stolen?

9   at whose Coronation was the sword borne between the Sovereigns?

10  whose crown fell off?

**• 8 •** (1937, 4) *Give the correct rhetorical terms for the following:*

1   If you don't do as I say, I'll … ?
2   Not so dusty?
3   Abso-bally-lutely?
4   His honour rooted in dishonour stood,
    And faith unfaithful kept him falsely true?
5   Cuckoo?
6   A thousand apologies?
7   He seized the throne?
8   The tumult and the shouting dies?
9   For ever – – – – never
    Never – – – – for ever?
10  She went straight home in a flood of tears and a sedan chair?

**• 9 •** (1937, 5) *Who propounded the following questions:*

1   Do cats eat bats?
2   What is truth?
3   Had Zimri peace who slew his master?
4   When shall we three meet again?
5   Is life worth living?
6   Who is Lottie Collins?
7   Who was then the gentleman?
8   How did the apple get inside the dumpling?
9   Who are the Yeomen?
10  Where is it? What shall I do?

• 10 • (1937, 7) *What are the following:*

1 St Anthony's Fire?

2 St Anthony's Nut?

3 St Barbara's Cress?

4 St Blase's Disease?

5 St George's Ensign?

6 St John's Bread?

7 St Paul's Cross?

8 St Mary's Well?

9 St Martin's Evil?

10 St Peter's Fish?

• 11 • (1937, 14) *What criminal in fact or fiction:*

1 might have given his name to the capital of Baden?

2 found wireless his undoing?

3 dressed himself in his victim's clothes?

4 was a qualified snake-charmer?

5 was the French Bluebeard?

6 was gyved?

7 called his victim an egg?

8 could not silence his victim's heart?

9 was the grandfather of Irad?

10 is the type of all criminals?

• 12 • (1937, 15) *What do you usually sing to:*

1 St Anne?

2 Rockingham?

3 Hanover?

4 Richmond?

5 Aurelia?

6 Eventide?

7 Melita?

8 Helmsley?

9 Nicæa?

10 Old Hundredth?

• 13 • (1937, 17) *To what royal personages do the following poems refer:*

1    Revered, beloved, -- O you that hold
       A nobler office upon earth
   Than arms, or power, or brain, or birth
       Could give the warrior Kings of old?

2    I would her liken to a crown of lilies
       Upon a virgin bride's adorned head
   With roses dight, and goolds, and daffadillies?

3    And thou Rochelle, our own Rochelle, proud city of the waters,
   Again let rapture light the eyes of all thy mourning daughters.
   Hurrah! Hurrah! a single field hath turned the chance of war.
   Hurrah! Hurrah! for Ivry and … ?

4    And he shouted, as the rifted
       Streamers o'er him shook and shifted
   'I accept thy challenge, Thor'?

5    The Roman soldier found
       Me lying dead, my crown about my brows,
   A name for ever! lying robed and crowned,
       Worthy a Roman spouse?

6    O, for a blast of that dread horn,
       On Fontarabian echoes borne,
   That to King Charles did come,
       When Rowland brave and Olivier …
   On Roncesvalles died?

7    When I was mortal, my anointed body
       By thee was punched full of deadly holes
   Think on the Tower and me: despair and die?

8    They were lovely and pleasant in their lives,
       And in their death they were not divided;
   They were swifter than eagles,
       They were stronger than lions?

9    O death, rock me asleep,
       Bring on my quiet rest,
   Let pass my very guiltless ghost
       Out of my careful breast?

10   Then the Queen she looked at Mary,
       'And what's your name?' she said?

**• 14 •** (1938, 1) *What schoolboy:*

1 knows who strangled Atahualpa?
2 makes a snail-like progress to school?
3 was 'cleaning the back-parlour window'?
4 laughed with counterfeited glee at his master's jokes?
5 said 'Tush' when thoroughly roused?
6 was leader of the Market Drayton gangsters?
7 sold his grandmother's letter for £4 10s?
8 ornamented his ancestors' portraits with beards and beer mugs?
9 protested that he would drink a bottle of wine every day?
10 was sent to a school 'at which there was no flogging'?

**• 15 •** (1938, 7) *What is meant by the following mining terms:*

1 stope?
2 winze?
3 rise?
4 crosscut?
5 poppet head?
6 whim?
7 Cornish pump?
8 kibble?
9 sollars?
10 adit?

**• 16 •** (1938, 8) *What vicar:*

1 was all things to all kings?
2 considered his six children a valuable present to his country?
3 administers merriment to his congregation?
4 had an infernal presentation?
5 was passing rich on a modest stipend?
6 composed *The Ivy Green*?
7 held the living of Puddingdale?
8 enjoyed the patronage of the Right Honourable Lady Catherine de Bourgh?
9 befriended Bella Gorry?
10 is a layman?

**• 17 •** (1938, 12) *Who:*

1   criticized her grandmother's appearance?
2   should have used Milton for blood-stains?
3   kept house for seven miners?
4   'didn't know it was so late'?
5   refused to become the Roast Beef of Old England?
6   was married at 115?
7   provided a capillary fire escape?
8   gate-crashed in the absence of her host?
9   roasted her hostess?
10  objected to his name being broadcast by fairies?

**• 18 •** (1938, 17) *Of what works by whom are the following the first words:*

1   This is the forest primeval. The murmuring pines and the hemlocks,
      Bearded with moss ...
    Stand like Druids of old?
2   Let fame, that all hunt after in their lives,
      Live register'd upon our brazen tomb?
3   No eggs! No eggs! Thousand thunders, man, what do you mean by no eggs?
4   A gentle knight was pricking on the plaine,
      Ycladd in mightie arms and silver shielde?
5   It is a truth universally acknowledged, that a single man in possession of good fortune, must be in want of a wife?
6   'What is truth?' said jesting Pilate, and would not stay for an answer?
7   When that Aprille with his showres sote
      The droghte of Marche had pierced the rote?
8   I was borne in the year 1632, in the city of York, of a good family, though not of that country, my father being a foreigner of Bremen, who settled first at Hull?
9   I sing the sofa, I, who lately sang Truth, Hope, and Charity?
10  There was never anything by wit of man so well devised, or so sure established, which in continuance of time hath not corrupted?

# 1939

1   in what war did the French request the English to fire first?
2   what war made old Caspar wonder what it was all about?
3   what war was started by the throwing of magistrates from the window?
4   what war caused red men to scalp each other by the shores of the Great Lakes?
5   in what war 'to battle fierce came forth all the might of Denmark's crown'?
6   what war was started by a deceptive telegram?
7   in what war was 'my boy George' shot by 'damned troopers'?
8   to the outbreak of what war did Mr Beecher-Stowe contribute?
9   in what war was *Dolly Grey* the marching song?
10  in what war did there fall upon men 'a great hail out of Heaven'?

• 2 •   *How much:*

1   did Schubert get for his *Winter's Journey* songs?
2   did Sapphira claim to have sold the land for?
3   did a copy of Cranmer's Great Bible cost?
4   did Moses Primrose take in exchange for the colt?
5   did Sam Weller receive as wages?
6   did the 'Old Lady' in *Henry VIII* say would hire her to be Queen?
7   did Augustus Moddle pay Mrs Todgers for his board?
8   is the estimated price of wisdom?
9   was owing to the unmerciful servant?
10  should a pinch of Kruschen cover?

**• 3 •**

1 who said 'Out of this nettle, danger, we pluck this flower, safety'?
2 who invented the safety-razor?
3 who was knighted as the inventor of the miner's safety-lamp?
4 who received a silver tankard and one thousand guineas as the inventor of the miner's safety-lamp?
5 where are the Islands of Safety?
6 who invented three-layered safety-glass?
7 whose poem on *Safety* was written in conditions quite the reverse?
8 how often must a theatre's safety-curtain be lowered by law?
9 whose motto is 'Safety First'?
10 who starred in the film *Safety Last*?

**• 4 •** *Who (in 1939) was:*

1 French Minister of Finance?
2 Polish Prime Minister?
3 British Chief of Air Staff?
4 Russian President?
5 German Commander in Chief?
6 German Naval Commander in Chief?
7 Russian Foreign Minister?
8 British First Sea Lord?
9 Polish Foreign Minister?
10 French Commander in Chief?

**• 5 •** *What line or lines:*

1 leads to marine horse-play?
2 is known as the Mason and Dixon?
3 leads to Goodge Street?
4 are Hymeneal guarantees?
5 was of exiguous carmine?
6 denotes financial gain or loss?
7 'Never go that way at all'?
8 protected Lisbon?
9 awaits your signature?
10 may be used for drying?

• 6 •  *Distinguish between:*

1  Tosi
2  Tosca
3  Tosti
4  Tosher
5  Tossia
6  Tostig
7  Toscaig
8  Tostado
9  Toselli
10  Toscanini

• 7 •

1  what affected a serpentine coiffure?
2  what snake incubates its eggs?
3  what snake's full title contains the words Di Capello?
4  who performed an infantile feat of boa-constriction?
5  from what snake did Mowgli gain his wisdom?
6  what snake found the bell-rope fatal?
7  the embrace of what snake does woman apparently not mind?
8  in what echelon sport does the serpent indulge?
9  what snakes are warned away from 'our fairy Queen'?
10  what serpent did Snow White's Queen emulate?

• 8 •  *To whom did the following nicknames apply:*

1  Schwammerl?
2  Cleopatra?
3  Duessa?
4  Afternoon?
5  Dickon?
6  Caliban?
7  Salamander?
8  Florizel?
9  Trimmer?
10  Candle-ends?

## • 9 •

1   who first awarded medals for conduct in battle?

2   after what battle were rank and file first decorated?

3   after what battle did medals first hang from a ribbon?

4   why do medals of the Peninsular War appear anachronistic?

5   what medal was so unattractive that it had to be replaced?

6   what medal is awarded for bravery in mines?

7   on what medal is inscribed 'Bravery in the Field'?

8   on what medal is the image of Britannia?

9   what medal ribbon is plain green?

10   what medal ribbon is plain maroon?

## • 10 • *Give screen names of the following film actors and actresses:*

1   Spangler Arlington Brugh

2   Gladys Smith

3   Charles Edward Pratt

4   George Augustus Andrews

5   Izz Iskowitch

6   Gretchen Belzer

7   Virginia Katherine Mc Math

8   Frederick Austerlitz

9   Joe Yule

10   Greta Lovisa Gustafsson

## • 11 •

1   who 'rode there so late, through night so wild'?

2   who galloped, who galloped, besides me?

3   whom did Drouet head off when he galloped through the woods?

4   who rode the Thirty Mile Ride to the Lamp-post on the Down?

5   who rode through the gloom and the light when 'the fate of a nation was riding that night'?

6   into what valley was a ride of 4½ miles taken?

7   who rode on Kyrat when he 'up the mountain pathway flew'?

8   who rode to the Ukraine bound to a wild horse?

9   who rode 'through the streets of Zacatin. To the Alhambra spurring in'?

10   to reach where was the gallant night directed to ride 'over the Mountains of the Moon'?

• 12 • *What sort of entertainment would you expect to be provided by or at:*

1. Hengler's?
2. Jarley's?
3. Barnum's?
4. Maskelyne's?
5. Astley's?
6. Vauxhall?
7. The Spaniards?
8. Ciro's?
9. Ranelagh?
10. Wonderland?

• 13 •

1. what Poet Laureate was called 'Our beloved Versificator'?
2. who was the first official Poet Laureate?
3. what Poet Laureate wrote a 'vulgar lampoon' on Flodden?
4. what Poet Laureate first received a 'tierce of canary wine'?
5. what Poet Laureate accepted £27 in lieu of canary wine?
6. what poet Laureate calls the Church of England 'the spotted panther'?
7. what Poet Laureate received 'this laurel, greener from the brows of him that uttered nothing base'?
8. what Poet Laureate wrote of Venice as holding 'the gorgeous east in fee'?
9. what Poet Laureate's 'long trick' is not yet over?
10. what Poet Laureate introduced telegraph wires into a congratulatory ode?

• 14 •

1. what grandmother was credited with facial enlargements?
2. who told his grandmother that he did not know what fear was?
3. what grandmother made her apology in 27 verses?
4. what grandmother was besieged by her grandson?
5. what grandmother, at her granddaughter's wedding, recalled that of Lady Tollinglower?
6. what grandmother's daughter-in-law was 'better to her than seven sons'?
7. what grandmother was saluted by her husband as a 'brimstone pig'?
8. who was Timothy's grandmother?
9. who was the Eaglet's grandmother?
10. in what feat are grandmothers supposed to be particularly interested?

**• 15 •** *What firm and what products do you associate with:*

1   Carlisle?
2   Cowley?
3   Hayes?
4   Isleworth?
5   Perth?
6   Port Sunlight?
7   Reading?
8   Somerdale?
9   Dagenham?
10  St John's?

**• 16 •**

1   who was the first Londoner to use an umbrella?
2   who were the 'Lords of the Umbrella'?
3   where is Umbrella Hill?
4   whose umbrella was solicited for exhibition in Italy?
5   whose grey umbrella served at home as a cupboard and on journeys as a carpet bag?
6   what is the botanical name of the umbrella tree?
7   where are white umbrellas used for white elephants?
8   who 'patches up your troubles, then goes on his way'?
9   what Commander-in-Chief took his umbrella on parade?
10  whose umbrella seemed not one umbrella but fifty?

**• 17 •** *What soldiers are referred to and by whom in the following lines:*

1   Lead out the pageant: sad and slow
As fits an universal woe,
Let the long long procession go …
The last great Englishman is low?

2   … Yet much remains
To conquer still; peace hath her victories
No less renowned than war: new foes arise?

3    O! more or less than man ... in high or low,
     Battling with nations, flying from the field
     Now making monarchs' necks thy footstool, now
     More than thy meanest soldier, taught to yield?

4    Now glory to the Lord of Hosts, from whom all glories are,
     And glory to our sovereign liege ...
     Hurrah! Hurrah! A single field has turned the chance of war.
     Hurrah! Hurrah! For Ivry and ... ?

5    ... But now behold
     How London doth pour out her citizens ...
     Go forth and fetch their conquering Caesar in?

6    Lightly they'll talk of the spirit that's gone,
     And o'er his cold ashes upbraid him;
     But little he'll reck if they let him sleep on
     In the grave where a Briton has laid him?

7    Last night, among his fellow roughs,
     He jested, quaffed and swore;
     ... ... ... ...
     Ambassador from Britain's crown
     And type of all her race?

8    If ye know the tract of the morning mist
     Ye know where his pickets are.
     At dusk he harries the Abazai ... at dawn
     he is into Bonair?

9    God and your arms be praised, victorious friends;
     The day is ours, the bloody dog is dead'?

10   Ungrateful country, France, for thee alone
     She lost the honour that her arms had won,
     (Such Caesar never knew, nor Philip's son)
     Resigned the glories of a ten year's reign,
     And such as none but -------'s arm could gain?

• 18 • *In 1939:*

1    what feline misunderstanding estranged France and Iran?

2    the centenary of the British seizure of what former possession of Solyman the Magnificent was celebrated?

3    what Bogey-man finished the course?

4    what painting was indifferently restored?

5    what orange blossom has budded?

6    who repeated Wolfe's conquest?

7    whose extension of labours recalls that of Jacob?

8    why would Gregory have renewed his prayers for the deliverance of the English 'De Ira'?

9    what has been stated to have suffered its prototype's fate in 1588 in being 'removed from the fight'?

10    who has been urged to leporine exercise?

# 1940–1941

• 1 • (1940, 1) *Who said:*

1   Fight on?

2   Backs to the wall?

3   Situation excellente: j'attaque?

4   O God of battles, steel my soldiers' hearts?

5   Patriotism is not enough?

6   At last I have these English in my grasp?

7   Peccavi?

8   If England is a small country, it is the easier to defend?

9   How goes the Empire?

10  You're a great people?

• 2 • (1940, 3)

1   across what river was Shenandoah's daughter to be taken?

2   what river flows through 'the old city's silence'?

3   what river's murmurs are transmuted into a Chopin Nocturne?

4   what Rivers' Regiment is described as *'suivant la route glorieuse'*?

5   what river has made the world dance?

6   what river was suggested for repeated ablutions?

7   what river would have risen before his time and flooded at whose nod?

8   of what river's navigation am 'I' innocent?

9   what river is named after the wife of the Judge of the Dead?

10  what river compasseth the whole land of Havilah?

### • 3 •   (1940, 6) *What schoolmaster:*

1   claimed to be a Tartar?
2   carried the day's disasters in his morning face?
3   did not spare the rod nor spoil the Westminster child?
4   inspired Tom Brown?
5   found Clifton a grind?
6   kept a school 'at which there was no flogging'?
7   was a 'surly devil'?
8   wrote of what pupil, 'her mind has no womanly weakness'?
9   stole the Eton spoons?
10   was beaten by his assistant?

### • 4 •   (1940, 7) *What do you mean by these nautical terms:*

1   soldier's wind?
2   Charlie Noble?
3   the bitter end?
4   Cape Horn Fever?
5   devil to pay?
6   dog watch?
7   salt beef squire?
8   sea grocer?
9   pusser's crabs?
10   whipjack?

### • 5 •   (1940, 10)

1   who might have rebuked her guests more mildly with the recommendation *desipere in loco*?
2   who claimed to be sea-sick *ad Calendas Graecas*?
3   who might have made his wedding motto *ad vitam aut culpam*?
4   of which of Dickens' works could he have said *Re infecta*?
5   what book's subtitle might have been *Per gradus*?
6   whose motto might have been *Video et taceo*?
7   which of Shakespeare's plays might be named *Ad libitum*?
8   what royal epicure might have accounted for his death by saying *Post hoc ergo propter hoc*?
9   what lady-in-waiting established an *imperium in imperio*?
10   whose gallantry has fulfilled the motto *Per ardua ad astra*?

**• 6 •**  (1940, 12)

1  what climatic conditions does Sir Roderic describe as suitable to ghosts?

2  what ghost did Falstaff impersonate?

3  what ghostly gate-crasher broke up the party?

4  what ghost had more 'gravy than grave' about him?

5  whose ghost propels what through streets of varied dimensions?

6  what ghost was saluted as 'Old Mole'?

7  what ghost 'stoops to folly and jests about a bodkin'?

8  how did the ghost prove his transatlantic tendency?

9  what equine ghost appears with a numerous company in stormy weather?

10  'It was a ghost … a spirit.'
'Whose?' they all cried.
'Gentlemen, this is the nineteenth of March.'


**• 7 •**  (1940, 16) *Who performed the feat of:*

1  leaping from one state to the other over the ice?

2  being shot from a cannon's mouth?

3  crossing the Niagara Falls on a tight-rope?

4  substituting an arm for a bolt?

5  saving her city by beheading her host?

6  performing a wagered circuit of 24,000 miles with 15 seconds to spare?

7  decoying her victim with a 'lordly dish'?

8  turning a gentleman's bathroom into a shambles?

9  slaying more at his death than in his life?

10  supporting a terrestrial burden?

- 8 • (1940, 17) *Who wrote in what work:*

1 Here and here did England help me; how can I help England?

2 O peaceful England, while I my watch am keeping,
Thou like Minerva, weary of war art sleeping?

3 Winds of the world, give answer! They are whimpering to and fro,
And what should they know of England who only England know?

4 Night sank upon the dusky beach and on the purple sea,
Such night in England ne'er had been, nor e'er again shall be?

5 But the might of England flushed
To anticipate the scene;
And her van the fleeter rushed
O'er the deadly space between?

6 Eleven men of England
A breastwork charged in vain;
Eleven men of England
Lie stripped and gashed and slain?

7 But the black North-easter
Through the snowstorm hurled,
Drives our English hearts of oak
Seaward round the world?

8 England, Queen of the waves, whose green inviolate girdle enrings thee round
Mother, fair as the morning, where is now the place of thy foemen found?

9 Work for her glory and strengthen her walls,
Live for her, die for her, glad if she calls;
Pray for her: strong she is, stronger shall be,
England the beautiful, England the free?

10 This precious stone set in the silver sea,
Which serves it in the office of a wall,
Or as a moat defensive to a house,
Against the envy of less happier lands;
This blessed plot, this earth, this realm, this England?

• 9 • (1940, 18) *In 1940:*

1    who has been 'lucky' in documentary research?

2    who might have substituted 'même' for 'fors' in Francis I's Pavia communiqué?

3    what lease has facilitated the 'ways of the destroyer'?

4    whose words might have been quoted: 'I do not say they cannot come. I only say they cannot come by sea'?

5    to whom might Strafford's death cry be applied?

6    what haphazard place has been bombed?

7    what table water is in disrepute?

8    what best-seller is recalled by the 'black-out'?

9    who might retort in their forefathers' words:

       'Then we might fight in the shade'?

10    what leading and tonic notes have formed an initial interlude?


• 10 • (1941, 1) *Who said:*

1    Woe to those who break treaties?

2    Rome shall perish, — write that word

     In the blood that she has spilt?

3    May the great God, whom I worship, grant to my country a great and glorious victory?

4    Come the three corners of the world in arms,

     And we shall shock them?

5    'Tis true that we are in great danger: The greater therefore should our courage be?

6    Pooh! Don't talk to me that stuff?

7    I think foul scorn that any Prince of Europe should dare to invade the borders of my realm?

8    He shall have seven feet of English ground for his grave?

9    No one is depressed in this house?

10    The battle is won; my life is of no consequence now?

• 11 • (1941, 3) *What executioner:*

1. should have announced 'No dogs admitted'?
2. insisted, according to Sam Weller, on 'reg'lar order'?
3. was 'stronger than his namesake … and tore away the gates of God's own temple'?
4. limited his functions to his domestic circle?
5. hid his sword in the straw?
6. kept a little list?
7. wore his victims' wardrobes?
8. was informed that his victim had 'vanished into air'?
9. had an audience of four?
10. profited by arboreal suspension?

• 12 • (1941, 5)

1. who sat on the royal wine-glass?
2. what royal head was likened to a pineapple?
3. whose death led to a temporary withdrawal of queens from packs of cards?
4. what rebellion failed to stop whose game of golf?
5. whose ears did Jane Lane box?
6. who refused to be considered a public meeting?
7. who declared that his Metropolitan had a nice taste in pigs?
8. who on his accession greeted his Prime Minister as a liar?
9. who stole his sister-in-law's peas?
10. who was the only person who could recall the tears shed by Elizabeth on the death of Mary?

**• 13 •** (1941, 7) *Fill up the ages:*

1   Rose a nurse of – – – – years.

2   Maud is not – – – – but she is tall and stately.

3   She may very well pass for – – – –
    In the dusk with the light behind her.

4   When I was – – – – I heard a wise man say.

5   Now to the widow of – – – –.

6   And all the days of Enoch were – – – – years.

7   Modest maiden will not tarry,
    Though but – – – – years she carry.

8   What Heaven vanished then,
    You were – – – – I was – – – –.

9   Whose – – – – winters freeze with one rebuke
    All great self-seekers.

10   The days of our age are – – – –.


**• 14 •** (1941, 8)

1   who wrote with the ink that trickled down his face?

2   who wrote, forming with his tongue imaginary characters to correspond with letters he was constructing?

3   who wrote 'from her doleful prison in the Tower'?

4   who claimed to write 'on a strip of ivory, two inches wide'?

5   whose postscript declined a warming-pan?

6   what family correspondence deals with the Wars of the Roses?

7   who 'studied too much for words of four syllables' in his letters?

8   whose letter of three lines made Henri IV foam at the mouth?

9   who ended his confidential letters with the injunction 'Now burn'?

10   who wrote to whom for his cloak, his books, but especially his parchment?

## • 15 • (1941, 9)

1    what income did Mr Micawber specify in his recipe for happiness?

2    what was the income of James I's Poet Laureate?

3    what was the stipend of Goldsmith's parson?

4    what was Mrs Lammle's annuity?

5    on what income did Mrs Norris set up housekeeping?

6    what was Nicholas Nickleby's pay as schoolmaster?

7    what was Solomon's yearly tribute to Hiram?

8    what was Mr Quiverful's stipend?

9    what is the guerdon of the finder and follower?

10    what was the National Revenue in 1939?

## • 16 • (1941, 11)

1    what British aircraft was given the Service number 201?

2    what bomber aircraft was ready to visit Berlin in November 1918?

3    what famous fighter aircraft came into service in the spring of 1917?

4    which was the first British single-seater tractor fighter?

5    in what way is the memory of Amy Johnson perpetuated?

6    what German first flew a glider over Ronaldsway?

7    how is the type of machine which conquered Everest still being kept in the public eye?

8    what Headmaster of which Public School was given the responsibility of organising the ATC?

9    how many times greater was the Air Force at the end of the last war than at the beginning?

10    what resident of the Isle of Man won the Schneider Trophy 1914?

• 17 • (1941, 14) *In swing language what are:*

1 hot fountain pen?

2 dog kennel?

3 alligator?

4 tin ear?

5 corn?

6 jam?

7 tailgate?

8 canary?

9 gentleman in the kitchen?

10 long underwear gang?

• 18 • (1941, 18) *In 1941:*

1 what 33 years' trek ended in Kenya?

2 who 'has joined the shades in the Parthenon'?

3 what mirthful Centenary has been celebrated?

4 who has been released from his Dutch exile?

5 the dropping of what pilot has been recalled?

6 where have the shades of Lord North and Washington hovered?

7 what overture has been recalled?

8 what quartet has replaced a piano solo?

9 who has been our Blitzstrahl aus blauem?

10 what new Rasselas has come home to his Happy Valley?

# 1942–1943

**• 1 •** (1942, 1) *Who:*

1 said of whom 'I am not afraid of a King of Spain, who has been up to the age of twelve learning his alphabet'?

2 called whom 'the bravest of the Gauls'?

3 bade his host 'Gain a reputation like the Huns of Attila'?

4 said of what nation 'She must free herself from a monarchy, Since it cannot give her liberty'?

5 said of whom 'When he died, little children cried in the streets'?

6 said 'Not by speechifying and majorities, but by blood and iron'?

7 said and where 'Stiffen the sinews, summon up the blood'?

8 said and where 'I was a grenadier before I was a marshal'?

9 said of whom 'I see a brilliant people and a beautiful city rising from this abyss'?

10 proclaims 'I am – – – – I am – – – –, there is Victory in the land'?

**• 2 •** (1942, 2) *Name the following:*

1 Our Mutual Friend

2 The Woman in White

3 The Little Duke

4 The Deemster

5 The Tenant of Wildfell Hall

6 Little Women

7 The Scarlet Pimpernel

8 A Gentleman of France

9 The Virginians

10 The Virginian

• 3 • (1942, 4) *Who travelled:*

1   in a boat propelled by knitting needles?
2   in a bowl?
3   in a harm-cheer in a shay cart?
4   in a pea-green boat?
5   in a converted Cucurbit?
6   in an undergirt ship?
7   on a baggage wagon, when not washing greens?
8   on a bull?
9   in the tiger?
10   on the tiger?

• 4 • (1942, 5)

1   where did the partridge roost?
2   what does Housman call the 'loveliest of trees'?
3   what leafy soubriquet is applied to Bucks?
4   under what did the rustic Vulcan set up his workshop?
5   over what does Kipling accord British dominion?
6   up what tree did the little publican shine?
7   what tree did the Maypole Inn choose to represent itself?
8   under what tree do the Earth and Heavens shelter?
9   what tree assumed regality?
10   what arboreal vegetation is boreal?

• 5 • (1942, 8) *Who said:*

1   'Who leans on the word of a woman is a fool'?
2   'Yes, a miracle! … a constant woman'?
3   'The man who can govern a woman can govern a nation'?
4   'A woman is only a woman, but a good cigar is a smoke'?
5   'Every woman is at heart a rake'?
6   'The woman is so hard upon the woman'?
7   'Women's weapons, water-drops'?
8   'Sweet is revenge – especially to women'?
9   'Rum creeters is women'?
10   'Her price is far above rubies'?

• 6 •  (1942, 11) *What University:*

1   possesses Goldsmith's name scratched on a table?

2   boasts a Gustavianum?

3   produced a son who stood there and could do no otherwise?

4   claims the Lord as its illumination?

5   suffered from a riot caused by lack of beer for supper?

6   embraces Botany Bay?

7   possesses a college founded by rival Queens?

8   was founded by Henry Wardlaw?

9   was founded by George II?

10   had as co-founder the author of *The Pleasures of Hope?*


• 7 •  (1942, 13) *In what work by whom is the Isle of Man referred to as follows:*

1   'Be off' I says, 'stir your stumps!'
    (These Foxdale lumps
    Is pirriful)?

2   He laid his hand on that stout bastion; hornwork, raven or demilune which formed the outworks to the citadel of his purple Isle of Man?

3   Arrived in Port St Mary, the two friends found themselves in a second Castletown on a smaller scale?

4   Once on the top of Tynwald's formal mound … would sit this Island's King?

5   … and even went as far as Douglas, IOM, to treat them to eighteen-penny glasses of champagne?

6   Let the mountain of Scoafell (Snaefell) conceal Dagnal and three hundred chosen warriors from the eyes of Raignald?

7   On either side of the bay was a bold headland, the one stretching out in a series of broken crags, the other terminating in a huge mass of rock, called from its shape the Stack?

8   Like him of whom the story ran, who spoke the spectre-hound in Man?

9   … old Billy Quilleash brought his boat-head to the wind in six fathoms of water outside Port Erin?

10   News of a tidy cargo of French brandy, German perfumes and Vallenceens lace snug on the northern shore of Ramsey Bay?

• 8 •   (1942, 14) *What scientist:*

1    is commemorated as a Father and a Brother?

2    loathed women and took to water?

3    made a mediaeval bonfire?

4    peered into the crystal, after leaving Mona's Isle?

5    is interested in money?

6    has his discovery carved in stone in Russia?

7    regarded fruit with a certain gravity?

8    was derided as an aerial jockey?

9    worked in his father's brewery?

10   was the object of a mob's disfavour in England?

• 9 •   (1942, 17) *In what work by whom do the following lines occur:*

1    God comfort thee! Why dost thou smile on, and kiss thy hand so oft?

2    Bold lover, never, never, never canst thou kiss,
     Though winning near the goal – yet do not grieve?

3    Kiss me, kiss me, kiss me, kiss me, Though I die of shame-a
     Please you, that's the kind of maid, Sets my heart a flame-a?

4    I kissed her slender hand, She took the kiss sedately?

5    The minister kiss'd the fiddler's wife,
     An' could na preach for thinkin' o't?

6    The coward does it with a kiss,
     The brave man with a sword?

7    Mercy and truth are met together: righteousness and peace have kissed each
     other?

8    Kiss-me-quick-my-loves in plenty,
     Comely maids of sweet and twenty?

9    And the sunlight clasps the earth,
     And the moonbeams kiss the sea –
     What are all these kissings worth,
     If thou kiss not me?

10   Dat it is not to de fashion *pour les* ladies of France, –
     I cannot tell vat is *baiser en* Anglish?

## • 10 • (1943, 1) *Who said of England or the English:*

1 'You English are mad – mad as March hares'?

2 'Every gale that blows from England is burdened with enmity'?

3 'There is nothing more fortunate than that these tribes make not one common cause'?

4 'We are without friends; Mr – – – – has alienated all other countries from us'?

5 'We are undone at home and abroad. We are no longer a nation'?

6 'We enjoin that all men in our kingdom have and hold the aforesaid liberties fully and wholly'?

7 'I shall lend credit to nothing against my people which parents would not believe against their own children'?

8 'It is lawful for Christian men to wear weapons, and serve in the wars'?

9 'Wake up England'?

10 'See my brave English – how they fight'?

## • 11 • (1943, 2)

1 what Emperor of India became a Buddhist?

2 what God left his footprint in trying to stamp out Buddhism?

3 where, and in whose honour, is the Qutb Minar?

4 where and what are the Towers of Silence?

5 what was Queen Victoria's Hindustani title?

6 who is 'His Exalted Highness'?

7 what Indian river assumes a maternal character?

8 to whom is the 'Dream in marble' a memorial?

9 what city does Kipling describe as 'Dower-royal' and why?

10 what are 'those cool waters where we used to dwell'?

## • 12 • (1943, 5) *What day of the week:*

1    saw the death of Hebdomadal?

2    fills its child with woe?

3    was Nomenclator in an insular domestic?

4    is annually sheer?

5    do I walk out with a Tar?

6    was it imperative for Royster Doyster to marry?

7    is canonised by toper?

8    in conjunction with itself denotes the Greek Kalends?

9    was a maid espied – with a comb and a glass in her hand?

10    is meetest for drink?

## • 13 • (1943, 6) *What conflagration:*

1    occurred during the duenna's visit to the second Mrs Tanqueray?

2    engulfed what aquiline prophet?

3    was requited by destruction by rodents?

4    destroyed the sister of an Empress?

5    destroyed what friend of the Fairchild family?

6    led to the closing of the New York Stock Exchange?

7    was amplified '7 times more than it was wont'?

8    only partially pleased Dennis the hangman?

9    imposed on the Grande Armée the role of Mother Hubbard?

10    was spontaneous?

## • 14 • (1943, 8)

1    what tank recalls the march from 'Atlanta to the Sea'?

2    what is a Co-ax?

3    how did the 'Valentine' get its name?

4    what Russian soldier has given his name to a tank?

5    ''Twas not the tanks that won the war, 'twas …'?

6    what tank recalls the reign of Charles I?

7    how does the spirit of Richard I live in this war?

8    to what reverend gentleman have the Germans taken an active dislike?

9    what tank has added fresh laurels to the name of an American President?

10    to whom is attributed the invention of the tank?

• 15 • (1943, 9) *What exhibitionist:*

1    featured in an aureate migration?

2    sought the bubble reputation even in the cannon's mouth?

3    was caricatured by Bob Sawyer?

4    was Charles II's pet acrobat?

5    immortalized Mrs 'Enry 'Awkins?

6    travelled from Omtario to New York State on hemp?

7    danced through a faun's afternoon?

8    juggled billiard balls from Odessa to London?

9    defeated Samson, Cyclops and Hercules?

10   said 'Shurrup'?


• 16 • (1943, 12) *Which Public School:*

1    arrays its cricket eleven in light blue shirts?

2    once decorated its walls with the slogan 'Bread or Blood'?

3    invests the word Pop with a significance other than that of a beverage?

4    is a memorial to one to whom his mother once referred as 'poor awkward Arthur'?

5    was described in fiction as 'Roslyn School'?

6    is privileged to cry 'Vivat Rex'?

7    endeavoured to educate Titus Oates?

8    was chosen as the Alma Mater of one of Thackeray's characters?

9    looks down on the others from a height?

10   proclaims itself in song to be 'the best school of all'?

• 17 • (1943, 13) *What Sexton:*

1    buried two Queens at Peterborough?

2    was stolen by goblins?

3    got into trouble for burying Polyneices?

4    digs his own grave?

5    is a Necrophorus?

6    is a follower of Sherlock Holmes?

7    dug up dead languages like a ghoul?

8    had a wife in league with the coffin-maker?

9    employed a 'little trowel'?

10    declared that a tanner would last 'nine year'?

• 18 • (1943, 18) *In 1943:*

1    how has the Orange Tree sheltered under a Maple Leaf?

2    what echo has there been of the US Grant?

3    whose Requiem would have appropriately included a Prelude?

4    what 4th edition has been proclaimed of the One and Indivisible?

5    to what regiment would Knox have lowered his trumpet?

6    what Armada signal has been used?

7    how did the Scarlet Pimpernel escape to happiness?

8    what Metropolitan Coronation has occurred?

9    how has Edward III delighted the Commons?

10    who might have said 'Wilt thou be gone? Sweet Valentine adieu'?

# 1944

**• 1 •** *What Sovereign:*

1   extenuated his vital tenacity?

2   regretted 'slaying his mother and two uncles'?

3   was a victim of epistaxis?

4   wished one of his generals to bite the others?

5   execrated Sorrel?

6   'spoke to the Almighty as one potentate to another'?

7   claimed that a post-mortem would be of geographical interest?

8   partly imitated White Ship etiquette?

9   was slung over the banisters?

10  objected that everything was something else?

**• 2 •** *What house in literature:*

1   indicates cardiac fracture?

2   seems to harbour puppets?

3   was big enough for Lucy Dale?

4   might describe a pedagogue's collapse?

5   was reluctant to admit the sunrise?

6   might be a Saxon armoury?

7   recalls Little Red Riding Hood?

8   has been bereft of 'Life and Thought, leaving door and windows wide'?

9   won its authoress a prize from a temperance league?

10  was first called 'The Peaks'?

**• 3 •**  *What painting by whom:*

1  bears the name of an overture?

2  shows the last journey of a man of war?

3  portrays the village blacksmith at work?

4  flattered its sitter?

5  shows a dissection?

6  bears a title from *The Bohemian Girl*?

7  included the wart?

8  shows 'the little street' where?

9  has been called 'the start of the hundred'?

10  has been called 'the lost potato'?

**• 4 •**

1  which is the Goliath of trees?

2  which is the Tom Thumb of trees?

3  which is the Methuselah of trees?

4  where is ebony green?

5  what is the most thickly forested country?

6  where does the English walnut spring from?

7  what tree is only found in fossil form in the Old World?

8  what could one of Longfellow's heroes have contributed to the telephone pole industry?

9  of what wood is parquet flooring usually made?

10  why would Mr Bagnet have found the subject of ships' pulleys embarrassing?

- 5 • *What Shakespearean character uttered the following in which play:*

1 'Without his roe, like a dried herring, O flesh, flesh, how art thou fishified'?

2 'Witches' mummy, maw and gulf
Of the ravin'd salt sea shark,
Root of hemlock digged i' the dark,
Liver of blaspheming Jew'?

3 'Why 'tis a cockle or a walnut shell,
A knack, a toy, a trick, a baby's cap'?

4 'And fools are as like husbands as pilchards are to herrings,
The husband's the bigger'?

5 'But fish not, with this melancholy bait,
For this fool's gudgeon. This opinion'?

6 'For yourself, sir, should be as old as I am, if, like a crab, you could go backward'?

7 'His face is all bubukles, and whelks and knobs and flames of fire'?

8 'If I be not ashamed of my soldiers, I am a soused gurnet'?

9 'For here comes the trout that must be caught with tickling'?

10 'She that in wisdom never was so frail
To change the cod's head for the salmon's tail'?


- 6 • *What London terminus:*

1 uprooted Stagg's gardens?

2 took its name from a Phrygian martyr?

3 stands on the site of a small-pox hospital?

4 might have been called 'Old Bethlehem'?

5 is a neighbour of London Stone?

6 commemorates a funeral journey's end?

7 may be gained from the playing fields of Eton?

8 recalls Pitt's sandwich-man?

9 would have been booked to by Tyburn spectators.

10 would probably have been the goal of Aldgate pump's nocturnal stroll?

• 7 • *Of what literary works and written by whom, are the following the second or alternative titles:*

1 *A Novel Without a Hero?*

2 *A History of a Father and Son?*

3 *'Tis Sixty Years Since?*

4 *A Pure Woman?*

5 *What You Will?*

6 *A Tale of Manchester Life?*

7 *A Metabiological Pentateuch?*

8 *The World of School?*

9 *The Story of a Simple Soul?*

10 *The Parish Boy's Progress?*


• 8 • *What Cook:*

1 suggested a fillet of fenny snake?

2 allowed political to oust culinary cares?

3 gave his name to the larder?

4 claimed to have discovered the refrigerator?

5 advised the capture of the lepus?

6 began his career with a special from Leicester to Loughborough?

7 had her pastries stolen by her son?

8 entered her oven?

9 poisoned the episcopal porridge?

10 found his discovery of the Sandwiches fatal?


• 9 •

1 what is the port of La Rochelle?

2 to what port do steamers green and gold sail?

3 what Oceanic port is named after an English Queen?

4 what French port borrowed its name from its opposite number?

5 what British port (in 1944) handles the greatest tonnage?

6 what is the port of Athens?

7 to what port do the stately ships go on?

8 what is the official residence of the Warden of the Cinque Ports?

9 what port gives access to Amsterdam?

10 what port is the desideratum during a hurricane?

QUESTIONS

## • 10 • *Whose biographer wrote:*

1   *Account of Corsica?*
2   *Wives and Daughters?*
3   *The Arrest of the Five Members?*
4   *The Ancient Spanish Ballads?*
5   *Irmingland Hall?*
6   *Elizabeth and Essex?*
7   *Midwinter?*
8   *The River War?*
9   *Sartor Resartus?*
10  *Hard Times?*

## • 11 • *What suicide:*

1   burnt Colchester?
2   fell upon his sword?
3   produced a post-mortem echo?
4   was unstrung by somnambulism?
5   destroyed himself in a public bath?
6   died to the strains of *The Star Spangled Banner?*
7   interrupted a race meeting?
8   leapt from the parapet of Saint Angelo?
9   placed a full confession in his right boot?
10  acted on the principle of *tel oncle, tel neveu?*

## • 12 • *With what Dutch town do you associate:*

1   Catriona?
2   Hugo Grotius?
3   William the Silent?
4   Peter the Great?
5   Oliver Goldsmith?
6   Thomas à Kempis?
7   Adrian VI?
8   Erasmus?
9   Francis Cludde?
10  Peace?

- 13 • *What baby:*
  1   was housed in *Typha latifolia?*
  2   had his heel seized by his twin?
  3   had his heel seized by his mother?
  4   would have troubled Serjeant Buzfuz?
  5   was chastised for sneezing?
  6   was a serpent constrictor?
  7   'Promised upon this land a thousand thousand blessings'?
  8   upset, by his death, the partition of an empire?
  9   had a daddy in the cotton fields?
  10  evinced a taste for chronometry?

- 14 • *What Irishman:*
  1   had his clothes eaten by rats when travelling to the USA?
  2   was promoted from Private to Colonel in a day?
  3   said 'We'll burn all English imports except coal'?
  4   'Tipped the wink' to his deformed little friend?
  5   expressed in music his desire to fall like a soldier?
  6   said that Mr Churchill was the Prince of Prime Ministers?
  7   'Went through life with a workman's hod'?
  8   was (in 1944) a BBC female impersonator?
  9   proved that one can be clergyman and author too?
  10  claimed that one can be clergyman and Irishman too?

- 15 •
  1   who first ran with the ball?
  2   who made 570 runs in a single wicket match?
  3   what game takes its name from the Tibetan for 'ball'?
  4   who refused to be hustled in his drawing to the Jack?
  5   what game was Leys the first school to play?
  6   whose game of what did a rebellion not interrupt?
  7   who played what with a flamingo?
  8   who should play with elliptical billiard balls?
  9   what game is also called shinty?
  10  who uttered an oath in the Tennis Court?

• 16 • *What notable character:*

1   spent his birthday in the cellar?
2   invented un-birthday presents?
3   was prohibited from cooking on her birthday?
4   celebrated a corsair's birthday every four years?
5   was born on the day of Frederick the Great's death?
6   had a birthday of Imperial significance?
7   was born on Christmas Day, as was her niece 35 years later?
8   returned 'from his travels' on his birthday?
9   wrote of his wife, on his birthday, that it was meet that 'the wretch' should have some enjoyment?
10  died on his birthday?

• 17 • *From what royal pens do the following emanate:*

1   For idleness is chief mistress of vices all,
    Then who can say but mirth and play is best of all?
2   Entre ses mains et en son plein pouvoir,
    Je mets mon fils, mon honneur et ma vie,
    Mon pays, mes sujets, mon âme?
3   O Death, rock me asleep,
    Bring on my quiet rest
    Let pass my very guiltless ghost
    Out of my careful breast?
4   Vénus était blonde, l'on m'a dit:
    L'on voit bien qu'elle est brunette?
5   Their brags did threat our ruin and decay;
    What came thereof the issue did declare:
    ... ... ... ...
    But how were all these things so strangely done?
    God looked at them from out His heavenly throne?
6   Vous nous faites de mal-faire défense
    Vous défendez de tuer, à chacun,
    Mais vous tuez sans épargner aucun?

7    Was never in Scotland heard or seen
    Sic dancing nor deray

    … … … …

    As was of wooers, as I ween,
    At Christ's Kirk on ane day?

8    Excellent sovereign, seemly to see,
    Proved prudence, peerless of price;
    Bright blossom of benignity,
    Of figure fairest, and freshest of days?

9    Nouvelles ont couru en France,
    Par maints lieux, que j'étais mort,
    Dont avalent peu de déplaisance
    Aucuns qui me haïsset à tort?

10   The daughter of debate, that eke discord doth sow,
    Shall reap no gain, where former rule hath taught still peace to grow?

• 18 • *In 1944:*

1    how many Times has the Thunderer pealed?
2    who has abdicated after a golden reign of 24 years?
3    what unpalatable 'mixture as before' has been swallowed?
4    how have the Principality's majority rights been deferred?
5    over whom has the curtain, that should have been the Queen's and not the Prince Consort's, fallen?
6    what *Te Deum* was a *Nunc Dimittis* manqué?
7    how has Charlotte Corday's progress been repeated?
8    what insular governorship has been rendered vacant?
9    what Julian feat has been repeated?
10   what diurnal importance has half an Etruscan thousand assumed?

# 1945

**• 1 •**  *What Peace or Treaty:*
1 produced a *Te Deum* from Handel?
2 'passeth' said Carson 'all understanding'?
3 was called 'the Ladies'?
4 was the first triumph of 'the Peacemaker'?
5 was coupled with honour?
6 should have deleted Mary's internal inscription?
7 set Congress dancing?
8 gave the Cape to the Dutch?
9 'had to pay to get the men to go away'?
10 is housed by Mme Tussaud?

**• 2 •**  *Whom do you specially connect with:*
1 an ear?
2 a nose?
3 teeth?
4 a rib?
5 a lady's mouth, for painting?
6 a left shoulder blade?
7 a fair round belly?
8 feet and ankle bones?
9 a little neck?
10 some neck?

• 3 • *What British Prime Minister:*

1  barred his windows?
2  promised rare and refreshing fruit?
3  invoked a boast of ancient Rome?
4  advised questioners to wait and see?
5  trained 'the most interesting mind in the world'?
6  chewed?
7  opined that a 'No Trespassers' notice would cost a crown or two?
8  is commemorated by a Pennsylvanian city?
9  suffered from an ambiguous Royal message 'His favourite flower'?
10  stated an unprecedented debit?

• 4 • *State the difference between:*

1  Magdalen and Magdalene
2  Bevin and Bevan
3  Queen and Quean
4  Thame and Thames
5  Manège and Ménage
6  Manet and Monet
7  Jenny Lee and Nancy Lee
8  Marat and Marot
9  Francis and Frances
10  Wimbledon and Wombledon

• 5 • *What garden or gardens:*

1  were suspended?
2  was viewed through a keyhole?
3  emitted Pison?
4  contained cockleshells?
5  received the body of a strangled king?
6  are traversed by cool waters?
7  was Maud's haunt?
8  gave its name to a sect?
9  contained Hera's apples?
10  and gallant walks are continually green?

**• 6 •** *What is the meaning of the following slang from the Services:*

1  shoot a line?
2  jankers?
3  erk?
4  pranged?
5  in the drink?
6  char?
7  wallop?
8  to Roman Candle?
9  brewed up?
10  wimpey?

**• 7 •** *With what introduction do you connect:*

1  'Dr – – – – I presume'?
2  'Harris, fetch me the brandy'?
3  'Sweetheart, I was unmannerly to take you out and not to kiss you'?
4  '– – – – is my name and – – – – my nater'?
5  'My Lord of Canterbury, we greet you well'?
6  'Hullo my covey, what's the row'?
7  'Out of the camp of Israel am I escaped'?
8  'I am that – – – – whom men call fair'?
9  ' Messieurs, je vous présente le roi d'Espagne'?
10  '– – – – mutton; mutton – – – –'?

**• 8 •** *Who was or is the Lady of:*

1  The Shawl?
2  The Lamp?
3  The Lake?
4  England?
5  Sorrows?
6  Shalott?
7  The Camelias?
8  The Snows?
9  Lyons?
10  Mann?

**• 9 •** *What Shakespearean character said the following, and in what play:*

1   But we will draw the curtain and show you the picture,
Look you, Sir, such a *one* as I was this present.

2   Here come *two* noble beasts in, a moon and a lion.

3   Come the *three* corners of the world in arms,
And we shall shock them:

4   Do not our lives consist of the *four* elements.

5   Full fathom *five* thy father lies;
Of his bones are coral made;

6   I think there be *six* Richmonds in the field;
Five have I slain instead of him.

7   Upon a lieu *seven* times removed;

8   You'll pay me the *eight* shillings I won of you at betting?

9   A tanner will last you *nine* year.

10   I will be bound to pay it *ten* times o'er,
On forfeit of my hands, my head, my heart.

**• 10 •** *Who officiated at the following weddings:*

1   Lammle — Akersham?

2   Knightley — Woodhouse?

3   Adriatic — Venice?

4   Hood — Marian?

5   Trundle — Wardle?

6   Arabin — Bold?

7   Bothwell — Stuart?

8   Wettin — Guelph?

9   Hapsburg — Tudor?

10   Tudor — Seymour?

## • 11 •

1 who introduced crushed bones into China?
2 what China ware should have been dear to Carlyle?
3 what China factory moved from St Cloud?
4 with what China do you connect shepherdesses?
5 who opened the Etruria works?
6 what Dutch town is the equivalent of the English Ware?
7 where does *Grès de Flandres* ware come from?
8 what dynasty produced the *Sang de Boeuf*?
9 what potting ground became a cemetery for foreigners?
10 what Railway Stock is known as Pots?

## • 12 • *Who or what is:*

1 Limbus?
2 Nimbus?
3 Thrombus?
4 Agabus?
5 Gibus?
6 Circumbendibus?
7 Phœbus?
8 Harquebus?
9 Erebus?
10 Cottabus?

## • 13 •

1 Take what said who?
2 Do not be indecisive in asking for what?
3 Neither a superfluity nor a scantiness of what?
4 Taking lessons for future beauty by means of what?
5 What keenness in battledress?
6 Three score lass three to choose from.
7 Your smile shows that you did – – – – what?
8 Produce what without ovoids, hazard, or inconvenience?
9 Prevent that submerging sensation with what?
10 My goodness my – – – –?

## • 14 •

1 what do kind hearts outvalue?
2 who is the saint of the flaming heart?
3 in what heart were Scotchmen imprisoned?
4 where does Bruce's heart repose?
5 and Edward I's?
6 and Richard I's?
7 what is the happy termination of the Valentia cable?
8 what is the facile synonym of Love in Idleness?
9 what is the Heart of Imperial significance?
10 'The sea hath its pearls, my heart hath – – – –'?

## • 15 • *What:*

1 bells instruct people to come and pray?
2 bells confer a capital right?
3 bell says 'I am – – – –, I am – – – –, there is victory in the land'?
4 bells have a fruity implication?
5 bells tinkle to Planquette's inspiration?
6 bells sound so grand on the River Lee?
7 bells did Trotty Veck insist could beat a Nor' Wester?
8 bell says 'Vivos voco – – – – Mortuos plango – – – – Fulgura frango'?
9 bells caused the man who was half a clown to laugh?
10 says London's Big Ben?

## • 16 • *Whose murderer:*

1 was called the 'Angel of the Assassination'?
2 came to the Isle of Dogs?
3 confessed to the use of a bow and arrow?
4 wore gyves upon his wrists?
5 denied the custody of his victim?
6 provided Jezebel with a query?
7 made wireless history?
8 anticipated the date of the Versailles Treaty for his exploit?
9 wished to marry his victim's sister?
10 had not been exposed by Gadshill?

• 17 • *From what poems, by whom, do the following lines come:*

1    Now joy, Old England raise
     For the tidings of thy might,
     By the festal cities' blaze,
     Whilst the wine cup shines in light?

2    When the oldest cask is opened
     And the largest lamp is lit;
     When the chestnuts glow in the embers
     And the kid turns on the spit?

3    O may this bounteous God
     Through all our life be near us,
     With ever joyful hearts and blessed peace to cheer us?

4    The time draws near the birth of Christ
     ... ... ... ...
     The Christmas bells from hill to hill
     Answer each other in the mist
     ... ... ... ...
     Peace and goodwill to all mankind?

5    How beautiful are the feet of those
     That preach the Gospel of Peace?

6    Peace, perfect Peace, death shadowing us and ours
     Jesus hath vanquished death and all its powers?

7    But O my country's wintry state
     What second spring shall renovate
     What powerful call shall bid arise
     The buried warlike and the wise?

8    A garden is a lovesome thing, God wot!
     ... ... ... ...
     The veriest school
     Of peace; and yet the fool
     Contends that God is not?

9         Yet much remains
     To conquer still; peace hath her victories
     No less renowned than war; new foes arise?

10  Let us then be up and doing,
     With a heart for any fate;
     Still achieving, still pursuing,
     Learn to labour and to wait?

• 18 • *In 1945:*

1   what Captain has handed over his Ship of State?
2   who wished to dispense with sponsors?
3   how has the *vox populi* become rubric?
4   who has lain a-thynkynge for 100 years?
5   to whom might London have exclaimed 'A Daniel come to judgment'?
6   what Queens have moved thousands?
7   what canine and infernal names have had a brumous and oleaginous connection?
8   what centenary has the ever-open door celebrated?
9   what alfresco concilium has become royal?
10  what Corellian work might be sub-titled 'Tube Alloys'?

# 1946–1947

**• 1 •**  (1946, 1)

1 who attended a midnight skating excursion?

2 whose gaoler should have exhibited a 'No instruments' notice?

3 who was braver than Miss Muffet?

4 who exploited his infant's muteness?

5 who rebuked his sister for marrying thrice?

6 who objected to being publicly décolletée before decollation?

7 who wrangled with whom up the aisle?

8 who preferred human to chevaline legs?

9 who considered enlarging his Burke to carry his Bouncing Bill?

10 who declared that either her guest or herself should leave the castle?

**• 2 •**  (1946, 2) *What is or was The City of:*

1 Refuge?

2 the Sun?

3 the Violated Treaty?

4 Saints?

5 Legions?

6 Brotherly Love?

7 Destruction?

8 the Tribes?

9 Beautiful Nonsense?

10 Lilies?

**• 3 •**  (1946, 7)

1   what fruity transmogrification has Vanbrugh's chef d'œvre achieved?

2   what fruit did Richard III reserve as dessert to whose execution?

3   whose eating of what fruit caused an annual descent?

4   what fruit grows there where whose lips do smile?

5   what fruit does what prophet blame for hereditary dental acidity?

6   what fruit was Mrs Norris assured by whom was 'insipid at best'?

7   whose royal head did the Mess symbolize at dessert by what fruit?

8   after what French Queen is what fruit named?

9   who purchased what fruit at Samarcand as a panacea?

10   affirmatively we are out of what?

**• 4 •**  (1946, 8) *Whose servant:*

1   poured beer into her master's gun?

2   'kept the wicket'?

3   assumed a niveous hue?

4   destroyed her master's masterpiece?

5   produced a pudding fit for a glass case?

6   rode Dapple?

7   served a brazen household?

8   married 'her dear master'?

9   was good and faithful?

10   ousted Sarah?

**• 5 •**  (1946, 9)

1   who founded a Club in the painted porch?

2   of what Club were the 48 members painted by Kneller?

3   what Club was founded by the Great Duke?

4   what Club would you join if interested in fat cattle?

5   what Club founder made the prefix of his name the suffix?

6   why has the Nihon-Jin-Kwai Club shut?

7   whom does the Gresham Club chiefly attract?

8   what Club is the arbiter of Bridge?

9   what Club was founded by Arthur?

10   what did Twemlow consider the best Club in London?

## • 6 •  (1946, 13)

1  what bed was 12 feet square?
2  whose bed became a lupine lair?
3  where were the beds so soft that the flowers slept?
4  what Welshman expiated his larceny in bed?
5  what bed was the seat of justice?
6  who could not lend what because he was in bed?
7  where did the martlet make its pendent bed?
8  whose bed-ward rush was checked by Slow?
9  who lent a narcotic bed?
10  who wrote of a 'terribly strange bed'?

## • 7 •  (1946, 15) *What women are referred to in the following:*

1  The Woman Thou gavest me?
2  'Peace Woman.' The Bishop jumped?
3  He has bowed to That Woman?
4  The Woman in White?
5  A Woman of no importance?
6  The Woman of Knockaloe?
7  The Moabitish Woman?
8  The Scarlet Woman?
9  'But you are such an unreasonable Woman' said Mr Benjamin Allen?
10  Little Women?

## • 8 •  (1946, 16) *Who was the more famous sister of:*

1  Fatima?
2  Helenus?
3  Stheno?
4  Anne of Wildfell Hall?
5  Aglaia?
6  Marie Christine of Saxony?
7  Laurence Hope?
8  Miss Barbary?
9  Bianca?
10  Mary Carey?

• 9 •  (1946, 17) *To what disaster do the following lines by whom refer:*

1  Avenge, O Lord, the slaughtered saints whose bones
   Lie scattered on the Alpine mountains cold?

2  A land breeze shook the shrouds
   And she was overset?

3  But the noblest thing that perished there
   Was that young faithful heart?

4  She with all a monarch's pride
   … … … …
   Rushed to battle, fought, and died?

5  The shrieks of death through Berkeley's roof that ring,
   Shrieks of an agonizing King?

6  While round the armed bands
   Did clap their bloody hands.
   He nothing common did or mean?

7  Tell it not in Gath
   Publish it not in the streets of Askelon?

8  Who knows if he be dead?
   Whether I need have fled?
   Am I guilty of blood?

9  Christ save us all from a death like this
   On the reef of Norman's woe?

10  But now the inly-working North
   Was ripe to send its thousands forth
   … … … …
   In Percy's and in Neville's right?

## • 10 • (1947, 1) *What Royal Marriage*:

1    united monarch and mendicant?
2    caused the Seine to burst its banks?
3    succeeded a wooing under the oak?
4    coincided with the royal obsequies?
5    meant a change of a crown for the bride?
6    witnessed the bridegroom 'hiccoughing out his vows of fidelity'?
7    saw a bride of seven?
8    brought death to its denouncer?
9    was preceded by the bride being dragged by her hair?
10    brought a bride to 'the heir of the Kings of the Sea'?

## • 11 • (1947, 3)

1    whose patient could furnish no grounds for antagonism?
2    whose case was diagnosed as ghostly rather than medicinal?
3    whose doctors (while taking their fees) pronounced what disease incurable?
4    who was the seraphic Doctor?
5    what is the piscatorial Doctor?
6    what is the vinous Doctor?
7    who refuted the medical opinion: 'She must be bled or she will die'?
8    whose patient ate five apples and a gingerbread cake, two minutes after an amputation?
9    who prescribed gruel to whom?
10    what Doctor raised Mrs Dombey to the peerage?

## • 12 • (1947, 4)

1    in whose crown did the Koh-i-noor first appear?
2    who first wore the Cullinan?
3    who was the Saint of the Iron Crown?
4    what state inaugurated the Crown of Rue?
5    who was crowned with a plain gold band?
6    what used to be woman's crowning glory?
7    where did one find the Crown of the East?
8    for what was the mural crown awarded?
9    who was crowned with a smoking wreath?
10    I'd crowns resign to call whom mine?

• 13 • (1947, 6)

1   who must go to church decently habited?
2   when shall the minister be discreet and wary?
3   what is the duty of Dames towards apprentices?
4   what is the security for those passing upon their lawful occasions?
5   what objections may precede the Benedictus?
6   where are threats uttered against those who mislead the blind?
7   when is the Canticle sung?
8   who authorizes the reading of Tobias?
9   when did Mr Sawyer's boy rush into Church?
10   what is the prayer book's last prohibition?

• 14 • (1947, 8) *What lunatic*:

1   flew kites?
2   was interested in apple-dumplings?
3   travelled with sepulchral luggage?
4   knew a lover by his sandal shoon?
5   wooed his love with vegetable marrows?
6   made his shoemaker swallow his shoes?
7   committed arson?
8   is adored by grateful science?
9   favoured Wagner?
10   produced the Hilarious Rustic?

• 15 • (1947, 9)

1   what Emperor took his name from his beard?
2   who had a grey beard and an eye that sparkled?
3   whose love was 'in their hearts, not in their beards'?
4   who was the 'bearded master'?
5   what barbal outrage did the Ammonites commit on David's envoys?
6   who considered his soldiers' beards too easy a purchase?
7   who dedicated his beard to Jupiter Capitolinus?
8   what Pope first discarded his beard?
9   who was the Tussaud Bluebeard?
10   who offered to act in a purple-in-grain beard?

- 16 • (1947, 10) *Who went to:*

1    Canossa?

2    Endor?

3    Normandie?

4    Azotus?

5    El Dorado?

6    Concord Town?

7    Dothan?

8    Munich?

9    Edmonton?

10   St Ives?


- 17 • (1947, 11) *What political figure uttered the following:*

1    'Let us squeeze the lemon till the pips squeak'?

2    'A rhetorician intoxicated with the exuberance of his own verbosity'?

3    'The House of Commons is full of ex-future Prime Ministers'?

4    'While we have good government, we have very bad people'?

5    'The Angel of Death has been abroad throughout the land; you may almost hear the beating of his wings'?

6    'The lights are going out all over Europe'?

7    'The Right Honourable Gentleman has been sitting on the fence so long that the iron has entered into his soul'?

8    'By God, Mr Chairman, I stand astonished at my own moderation'?

9    'I stand here, not only astonished at our moderation, but almost aghast'?

10   'The French don't like us? Why should they?'

• 18 • (1947, 17) *In reference to what marriage did who write the following*:

1   O stay, O stay, thou gallant youth
    She standeth by thy side –
    She's here alive, she is not dead,
    But ready to be thy bride?

2   Archly the maiden smiled and, with eyes over-running with laughter,
    Said in a tremulous voice, 'Why don't you speak for yourself John'?

3   Who'll come to my wedding?
    All those who love the blue sky above,
    And the green grass to lie upon, 'tis better than bedding?

4   So passed the strong heroic soul away,
    And when they buried him, the little port
    Had seldom seen a costlier funeral?

5   O perfect love, all human thought transcending,
    Lowly we kneel in prayer before Thy throne.
    That theirs may be the love which knows no ending,
    Whom Thou for evermore dost join in one?

6   Comes the pretty young bride, a-blushing, timidly shrinking –
    Set all thy fears aside, cheerily pretty young bride,
    Brave is the youth to whom thy lot thou art willingly linking?

7   My beloved spake, and said to me,
    'Rise up my love, my fair one, and come away,
    For, lo, the winter is past, the rain is over and gone'?

8   – – – – The eldest child of Liberty
    … … … …
    And when she took unto herself a mate,
    She must espouse the everlasting sea?

9   So stately his form, and so lovely his face,
    That never a hall such a galliard did grace?

10   It is I. O Love! What bliss!
    Dost thou answer to my kiss?
    O sweetheart! What is this
    Lieth there so cold?

# 1948–1949

• 1 • (1948, 1) *What Royal infant:*

1 was 'not a little girl'?

2 took seizin of the rushes?

3 was born in Sanctuary?

4 was as like its Father as 'cherry is to cherry'?

5 was also named Jedidiah?

6 was nearly named Cadwallader?

7 was exploited as having no English?

8 was not the lass with whom it went?

9 had his peace of mind broken more than Serjeant Buzfuz allowed?

10 elicited from Punch the lines:

'Huzza! We've a little Prince at last,

A roaring Royal boy'?


• 2 • (1948, 2) *Who was or were:*

1 King of King's?

2 Queen of Queen's?

3 Queens of Queens'?

4 Lord of Lord's?

5 Duke of Duke's Meadow?

6 Earl of Earl's Court?

7 Regent of Regent Street?

8 Bishop of Bishop's Stortford?

9 Prince of Prince's Risborough?

10 Canons of Canonbury?

• 3 •   (1948, 3) *What window:*

    1    was really in Kirriemuir?
    2    betrayed the Royal Corpulance?
    3    admitted the morning peeper?
    4    released the tresses?
    5    preceded a sneeze into the sack?
    6    was fatal to the Queen-Dowager?
    7    was called an Ancient Light?
    8    showed a many towered view?
    9    framed an 'arrum'?
    10   provided work for the Head boy?


• 4 •   (1948, 4)

    1    what is a Knight of the Pestle?
    2    who was the Night of the Burning Pestle?
    3    what is a Knight of Labour?
    4    what was a Knight of Industry?
    5    what is a Knight of St Crispin?
    6    who was the Knight of the Swan?
    7    what is a Knight of the Carpet?
    8    what is a Knight of the Spigot?
    9    what is a Knight of the Stick?
    10   who was the Knight of the Rueful Countenance?


• 5 •   (1948, 7)

    1    what's for Remembrance?
    2    what begin to ope their golden eyes?
    3    every morn I bring thee what?
    4    from what has a splendid tear fallen?
    5    what folds all its sweetness up?
    6    what grows on the bank?
    7    who'll buy what?
    8    the fairest Queen, it is I ween … ?
    9    what stand like Druids of eld?
    10   a day beside what is a day of days?

**• 6 •** (1948, 10) *To what Samuels are the following sayings attributable:*

1 No, No; reg'lar rotation, as Jack Ketch said?

2 Foreigners always spell better than they pronounce?

3 Up and to Church, and a lazy sermon?

4 In hac domo quam a vermiculis accepi confratibus meis jaceo Sam ... vide ac ride palatium episcopi?

5 Was there anything, Sir?

6 Claret is the liquor for boys?

7 Oh Sleep, it is a gentle thing,
Beloved from pole to pole?

8 What makes all doctrines plain and clear?
About two hundred pounds a year?

9 Chops and Tomata sauce?

10 To obey is better than sacrifice and to harken, than the fat of rams?


**• 7 •** (1948, 12)

1 what sprang from the forehead of Jupiter?

2 who was born and bred in a briar bush?

3 what new-born boys are presented with arrows?

4 who rose from the ocean?

5 what twins emerged from one egg?

6 who was born with a caul?

7 whose birth altered the Shakespearean ship's course?

8 who was fed from birth on the sap of the ash?

9 whose stunted arm was due to inattention at birth?

10 who growed?

**• 8 •**  (1948, 15)

1    who telegraphed to whom 'He's up'?

2    what telegram drew from the *Saturday Review*, 'Germania delenda est'?

3    whose laureate telegram reduced the Royal recovery to bathos?

4    what Telegraph was described as 'long winded and redundant'?

5    on what occasion was the Royal wrath not expressed in code?

6    what telegram was a *casus belli*?

7    how did Napier anticipate telegraphese?

8    how does the Chappe Telegram survive today?

9    who thought that telegraphy could not reach the *Montrose*?

10   whose telegram proved too gauche?

**• 9 •**  (1949, 1) *Complete the following items in Hatch, Match and Dispatch:*

1    At Blunderstone, to the widow of – – – –, a son.

2    At Highbury, – – – – of Donwell Abbey to – – – –, daughter of – – – – Woodhouse.

3    On May 19th on Tower Green, suddenly – – – – late beloved wife of – – – –.

4    In Westminster Sanctuary to – – – – wife of – – – – a son.

5    On the seventeenth instant, at St James' Church, Piccadilly – – – – of Sackville Street, Piccadilly to – – – – daughter of the late Horatio Askersham.

6    In a conflagration – – – –, in the absence of her aunt.

7    On Jan 31st, at Lichtenthal, Vienna, to Elizabeth wife of – – – –, a thirteenth child, a son.

8    At the Chapel of St Peter, Colonel – – – – to – – – –, late fiancée of Mr J Point.

9    On Sept 8th at Cumnor Place, through a mishap – – – – beloved wife of – – – –.

10   Since it is – – – – who was alive and is dead, there's no more to be said.

## • 10 • (1949, 2)

1     what is the Whig Bible?

2     what Prophet ends his book with a curse?

3     which and what are the Psalms of Ascents?

4     what is the Hexateuch?

5     which Prophet is the creator of Gog and Magog?

6     who confesses to being black but comely?

7     which Epistle is 'not an abolitionist pamphlet'?

8     what is the Vinegar Bible?

9     what is the Biblia Pauperum?

10     what in bible Literature is 'Q'?

## • 11 • (1949, 4)

1     what feature of *Punch* recalls a mésalliance?

2     what month did *Punch* describe as turning Traitor?

3     what did the Peebles visitor's London pleasures cost?

4     what is *Punch*'s example of saponaceous thrift?

5     what advice does du Maurier make the widow give the neglected wife?

6     what master mariner does Tenniel portray as relieving whom of his licence?

7     who illustrated the *Diary of Toby, MP*?

8     who would admit only partial deterioration?

9     to what interview does Bernard Partridge affix the word 'Unconquerable'?

10     what is *Punch*'s hymeneal advice?

## • 12 • (1949, 5)

1     who took her stand on a purple cauliflower?

2     who found the right side of the mushroom depressing?

3     who reduced his sister-in-law to tears by eating all the peas?

4     what is a potato-bogle?

5     who darkened the sky with a shower of onions, turnip-radishes and other small vegetables?

6     how did Rice cause a Cabbage-patch to flourish?

7     who envied what their husks?

8     what do the French mean by a Gros Légume?

9     who addressed whom as 'Young brockiley sprout'?

10     whose sobriquet was derived from the natural order *Cruciferae*?

• 13 • (1949, 6) *What (or whose) swindle:*

1 caused the suicide of the PMG?

2 bubbled in Dixie?

3 caused whom to write 'Jolly', feebly, on a slate?

4 brought the Rowley Poems into disrepute?

5 involved the magic mirror?

6 was shared in by husband and wife?

7 was perpetrated against the Delft Master?

8 led to a suicide in a hot bath?

9 is guarded against by the Counterfeit Medals Act?

10 might have called for a Counterfeit Gloves Act?

• 14 • (1949, 9)

1 what service witnessed a display of tabouret work?

2 whose sermon carried the congregation to the edge of the precipice?

3 where did the Upper Ten flock to hear whom castigate the sins of Society?

4 who preached where on the dispersion of rooks?

5 what wedding was interrupted by the apparition of whose face at successive windows?

6 at whom was aimed the sermon on the text 'I have married a wife'?

7 what service was 'abruptly suspended, while the multitude wept like children'?

8 who attempted a gate crash in pursuit of a Crown?

9 who admonished the preacher to keep his arithmetic to himself?

10 who came to the village church, and sat by a pillar alone?

## • 15 • (1949, 10) *What Princess:*

1    was the first Princess Royal?

2    though of German origin became a Savoyard?

3    laid down the style regnal?

4    was made to kiss a rebel?

5    looked, decapitated, through her friend's window?

6    was proxy-wedded with a bootless calf?

7    partly recalls 'the sweetest blossom that in the garden grows'?

8    was lampooned with a jack-boot?

9    gave Mason a plot?

10    wrote on a window:

> 'Much suspected – of me
> Nothing proved can be
> Quoth – – – –, prisoner'?

## • 16 • (1949, 11)

1    what clearance scheme was contracted for, for 1000 guilders?

2    what were the pounds when the demd total added 4s. 9½d.?

3    whose person was valued at 20 pieces of silver?

4    whose at one groat?

5    who resented being priced at 1s. 8d. instead of 2s. 3d.?

6    what 'No thoroughfare' notice would have cost 3 crowns?

7    against what ½d. patent did W B Draper protest?

8    who paid whom £3000 a year for the substitution of fraternal for conjugal rights?

9    who punished absenteeism with a 1s. fine, instead of greater fuel production?

10    who considered that an annual expenditure of £20 ought and six, resulted in misery?

• 17 • (1949, 14)

  1    who tried to drown himself at the Custom House?

  2    what may Customs Officers be legally required to wear?

  3    who in what novel describes a fight with smugglers in Ramsey Bay?

  4    who considered Excise a hateful tax collected by wretches?

  5    when does Kipling advise you to watch the wall?

  6    who's awa' wi' the Exciseman?

  7    who smuggled his wife in a wooden box pierced with holes?

  8    who advised the smuggling of whom in a pianner forty, vun as von't play?

  9    what smuggler feared neither dog nor devil?

10    whose effigy as a fat woman was burnt in protest against Excise?

• 18 • (1949, 16) *Who sang:*

  1    tirra lira?

  2    both high, and low?

  3    so high, so low?

  4    as she went along?

  5    lyrics to the rose?

  6    praises among the nations?

  7    in the village choir?

  8    songs of love and songs of longing?

  9    what at Hastings?

10    Amen (at the door)?

# 1950

## • 1 •

1   whose son-in-law kept the family flocks?
2   whose step-mother combined stirrup-cup and dagger?
3   who was the mother of the Gracchi?
4   who was the mother of the modern Gracchi?
5   whose uncle was coupled with whose prophetic soul?
6   who was our cousin of Scotland?
7   whose father's wife was old and harsh with years?
8   whose grandchild sported with an osseous bowl?
9   whose mother-in-law changed her name from Pleasant to Bitter?
10  whose grandmother said 'William's faults come from conceit'?

**• 2 •** *Fill up the blanks in the following Personal Column:*

1     Wanted urgently, a reliable mount, in exchange for extensive hereditary estate. Apply – – – –.

2     Lost in the Wash, Jewels of value. Finders apply to – – – – Newark Castle.

3     You want the best poisons? We have them. Apply A– – – – B– – – – Mons Vaticanus.

4     T– – – – C– – – –. Meet Chertsey 1 am. Bring jemmies. B– – – – S– – – –.

5     Italian gentleman, keen on discovery. Go anywhere. Patronized by Royalty. Apply C– – – – C– – – – Valladolid.

6     Cellar wanted for November. Westminster District. Large rent guaranteed. Apply – – – – – – – –.

7     Privated Detective Agency, Shadowing, Deduction. Dr – – – – says 'My dear – – – – you amaze me.'

8     Room to let in Scottish Castle, owing to sudden vacancy. Porter kept. Moving view of woods. Apply – – – –.

9     Executions undertaken. Many unsolicited testimonials. Apply J– – – – K– – – –, T– – – – Tree.

10    Secluded Island residence offered. Off the Orinoco. Burglar proof. Devoted domestic staff. Apply – – – –.

**• 3 •**

1     what race would not be acceptable in Moscow?

2     in what race did a poorly directed banner result in a lady's death?

3     from where was the race run by a Boomer started?

4     what racing success cheered a King's deathbed?

5     who raced a Berlin to Varennes?

6     who was lost in the Race of Gatteville?

7     who won the Caucus Race?

8     where is the Portland Plate run?

9     in what race was Mrs Jarley interested?

10    to whom is the race not?

• 4 • *What is the Land of:*

1   Oc et No?
2   Handsome Women?
3   Lost content?
4   The great departed?
5   Love and land of mirth?
6   Wandering?
7   Blue Laws?
8   The Leal?
9   Promise?
10  Always Afternoon?


• 5 •

1   what proportion of the wedding guests was stopped?
2   how many people went into the Ark?
3   how many people came out of the Black Hole?
4   how many little maids 'won't have to wait very long they say'?
5   to how many members is the Order of Merit limited?
6   how many children had Count Abensberg?
7   how many players are there in a baseball team?
8   this night the Queen will 'hae' how many Marys?
9   how many of us in the Church-yard lie?
10  'With one man of her crew alive
    That went to sea with – – – –' ?

**· 6 ·**

1   from whose reign does the 'Contested Election' date?

2   who told a new Parliament that liberty of speech extended no further than 'Aye' or 'No'?

3   who was returned for Pocket Breaches?

4   who was not returned for Eatanswill?

5   who was expelled and returned for Middlesex?

6   whose 'Benefit of Clergy' did not prevent his Parliamentary disqualification?

7   for what seat was Mr Nearthewinde political agent?

8   what 'grassy mound' returned two members of Parliament?

9   to what cave were the opponents of Reform in 1866 relegated?

10  who was the correspondent of the Red Letter Election?

**· 7 ·** *Who met in single combat:*

1   Paris?

2   Wellington?

3   Castlereagh?

4   Slammer?

5   Robin Hood?

6   Laertes?

7   Lovel?

8   Rustum?

9   Miss Pross?

10  The Red Knight?

**· 8 ·**

1   who escaped with the skin of his teeth?

2   whose ultimatum was 'Your money or your teeth'?

3   whose tooth did treble duty?

4   who extracted a bishop's tooth in what riots?

5   where is the Tooth of the South?

6   whose councillors offered to have a tooth out as an encouragement?

7   what dental adornment can architecture boast?

8   whose tooth is less noxious than unthankfulness?

9   what Blue Tooth was father of a Split Beard?

10  who, being in liquor, struck out four, two singles and two doubles?

## • 9 • *Identify the Man of:*

1 Blood.
2 Blood and Iron.
3 Brass.
4 December.
5 Destiny.
6 Straw.
7 Sin.
8 Wrath.
9 Ross.
10 The Hill.

## • 10 •

1 who was, by implication, half-baptized?
2 who resolved to be new-baptized; ... 'henceforth I will never be ...'?
3 on whom was Alexandrina forced, as a first name?
4 in confirmation of what name did the dumb speak?
5 whose name was Mary too?
6 who objected to being called Mary, when her name was Miss – – – –?
7 whose two daughters escaped the name of Grissel?
8 at what Royal christening was there an unfortunate omission in the invitations?
9 who received her name 'for she was born at sea'?
10 whose name stood between Swubble and Unwin?

## • 11 • *Which Anne:*

1 became a Constable?
2 quarrelled with a Freeman?
3 mounted the watch-tower?
4 would not be queen for all the mud in Egypt?
5 gave Dumas a heroine?
6 insisted on refreshment before retiring?
7 came from Shottery?
8 came from Maxwellton?
9 came from Nazareth?
10 added lustre to Trafalgar Day?

# 1950

- 12 • *At what execution:*

1  did the two Gregories officiate?
2  did the victim squirm and struggle and gurgle and guggle?
3  did the victim rend her clothes, crying 'Treason, Treason'?
4  was it argued that anything that had a head could be beheaded?
5  had a sea green jaw to be first operated on?
6  did admirers sing 'would I might be hanged,' 'And I would so too'?
7  was barbigerous innocence affirmed?
8  was the gallows 50 cubits high?
9  may a silken rope be claimed?
10  might the victim have exclaimed 'Well I *am* hanged'?

- 13 •

1  who handled his reins *molto con fuoco*?
2  whose moral decline occurred *poco a poco*?
3  what headland faded *noblimente*?
4  when did Elijah urge a *crescendo*?
5  whom did we lay down from the field of his fame *lento e dolente*?
6  what rubicund monarch reiterated her injunction '*Piu presto*'?
7  whose song of the shirt had a nightly *da capo*?
8  what wind is desired to blow *dolce e piano*?
9  who repeated his intention of living *giocoso giocoso*?
10  in whose garden might the roses' entertainment be marked *tutti*?

- 14 •

1  what is a syzygy?
2  who composed the Seven Planets in seven movements?
3  against whom did the stars in their courses fight?
4  what Saint wears a star on his forehead?
5  what star is connected with the Lady of Eleven o'clock?
6  what is the distinction between Stars and Stripes?
7  to what star did Wulfram sing?
8  what Arch stands in the Starry Place?
9  of what star had Justice Darling never heard?
10  what star did Locke give to the world?

## • 15 •

1   where is only man vile?

2   where do we sing the glorious conquest?

3   Ah me! That I should stay where?

4   from where comes the cry of myriads as of one?

5   where did the reaper band go forth?

6   what excels all noble cities?

7   where rushed down the fires in sudden torrents?

8   whose days are long forgiven, unforgotten is the pain?

9   what rolled between the Jews and the sweet fields?

10   whose daughter shall be there with a gift?

## • 16 •

1   who painted the *Light of the World*?

2   who wrote the *Light of Asia*?

3   who claims the Lord's Illumination?

4   what is the *Ville Lumière*?

5   who was the Light of the Age?

6   what was the Light that failed?

7   how long is a Light-Year?

8   what legally is Light and Air?

9   who died desiring more light?

10   who died with the question, 'Is the light a-comin'?

## • 17 • *Who wrote of whom the following lines:*

1   O – – – –! To thee a streaming flood of woe,
    Sighing we pay, and think e'en conquest dear?

2   His form was of the manliest beauty,
    His heart was kind and soft?

3   O Mary, at thy window be,
    It is the wished, the trysted hour?

4   He spurred to the fort of the proud Castle rock
    And with the gay Gordon he gallantly spoke?

5   By each gun the lighted brand
    In a bold determined hand,
    And the Prince of all the land
    Led them on?

6   The Assyrian came down like the wolf on the fold,
    And his cohorts were gleaming in purple and gold?

7   And straight against that great array
    Forth went the dauntless three?

8   These to His Memory – since he held them dear,
    Perchance as finding there unconsciously
    Some image of himself – I dedicate – ?

9   He long lived the pride of that countryside,
    And at last in the odour of sanctity died?

10  Then he flung away his sail, and oars, and rudder,
    And he took her in his arms so tenderly,
    And they drifted on amain, and the bells may call in vain?

## • 18 • *In 1950:*

1   whose Pro-fumosity has created whom Lord Festival?
2   what has brought the orbs to the urbs?
3   what immortal has shown her mortality?
4   who has outrivalled Prince Housain and Axmunster?
5   who have prayed, face to the wall?
6   what bereavement has occurred in the House of Pontecorvo?
7   who has ceased to roam by the bonnie banks of Clyde?
8   who found that the Ayes had it, but inadequately?
9   whose after-dinner speech sped the parting guest?
10  who was told to chuck it?

# 1951

**• 1 •** *In 1851:*

1   what change of rôle was witnessed on the French stage?

2   what British Foreign Minister witnessed it too sympathetically?

3   what Anglo-German King died?

4   what Chancery suit began in a fog?

5   who proclaimed operatically the inconsistency of women?

6   at what London terminus did Cantabs arrive?

7   what Public School welcomed Clerical sons?

8   what assessor of a *situation excellent* was born?

9   who conducted at Covent Garden?

10   at what did Prince Henry first sing Amen?

**• 2 •**

1   what Exhibition induced fears in whom that the *entente* might be worn threadbare?

2   what Exhibition was marred by what assassination?

3   with what monument did the Dijon engineer commemorate what Exhibition?

4   what Exhibition was described as 'calm and classical'?

5   to what Exhibition did Offenbach contribute – with what?

6   what Exhibition is connected with what ducal gardener?

7   who complained that what Exhibition had been only half described?

8   what Exhibition was opened 'by wireless'?

9   what Tantalus Exhibition is for export only?

10   what is the Exhibition of domestic content?

**• 3 •**

1 what is Odic Force?

2 what is Aira Force?

3 what Force raised water to the Hanging Gardens?

4 what Force was instituted in 1814?

5 what Force startled Newton?

6 what Force clothes the Diane chasseresse?

7 what Force does Billiards afford?

8 of what Force did Verdi write?

9 what is the French House of Force?

10 what Force raised Sunny Jim?

**• 4 •**

1 what divides men of Kent from Kentish men?

2 what Kentish knight 'Stood for his King'?

3 what Kentish rebel kissed what Kentish maid?

4 what Kentish Duke added Strathearn to his title?

5 what Kentish watering place inspired what artist?

6 what Kentish coastal feature recalls 'the dread summit of this chalky bourn'?

7 what Kentish Queen eased the first Archbishop's task?

8 what is Kentish fire?

9 what Kentish railroad was credited with smashing and turning over?

10 'Kent, sir – everyone knows Kent – ' Why?

**• 5 •** *Where would you study:*

1 What they are saying?

2 Misleading cases?

3 Points from letters?

4 Inside information?

5 Far and near?

6 Sitting on the fence?

7 Marginal comment?

8 Atticus?

9 Profile?

10 Sportlight?

### • 6 •

1  from whose name is derived that of succeeding tombs?
2  to whom did we carve not a line nor raise a stone?
3  where is Tombland?
4  who directed her tomb to be inscribed 'By the wrath of God, Queen of England'?
5  whose tomb is described as a 'dream in marble'?
6  who rests in a porphyry sarcophagus *aux bords de la Seine*?
7  who forbade 'Mr' or 'Esquire' on his tomb?
8  whose family tomb was forced to open its rotten jaws?
9  whose tomb was the cave of Machpelah?
10  'Drive him fast to his tomb; this from – – – –'?

### • 7 •  *What Thomas was:*

1  turbulent?
2  rhythmical?
3  cold?
4  cast and was once Mary?
5  inquisitive?
6  larcenous?
7  dubitant?
8  long?
9  pensive?
10  this and that?

### • 8 •

1  who played the organ at Salisbury?
2  what made the banjo strings play out of tune?
3  who questioned Ben Bolt in a hypnotic condition?
4  who entertained her guests with an improved grand piano and an improvable voice?
5  what hired musician meditated an attack on the bridegroom?
6  what did we do with our harps?
7  who with what made the trees bow their heads?
8  who used saucers for castanets?
9  what air made the place start swaying?
10  who was inventress of the vocal frame?

• 9 • *In what works do the following perform what eponymous function:*

1 Backbite?
2 Poundtext?
3 Filgrave?
4 Howler?
5 Dauntless?
6 Prosee?
7 Worldly Wisemen?
8 Shallow?
9 Bones?
10 Froth?

• 10 • *Whose murderess:*

1 visited Horsemonger Lane in black satin?
2 disregarded bathroom etiquette?
3 gave him eels boiled in broo?
4 practised window dressing?
5 left him with the Roman pointing from the ceiling?
6 first offered refreshments on superior plate?
7 did not stop short at parricide?
8 expressed her opinion that he was dying?
9 never heard the roll of the tumbrils 'nor anything else in this world'?
10 turned quaternity into a trinity overnight?

• 11 • *What person or class do you connect with:*

1 GOM?
2 VIP?
3 PVPMPC?
4 DP?
5 AL?
6 WG?
7 BP?
8 RLS?
9 K of K?
10 Three B's?

**• 12 •**

1. whose tiny hand was frozen?
2. who was not a beauty, not a lady?
3. whom did bright eyes fondly regard?
4. who counselled himself to laugh?
5. for whom was room demanded?
6. who had sighed to rest him?
7. who shall we notice one fine day?
8. who were the Star of Renown and the Flower of the Earth?
9. whose heart softly awoke?
10. who depended for apparent juvenility on the position of the light?

**• 13 •** *Who sailed (most famously) in the:*

1. *Castor and Pollux?*
2. *Royal George?*
3. *Mora?*
4. *Montrose?*
5. *Screw?*
6. *Pelican?*
7. *Hampshire?*
8. *Empress of Scotland?*
9. *Bacchante?*
10. *Cautious Clara?*

**• 14 •** *Who or what:*

1. made a lunatic vault?
2. belied the promise of caudal completeness?
3. found rationing a problem in canine feeding?
4. would have saved a crown by domestic plumbing?
5. obviated washing up?
6. could sing after the ordeal by fire?
7. let fear triumph over entomology?
8. insisted on ranine courtship?
9. was premature in his East Anglian progress?
10. was recalled from the northern suburbs?

• 15 • *Of what tragedies were the following the scene:*

1  Gallion's Reach?

2  Sarajevo?

3  Silvertown?

4  Tay Bridge?

5  Kabul?

6  Algoa Bay?

7  Les Couronnes?

8  The Longstone?

9  Marche les Dames?

10  Phoenix Park?

• 16 • *Who stigmatized whom as:*

1  Bald head?

2  Cream faced?

3  Butcher's cur?

4  Twining serpiant?

5  Full of all subtilty?

6  Proud Prelate?

7  Cornet of Horse?

8  Unkind, untrue, unknightly?

9  Imperfect ablutioner?

10  Vermin?

• 17 • *On what revels did who write the following:*

1 There was a sound of revelry by night
   And Belgium's capital had gathered then
   Her beauty and her chivalry?

2 Sweet remembrancer!
   Now, good digestion wait on appetite,
   And health on both?

3 We'll usher him in with a merry din
   That shall gladden his joyous heart,
   And we'll keep him up, while there's bite or sup,
   And in fellowship good, we'll part?

4 Then fill up your glasses as quick as you can,
   And sprinkle the table with buttons and bran;
   Put cats in the coffee and mice in the tea – ?

5 The feast was over in – – – – tower,
   And the ladye had gone to her secret bower?

6 The feast was over, the board was cleared,
   The flawns and the custards had all disappeared?

7 Bacchus, ever fair and young,
   Drinking joys did first ordain;
   Bacchus' blessings are a treasure,
   Drinking is the soldiers' pleasure?

8 I said to the rose, 'The brief night goes
   In babble and revel and wine.'?

9 Then on pemmican they feasted,
   Pemmican and buffalo marrow,
   Haunch of deer and hump of bison ...
   And the wild rice of the river?

10 For eatin' and drinkin' there's heaps of bin-jean,
   And milk for the women and jough for the men?

• 18 • *In 1951:*

1    how has Joab's task been repeated?

2    what made a 'fence' of Arbroath?

3    where has the Playboy's play been stopped?

4    who did not find the simian graft infallible?

5    where did Cavaliers and Roundheads re-open the feud?

6    who has emulated Blondin?

7    who has shaken Manyfingers?

8    who has made a final return to her capital?

9    what wilderness is no longer Paradise enow?

10    how has St Crispin re-edified the Cinque Ports?

# 1952–1953

• 1 •  (1952, 1) *What Queen Regnant:*

1   was 'entirely English'?
2   came from Earth's uttermost parts?
3   was a male impersonator?
4   had 'never undressed before so much company'?
5   styled herself Queen of England, Spain, France, Sicily, Jerusalem, and Ireland?
6   lay 'robed and crowned worthy a Roman spouse'?
7   died on the crossing?
8   preserved her gravity?
9   allowed her treasurer to worship at Jerusalem?
10  was 'mere English'?

• 2 •  (1952, 2) *Who on accession said the following:*

1   'I will work as long as there is breath in my body'?
2   'It must have been my fault that I did not come home sooner'?
3   'I glory in the name of Briton'?
4   'Dat is one big lie'?
5   'Great God of Heaven say Amen to all'?
6   'When France is satisfied, the world is tranquil'?
7   'I will add to your yoke ... I will chastise you with scorpions'?
8   'It is a fine day'?
9   'Let me be by myself for an hour'?
10  *'A Domino factum est illud'*?

· 3 ·   (1952, 3)

  1    whose crown got onto her head without her knowing it?

  2    whose Knighthood was watched by the Spanish Ambassador?

  3    to whom was imputed consecration at the Nag's Head?

  4    who said to whom 'My Lord of Canterbury, we greet you well'?

  5    who cloaked his Kingship with the finding of the asses?

  6    who conferred Knighthood on the joint?

  7    whom would a 'threepence bow'd' have hired as Queen?

  8    who kissed hands at Biarritz?

  9    who was said to have played most foully for his throne?

10    whom can a breath make, as a breath has made?

· 4 ·   (1952, 4)

  1    what Mayor was a Queen's great-grandfather?

  2    what Mayor called the tune?

  3    what Mayor was adjured not to desert the nail and saucepan business?

  4    where must we look for Hardy's Mayor?

  5    what Mayor offered his besieged townsfolk his body to eat?

  6    what Mayor gave Richard his opportunity?

  7    what bells gave Richard his opportunity?

  8    to what Lord Mayor is Bill Sikes partial?

  9    who was the Mayor of the Palace?

10    what Lord Mayor represented S. Worcs?

· 5 ·   (1952, 6)

  1    who came to the dark tower?

  2    what tower slew eighteen?

  3    what place had a multiplicity of towers?

  4    what name was 105 North Tower?

  5    what tower foreshadowed Lake Success?

  6    what tower has a penchant for the south?

  7    what tower has the shape of a 'curved pyramid'?

  8    who bring their dead to the silent towers?

  9    on what 'lofty tower' did Longfellow stand?

10    Tower, Tower, Tower – – – –?

## • 6 •  (1952, 8) *Who in what song:*

1  claimed Hebraic Matriarchy?

2  serenaded a Royal captive?

3  uttered a threnody on an imbecile quadruped?

4  warbled alone in her joy?

5  treated of love and longing?

6  enquired particulars of the Duke of Milan's daughter?

7  celebrated the immersion of horse and rider?

8  sang in effect 'glitter flittermouse'?

9  demanded particulars of the yew-stave?

10  urged himself to proceed with his make-up?

## • 7 •  (1952, 12) *On what sea journey:*

1  was a pictorial effect presented by ship and sea?

2  did MacDowell found what Sea-piece?

3  was the smoke blown now west, now south?

4  did the commander turn executioner?

5  were the nymphs according to Milton guilty of inattention?

6  were land and sea stated to be equidistant from heaven?

7  did the centurion alone survive?

8  did the butcher alone survive?

9  did neither sun nor stars appear in many days?

10  did the bowsprit get mixed with the rudder?

## • 8 •  (1952, 15)

1  whose Poll was kind and fair?

2  who shipped at Wapping for a sailor?

3  to whom did son George quaff?

4  who had a sweetheart in England (and one in the Isle of Man)?

5  whose cornual performance encouraged early rising?

6  to whom do the pipes call from glen to glen?

7  whose orisons must not a whisper interrupt?

8  who is my darling?

9  who was an authority on conchology?

10  who persists in an undulating progress?

• 9 • (1952, 17) *Name the authors of the following and to whom they are referring:*

1 Lay her i' the earth,
   And from her fair and unpolluted flesh,
   May violets spring?

2 He is gone on the mountain,
   He is lost to the forest,
   Like a summer-dried fountain,
   When our need was the sorest?

3 One piercing neigh
   Arose, and on the dead man's plain,
   The rider grasps his steed again?

4 They tolled the one bell only,
   Groom there was none to see,
   The mourners followed after,
   And so to church went she?

5 Mighty victor, mighty Lord,
   Low on his funeral couch he lies?

6 Say ye, O gallant Hillmen,
   For these, whose life has fled,
   Which is the fitting colour,
   The green one or the red?

7 In their death they were not divided,
   They were swifter than eagles,
   They were stronger than lions?

8 Thou, to whom all griefs were known;
   Who wert placed upon the bier
   In happier hour than on a throne?

9 We carved not a line, and we raised not a stone –
   But we left him alone with his glory?

10 There those three Queens
    Put forth their hands ... and wept
    ... ... ... ...
    And on the mere the wailing died away?

• 10 • (1953, 1) *At the Coronation:*

1   who disappeared?

2   who averted a traffic jam?

3   what ecclesiast made his début?

4   what ancillaries diversified the waiting?

5   who played the organ?

6   what did Parry provide?

7   what sword was pointless?

8   what hill was sanded?

9   who sent the Armills?

10   who brought a Friendly greeting?

• 11 • (1953, 3)

1   who was the widow of Prasutagus?

2   whose widow was Penelophon?

3   who married the widow of the dead and gone Mr Clarke?

4   what widow was the daughter of Phanuel?

5   whose widow did Mr Hoggins degrade from the peerage?

6   what widow is a weaver?

7   who married the Warden's widowed daughter?

8   to whom was the widow's hospitality inexhaustible?

9   who married Harry of Monmouth's widow?

10   what widow does Kipling place where?

• 12 • (1953, 6)

1   who encountered opposition on the beach?

2   who clawed up what beach?

3   who poured water on a sand-removal scheme?

4   what shall we do on these yellow sands?

5   who was welcomed ashore by a serpent?

6   what beach did Farmer George popularize?

7   who was begged to land in Devon and not in Dorset?

8   on what beach does Heber locate a cry for deliverance?

9   from what littoral does Albion derive her name?

10   what beaches should be forever England?

## • 13 • (1953, 7)

1. what garden saw the allocation of the pale and purple rose?
2. of what garden was Ladon the Cerberus?
3. what garden evokes manual pallor?
4. who was invited to the garden gate?
5. what was the first English Garden City?
6. what gardens were erected for Amytis?
7. what garden was more fatal to a King than gunpowder?
8. whose reluctance to surrender his garden gained him whose reprimand 'Proud Prelate!'?
9. where does who locate Allah's Garden?
10. who hath a garden?

## • 14 • (1953, 10)

1. who cured her cold by sitting with her head in boiling water for 20 minutes?
2. what medicine was labelled 'Drink me'?
3. for what was septenary immersion prescribed?
4. who had more need of spiritual than of medical attention?
5. who recommended a little gruel as an after-journey freshener?
6. who drew forth the poison with her balmy breath?
7. what was the best cure for headache and prevented the hair from turning grey?
8. who prescribed wine in moderation for stomachic reasons?
9. what disease was pronounced incurable as the doctors received payment?
10. what result attends diurnal pomaceous treatment?

## • 15 • (1953, 12)

1  of what ship was John Macpherson Captain?

2  ahead of what saucy ship did the *Belle Poule* lie?

3  what ship sprang no fatal leak?

4  what ship was likened to a lame duck?

5  what liners ply to Brazil *ad lib*?

6  who wrote her own name 'round about the prow'?

7  what ship 'bethought herself and went'?

8  what northern ship feared capture by the Porte?

9  of what ship was the Captain punctilious in matinal greetings?

10  'For the bread that you eat and the biscuits you nibble,
    They are brought to you daily by all us – – – – – – – –'?

## • 16 • (1953, 14)

1  over what canals did who make and break his fame?

2  what canal flows through the Tongue of Yes?

3  what canal ends at the Y's mouth?

4  what canal contains Neptune's Staircase?

5  what canal shares its name with the Brick Lane Temperance Association?

6  who repeatedly painted the Grand Canal?

7  what canal was opened with an international naval procession?

8  how do we name canal excavators?

9  what canal suffered aerial vacuation?

10  who lived 'by the side of the sleepy canal'?

## • 17 • (1953, 16) *Whose foreign servant:*

1  bowled his master for 570 runs?

2  took his name from the Mohammedan Sabbath?

3  was admitted by his master to be his superior?

4  declared his isle to be full of noises, sounds and sweet airs?

5  presumed spontaneous development?

6  recommended the man of God?

7  reiterated 'All you want, you shall have'?

8  died from 56 wounds?

9  went to bed with the crown jewels?

10  shot the family lawyer?

• 18 • (1953, 17) *To what Queens does Shakespeare allude in the following:*

1    Age cannot wither her, nor custom stale
     Her infinite variety?

2    Never harm,
     Nor spell nor charm
     Come our lovely lady nigh:
     So, good-night, with lullaby?

3    The rude sea grew civil at her song,
     And certain stars shot madly from their spheres,
     To hear the sea-maid's music?

4    Take her, fair son; and from her blood raise up
     Issue to me; that the contending Kingdoms
     Of France and England …
     May cease their hatred?

5    She should have died hereafter;
     There would have been a time for such a word,
     Tomorrow, and tomorrow and tomorrow – – – –?

6    Clarence and Gloster, love my lovely queen;
     And kiss your princely nephew, brothers both?

7    That man i' the world who shall report he has
     A better wife, let him in naught be trusted,
     For speaking false is that?

8    You are the queen, your husband's brother's wife;
     And – would it were not so! –
     You are my mother?

9    Do, child, go to it' grandam, child,
     Give grandam kingdom, and it' grandam will
     Give it a plum, a cherry and a fig?

10   She shall be, to the happiness of England,
     An aged princess; many days shall see her,
     And yet no day without a deed to crown it?

# 1954–1955

**• 1 •**   (1954, 1)

1   what march brought the jubilee?

2   what jubilee has recalled the King of Paris?

3   under what alias did Bytown celebrate its jubilee?

4   what jubilee entailed thirty visits to St Peter's?

5   from what jubilee did the captains and kings depart?

6   whose death from exhaustion would Miss Nipper have considered a jubilee?

7   what jubilee celebrated 'a very ordinary fellow'?

8   who celebrated his jubilee 'low on his funeral couch'?

9   what Romanic jubilee will St Martin's Lane celebrate this Christmas Eve?

10   in what 'jubilee' year were sowing and reaping forbidden?

**• 2 •**   (1954, 3)

1   what scent is like to the damask rose?

2   what did the cardinal's scent-bearers carry?

3   where do the spicy breezes blow?

4   whose garments smelt of myrrh, aloes and cassia?

5   what spice does Marvell give as Cromwell's highest ambition?

6   what floral tribute smelt of the recipient?

7   what perfumes did Lady Macbeth reject?

8   what was Maud invited to inhale?

9   what intoxicates the hot and quivering air?

10   with what did Jorrocks perfume his cupboards?

• 3 •  (1954, 5)

1   who ate what with a runcible spoon?
2   who drank from a small brass pipkin?
3   who mended the watch with breadknife and best butter?
4   who served butter in a lordly dish?
5   who sat on his wine glass?
6   who ate peas with two-pronged, black-handled forks?
7   where were broken teacups wisely kept for show?
8   who might have seized the grapes with lazy tongs?
9   to what attacks were the cooks' own ladles subject?
10  with what host is elongated cutlery advisable?

• 4 •  (1954, 7)

1   what ambassador claimed to lie abroad for his country?
2   who presented his ambassadors pictorially?
3   what ambassador does Shakespeare introduce as Capucius?
4   what ambassador helped Congress to dance?
5   what ambassador caused Elizabeth to 'scour up her old Latin'?
6   what ambassador was 'Soveral überall'?
7   who called for stools for what ambassadors?
8   whose ambassador comes 'A latere'?
9   what ambassador's mission failed?
10  what did Agatha Christie entrust to the Ambassadors?

• 5 •  (1954, 9) *In what duel:*

1   was a principal called 'Good King of cats'?
2   was the challenge 'Gauntlet or Gospel'?
3   did a principal cry, 'That's not the man'?
4   did war minister challenge foreign secretary?
5   did embryo president and premier meet?
6   were swords smiled at and weapons laughed to scorn?
7   did the last great Englishman borrow the doctor's pistols?
8   was an exchange of arms the courteous result?
9   was the height of one principal six cubits and a span?
10  was the height of one principal two leagues or more?

## • 6 • (1954, 11)

1 whose warnings earned the reproach 'foolish, dreaming, superstitious girl'?
2 what warner had coals of fire heaped on his head?
3 concerning what manxome foe was a warning delivered?
4 what gerundival warning was applied to Dido's domain?
5 what coppersmith was the subject of whose warning?
6 whose warning was answered far up the height?
7 what warner was drupaceous?
8 who had been repeatedly warned to cling to his nanny?
9 whose warning had as its refrain 'Ride your ways Ellangowan'?
10 who was warned from the cerulean penetralia?

## • 7 • (1954, 12)

1 who whispered to his arrow 'Swerve not'?
2 who shot an arrow beyond the stone Ezel?
3 whence did the swan-neck retrieve the arrow?
4 where did my arrow fall?
5 what toxophilites have scored a chiliad?
6 who was the archer of Uri?
7 what Arrow was seized by a mandarin?
8 where was the shaft cut?
9 what archer was borne on a Tittlemouse?
10 what is the arrow's Masonic lodge?

## • 8 • (1954, 15)

1 whose cheek was wormeaten?
2 whose nose was sharp as a pen?
3 whose eyes were as big as millwheels?
4 whose beard was like the pard's?
5 whose brow was like the snowdrift?
6 whose breath was rude?
7 whose lips were from cherry-isle?
8 whose grin was canine?
9 whose face was like tan?
10 whose head might have earned him the nickname 'Chunks'?

## • 9 • (1954, 16)

1     whose imprisonment preceded trial and crime?

2     at what prison was what hangman hanged?

3     from what prison did Mme Veto make her exit?

4     what prison was its county's heart?

5     whose mother wrote from her doleful prison in the Tower?

6     whose daughter sat on her prison's wet threshold?

7     at what prison was aerial dancing deprecated?

8     where did the prisoner dissuade the keeper from suicide?

9     from what prison was the prisoner sacked?

10    where do iron bars apparently make a cage?

## • 10 • (1955, 3) *Fill in the blanks:*

1     Wanted. Smart lads to train in easy, light-fingered occupation. Apply Mr – – – –.

2     Can any housewife recommend a prompt remover of bloodstains from keys. Urgent. F – – – –.

3     To let, that compact one-room flat known as – – – – – – – –. Four feet by four feet. Private entrance from river. One minute's walk from Green.

4     Book now for Autumn Cruise in that fine Whaler the – – – –, leaving Plymouth Sept 6th.

5     Warming pan for sale. Owner going abroad. Apply – – – – – – – –.

6     Cake-makers! Have you an electric toaster? Avoid risk of burning. – – – – – – – – says 'If only I had had one.'

7     Comfortable accommodation in Eastcheap – Patronized by Royalty. Mrs – – – – Manageress.

8     On your last night at Rome, do not fail to sup at V– – – – B– – – –.

9     Nurse (not SRN) offers Life and Death Services. Can bring own umbrella. Apply Mrs – – – –.

10    Wanted, two Bridge partners. Apply – – – –.

## • 11 • (1955, 5)

1  what clouds rained ridicule on Socrates?
2  who espied a 4-inch cloud?
3  what fishy name is applied to the cirro-cumulus?
4  what is the nebular name for mares' tails?
5  who confirmed a camelious hump in a cloud?
6  who describes whom as 'clouds without water'?
7  who was the Cloud-Assembler?
8  till when should fracto-cumulus extroversion be practised?
9  what form the deep thunder clouds?
10  what clouds are transitory?

## • 12 • (1955, 7)

1  what American Indian was the child of the west wind?
2  against what Red Indian murderer did Tom Sawyer testify?
3  what American Indian was baptised Rebecca?
4  what American Indian was President of Mexico?
5  of what party is the Wigwam the headquarters?
6  Montezuma was the last of the – – – –?
7  to whom did Valmond come?
8  what Indian tribe was personified in Peter the Painter?
9  who imagines every schoolboy an authority on Atahualpa?
10  who accused whom of having as much politeness as a wild Indian?

## • 13 • (1955, 8)

1  to what recruiting ground did lads in their hundreds come?
2  where are there violets now in plenty?
3  in the suburbs of what town did Jockie kiss Jenny?
4  where do the bells sound so grand?
5  where do the bells count up to six?
6  where was a fish-hawking business inherited?
7  where had the singer seen diamonds?
8  with what town was telephonic communication difficult?
9  what did Charles Edward consider a 'noble town'?
10  what town of all towns am I glad to leave behind?

**• 14 •** (1955, 11) *What light periodical:*

1    is the bonne bouche of a vegetarian regime?

2    could have replied to a query as to its editor, 'The answer is a lemon'?

3    accompanied the vicar's daughter to Lincoln?

4    launched Weary Willie and Tired Tim?

5    had a half-day?

6    portrayed the Gibson girls?

7    incensed the spiritual peers?

8    shares honours with Rossini?

9    shares honours with Offenbach?

10   knows them all?

**• 15 •** (1955, 12)

1    in what play did the lady protest too much?

2    who went to see *The Second Mrs Tanqueray*?

3    where was Lover's Vows considered improper?

4    about what work did a foreign royal visit cause a how-de-do?

5    what play had a gallinaceous cast?

6    what play showed a fat man in love, to please Elizabeth?

7    in what play did the divine Sarah break her leg?

8    in what play was a purple-in-grain beard suggested?

9    in what play was Mr Wopsie asked for *Rule Britannia* on the recorders?

10   what play was a Tragedy Rehearsed?

**• 16 •** (1955, 13)

1    what royal yacht embraced the fate *Revenge* shunned?

2    what royal yacht club is 'exclusion itself'?

3    what royal vessel departed to a sound of wailing?

4    who raced in the *Meteor*?

5    who travelled in the *Standart*?

6    on what royal yacht did Queen Victoria make her last voyage?

7    whose royal barge had perfumed purple sails?

8    what royal owner demanded a 'skeely skipper'?

9    what royal yacht took its name from a high Württemburg mountain?

10   what royal yacht recalls the line 'Ye made one light together'?

## • 17 • (1955, 14)

1    what witch caused a king to faint?
2    what witch knew that love was wanted by a queen?
3    what witches should have sported a red rose?
4    who was the witch of the wood?
5    what witch died with 'Proud Maisie' on her lips?
6    what witch burnt the wrong baby?
7    what witches water the Yggdrasil daily?
8    where was Faust invited on 1 May?
9    what witch lived in sweet cottage?
10   who predicted smog?

## • 18 • (1955, 16)

1    where was the *Hesperus* wrecked?
2    where did the deck burn?
3    what should be viewed by the pale moonlight?
4    where did Joris announce 'Yet there is time'?
5    where was Boadicea flogged?
6    where did Barbara Frietchie take up the flag?
7    where was Kempenfelt's work of glory done?
8    where lay a youth to fortune and to fame unknown?
9    where did Blondel sing?
10   where did Blondin walk?

# 1956–1958

• 1 •  (1956, 1) *How would Salic Law have:*

1   prevented an internal localization?
2   denuded the statuary at St Paul's?
3   obviated a nine days' wonder?
4   deprived Henry VIII of a bride?
5   rendered unnecessary the transfer of a king's heart and stomach?
6   granted a monopoly of the throne?
7   obscured the royal mirthlessness?
8   reduced the monstrous regiment?
9   made one less Lady of the Garter?
10  rendered less important the visit of Balkis?

• 2 •  (1956, 3) *What son of what mother:*

1   went to Avalon?
2   was no pastry cook?
3   visited Medusa?
4   visited Porto Ferrajo?
5   took seizin of the rushes?
6   had a little coat annually?
7   dispensed with her permission to court?
8   could be nursed by no other?
9   gat eels boiled in broo?
10  was stung by a wasp?

## • 3 • (1956, 5)

1    what card game hails from Old Man River?

2    in what game is 'Two for his heels' heard?

3    what is the French knave?

4    who (according to Hollywood) cheated Henry VIII at cards?

5    what game is not played alone?

6    what is the curse of Scotland?

7    what game involves a royal marriage?

8    who found 'Death, always Death' in her cards?

9    who recorded her victory by placing a battered halfpenny under the candlestick?

10    what was Tchaikovsky's trump?

## • 4 • (1956, 6)

1    in what song is strangulation preferred to separation?

2    where does the gold fin not wink?

3    what song promises Kashmiri stories and Arabian nights?

4    what song implies emigration of Adam and Eve?

5    what song puts a stop to nocturnal wandering?

6    whence were the coloured counties seen?

7    where does the splendour fall?

8    where did the shadow of a cross arise?

9    what song-cycle develops as a duet?

10    what stirred?

## • 5 • (1956, 7) *What sequel to what:*

1    moves from Highlands to Lowlands?

2    inducts Mr Quiverful?

3    proceeds from maidenhood to matronage?

4    opens with the fall of the mighty?

5    revives the two Samuels?

6    treats of perennial boyhood?

7    recalls a former treatise?

8    unites Christian and Christiana?

9    extols English archery?

10    jumps two decades?

**• 6 •**  (1956, 8)

1   what carpenter was the son of Heli?
2   what carpenter is known as Chips?
3   what murine accessory is found in carpentry?
4   what carpenter said nothing but 'Cut us another slice'?
5   for what should a carpenter apply to the Grey Sisters?
6   what is a thornback?
7   between what carpenter's legs did Pip see some miles of open country?
8   what carpenter was one of the hempen homespuns?
9   what carpenter was of vindictive reputation?
10  what carpenter used his augur founderously?

**• 7 •**  (1956, 9)

1   who was the organist of Cloisterham?
2   what organ's keys needed adjusting?
3   who called the organ a box of whistles?
4   where, says Longfellow, do burnished arms rise like a huge organ?
5   who writes of the organist in heaven?
6   to what institution did Handel present an organ?
7   what organ was built to commemorate Handel?
8   what heretical organist did Gardiner save from the stake?
9   who is the organ's patroness?
10  of what organ is Pan the patron?

**• 8 •**  (1956, 10)

1   who was the 'pride and sorrow of chess'?
2   who introduced to England 'The Game and Playe of Chesse'?
3   what is a gambit?
4   what gambit recalls the Hungarian tragedy?
5   what variation is patriarchal?
6   what does 'J'adoube' mean?
7   where recently has a Bolshevik won a tournament commemorating a White Russian?
8   what English chess tournaments recall William I and George V?
9   whom did Elizabeth call a 'pawn who might well checkmate her'?
10  what pawn was called 'my imperial kitten'?

## • 9 • (1956, 12)

1     what does Gilbert shelter under an oak?

2     what was found intact in an oak?

3     whose heartwood is oaken?

4     what shares the oak's septentrional predilections?

5     who shared the oak's hospitality with Charles II?

6     when is the oak guilty of inhospitality?

7     what oak became a gallows?

8     who walks round an oak with ragged horns?

9     who found the oak boughs too low?

10    why the Oaks?

## • 10 • (1956, 13)

1     what wind does Kingsley apostrophise?

2     what 'tempestuous wind' drove the ship of Alexandria?

3     what wind makes the yellow roses droop?

4     where does the sailor encounter the brave west wind?

5     who writes of the weary west wind?

6     what 'gigantic storm wind' descends on the Atlantic?

7     what wind suggests the poetry of Provence?

8     what wind was of Calvinist tendency?

9     what wind has a medical connection?

10    who bagged the contrary winds?

## • 11 • (1956, 14) *What English county town, past or present:*

1     welcomed Monmouth?

2     expiated welcome?

3     compromised Miss Witherfield?

4     houses Jane and William?

5     received a troop of horse?

6     sent back Charlie?

7     saw its burghers roused?

8     might be named 'The Hump'?

9     was the Selenite's goal?

10    had a use?

• 12 • (1956, 15) *What garment was a:*

1    wimple?

2    rail?

3    biggen?

4    baldric?

5    pelerine?

6    paduasoy?

7    sacque?

8    fontange?

9    houpelande?

10    pourpoint?


• 13 • (1957, 2) *What seaside resort:*

1    is so bracing?

2    enjoyed a late-season invasion?

3    is pavilioned in splendour?

4    witnessed Miss Musgrove's fall?

5    provided music for the Royal dip?

6    had its sands painted for Queen Victoria?

7    recruited the *Revenge*?

8    had to fear burglaree varied by piracee?

9    has been denied its suffix '-on-Sea'

10    unites palm and pine?


• 14 • (1957, 4) *Identify the following vicars:*

1    of Bray.

2    of Wakefield.

3    of Auburn.

4    of Haworth.

5    of Puddingdale.

6    of Hunsford.

7    of Eversley.

8    of Lutterworth.

9    of Mirth.

10    of Hell.

• 15 • (1957, 6) *What associations have the following:*

1    Tanglewood?
2    Gopher wood?
3    Polygon wood?
4    Poon wood?
5    Sherwood?
6    Redwood?
7    Ravenwood?
8    Lowood?
9    Longwood?
10   Broadwood?

• 16 • (1958, 1) *What Prince of Wales:*

1    rehearsed his coronation?
2    was given molinary encouragement?
3    was lion-like?
4    was pavilioned in splendour?
5    evoked the epitaph:

      'Who was alive and is dead –
      There's no more to be said'?

6    told England to wake up?
7    was Sobieski's son-in-law?
8    was born in sanctuary?
9    was to become king of Paris?
10   inspired the fulfilled prophecy,

      '... shall come again'?

• 17 • (1958, 2) *Who wrote a letter or letters from:*

1   my doleful prison in the Tower?

2   my Hermitage?

3   Patmos?

4   Pampérigouste?

5   Rosings?

6   Tusculum?

7   Vailima?

8   Strawberry Hill?

9   Corinthus?

10  the Blue Boar?

• 18 • (1958, 7)

1   when does the shepherd light up?

2   when does he become convivial?

3   what shepherd had cold fingers?

4   what colours does the Highland shepherd wear?

5   in what almanac does Colin Clout figure?

6   whose carelessness led to gregarious docking?

7   what shepherd fell in love with whose foulness?

8   who regretted her shepherd's delights?

9   what shepherd went to Dothan?

10  what Sheppard went to Tyburn?

# 1959–1960

## • 1 • (1959, 1)

1 'An election, – – – –, we will behold and minutely examine a scene so interesting to every Englishman.'

      Where was it?

2 what submarine borough returned two members?

3 what was 'His Majesty's bouncing Bill'?

4 what borough returned the Cornet of Horse?

5 what borough returned Veneering?

6 who was Barchester's political agent?

7 who were the Potwallopers?

8 who conducted the Midlothiam campaign?

9 who survived the Middlesex elections?

10 who was the Great Elector?

## • 2 • (1959, 2)

1 what is the Island of the Moon?

2 whose moon knew no wane?

3 what felspar did Sergeant Cuff investigate?

4 what lunar sea connotes fertility?

5 in what guise does the moon hunt the clouds?

6 whose French expedition forestalled the Russians?

7 who lost his bearings in East Anglia?

8 what presented moonshine?

9 what land is found 'over the mountains of the moon'?

10 who raked?

· 3 ·   (1959, 3) *What park:*

1   afforded a king his last walk?
2   surveys the Blue Danube?
3   saw a lordly murder?
4   saw a doubly fatal ducal duel?
5   received Caroline's ophidian addition?
6   is watered by Hacking?
7   is intersected by the New River?
8   was tyrannized by Mrs Norris?
9   does not reach the Channel?
10   did not reach Timbuctoo?

· 4 ·   (1959, 5) *What time:*

1   is St Martin's finest hour?
2   was Kate Nickleby born?
3   do I fly to the lone vale?
4   saw the murine collapse?
5   do the Christchurch bells call to prayer?
6   did Phileas complete the circuit?
7   steps forth the great leader?
8   is morning at?
9   did Cassius say the clock had stricken?
10   did Chu Chin Chow appoint for kissing?

· 5 ·   (1959, 6)

1   with what did Silchester meet the central-heating problem?
2   how does the psalmist suggest a plumbing nuisance?
3   what is the plumber's badge?
4   who was the Elizabethan courtier plumber?
5   what is a turnpin?
6   what stopgap did the Dutch boy use?
7   what mineral comes from Les Baux?
8   how does Rotorua dispense with the plumber?
9   when is a smudge useful?
10   what is the plumber's usual omission?

## • 6 •  (1959, 7)

1    why is a tournament so called?

2    what tournament was rained off?

3    whom did a dropped handkerchief lead from the tournament to the scaffold?

4    who was the hero of the tournament at Ashby-de-la-Zouch?

5    who wrote of the gentle knight pricking on the plaine?

6    who wrote of 'The gravelled ground – on foaming horse with swords and friendly hearts'?

7    what tournament placed Mary Stuart on the throne?

8    what tournament was held in the Wartburg?

9    at what tournament did many carry on their backs 'their mills, forests and meadows'?

10    what tournament was fought for possession of a coming queen?

## • 7 •  (1959, 8)

1    how was the cubit determined?

2    what houseboat was 30 cubits in height?

3    what room's dimensions offered scant comfort?

4    in what shipwreck did successive soundings register 20 and 15 fathoms?

5    what eyrie is 984 feet up?

6    what standard determined the distance to the maypole?

7    whose spear's head weighed 600 shekels of iron?

8    what linear seizure results from an uncial surrender?

9    what weight of carrion was assessed at 3000 ducats?

10    how many feet had Harald Hardrada?

## • 8 •  (1959, 9) *What massacre:*

1    shocked Dr Manette?

2    inspired Brueghel?

3    is commemorated by an angel?

4    commemorated a wedding?

5    changed the affix of Water to Peter?

6    made the vale weep?

7    demanded revenge for the slaughtered saints?

8    inspired Verdi?

9    provoked the Curse of Cromwell?

10    is frequently seen at Westminster?

**• 9 •** (1959, 10) *What Catherine:*

1    brought home the pope?
2    was the banker's daughter?
3    was the Barlass?
4    was kissed by Pepys?
5    was not born 'an heroine'?
6    was the first Queen of Ireland?
7    was Kate of Kate Hall?
8    succeeded Eudoxia?
9    reduced the duty on port?
10   should antedate her festival by twenty days?

**• 10 •** (1959, 11)

1    what key is occidental?
2    what key is Salamancan?
3    who made keys for the Prentice Knights?
4    what German key is labial in England?
5    what key is not Manx?
6    who reached a high key by dieting?
7    what key called for Milton?
8    what keys postulated a walkie-talkie?
9    what Fleet inmate had the key of the street?
10   'Pass Keys.' 'Whose Keys?'?

**• 11 •** (1959, 12)

1    what was the first body of male nurses?
2    what nurse would Queen Victoria have welcomed at the War Office?
3    what nurse was recommended by St Bartholomew's Hospital?
4    what councillor of blood died in his nurse's arms?
5    what nurse came home to Norwich?
6    what nurse assisted nature in the Plague?
7    what nurse had a merry husband?
8    who prayed that his nurse might be made good?
9    what nurse might have prescribed cocoa?
10   what Tennysonian nurse sounds pensionable?

## • 12 • (1960, 1)

1 how has the Royal Society yielded precedence to the General Letter Office?

2 where were the early meetings of the Royal Society held?

3 what founder member passed from natural philosophy to monumental fame?

4 who catalogued the stars for navigators?

5 who was President of the Royal Society for twenty-four years?

6 what president of the Society left on the map the name of his favourite study?

7 what apprentice from Staithes went to observe a transit of Venus?

8 what ex-bandsman was relieved from the intolerable waste of time of giving music lessons?

9 what native of Berkeley had a deep interest in cows?

10 whose researches led to the success of the first transatlantic cable?

## • 13 • (1960, 6) *Which hymnographer:*

1 travels o'er crag and torrent?

2 pours contempt on his pride?

3 desires a plurality of tongues?

4 calls righteousness His royal harbinger?

5 exhorts to walk uncowed?

6 calls temptation His jewels?

7 declares the dreaded clouds big with mercy?

8 prays deliverance from sleep and from damnation?

9 calls our land a garden fenced with silver sea?

10 includes an hobgoblin?

## • 14 • (1960, 8) *What Ben:*

1 was cracked?

2 had a quintuple portion?

3 looks down on the Ptarmigan?

4 laid down his arms?

5 insisted that he would be heard?

6 shows commercial solidarity?

7 has Uist on both sides?

8 brought the death of Wolfe to life?

9 is alias Cobbler?

10 is overseer of the Sudries?

**• 15 •** (1960, 10)

1   who did seven years and then had it doubled?

2   who were the apostolic gardeners?

3   who were neither hot nor cold?

4   whom did the king delight to honour?

5   who did chide what brother's pride?

6   what king was greeted with the national anthem?

7   whose knees smote one against another?

8   which fools were bewitched?

9   who were liars and slow bellies?

10   whose grandson was told to fight the good fight?

**• 16 •** (1960, 11) *Identify the birds and give the source of the allusion:*

1   That's the wise – – – –; he sings each song twice over.

2   The bird in the wilderness.

3   Thou hast no sorrows in thy song,
     No winter in thy year!

4   Perhaps the selfsame song that found a path
     Through the sad heart of Ruth...

5   Light vanity, insatiate – – – –,
     Consuming means, soon preys upon itself.

6   All ye highflyers of the feathered race,
     – – – – and – – – –
     Here's the top peak!

7   Sweet – – – – sits in the bush,
     Singing so rarely.

8   The bird that never was.

9   What did Passer do to Erithacus, and with what?

10   Who knew which bird from a handsaw when the wind was southerly?

• 17 • (1960, 12) *What scientist is indicated by the following:*

  1  fruit juice for sailors?
  2  his missing link is missing again?
  3  preferred diptera to his namesake's dubloons?
  4  suffered pseudocarpial percussion?
  5  must have had a great sense of humours?
  6  salopian who studied balanus?
  7  saved the life of Joseph Meister?
  8  expert on gases, he lost his head in a crisis?
  9  discovered nature's substitute for Echo satellite?
  10  pinchbeck or sterling? His bath provided the answer?

• 18 • (1960, 14) *What mouse or mice:*

  1  had a beautiful view?
  2  left whose last buttonhole undone?
  3  fandangoed in the attics?
  4  was domiciled with a bent tanner?
  5  felt the pinch?
  6  was sacrificed to make a Roman victory?
  7  never came back?
  8  felt the draught in December?
  9  provides the motive power?
  10  has been diplomatically trapped for eight years?

# 1961–1962

**• 1 •** (1961, 1) *What is the Authorized Version of the following:*

1   Do not bring us to the test?
2   Now we see only puzzling reflections in a mirror?
3   Do not keep thinking how wise you are?
4   … whom you had done to death by hanging him on a gibbet?
5   We must not tear this; let us toss for it?
6   Each day has troubles enough of its own?
7   For coat of mail put on integrity?
8   God … does not live in shrines made by men?
9   The arrogant of heart and mind he has put to rout?
10  The worker earns his pay?

**• 2 •** (1961, 3)

1   who was Lord of the Golden Age?
2   who strangled serpents in his cradle?
3   who was old Noah's counterpart?
4   what traveller greeted what seer across a gory trench?
5   who taught men the use of fire?
6   who lost her freedom for seven pomegranate seeds?
7   who was the alchemist of the Pactolus?
8   who was the fabricator of equine statuary?
9   which of the seven should have been the beneficiary?
10  whose bride had not then a nebulous reputation?

**· 3 ·** (1961, 5)

1 who was allotted the task of asking for more?
2 who made what record score for a single-wicket match?
3 who was forced to advertise a mordant tendency?
4 what prisoner never lost his Grip?
5 who was the legendary founder of Bath Spa?
6 who was the angel of the Marshalsea?
7 who ended as a Port Middlebay magistrate?
8 what was the name of the Aged Parent?
9 what cause came to a Deadlock?
10 whose final flagellation was administered with an umbrella in a hackney coach?

**· 4 ·** (1961, 7) *What comic character:*

1 craved no crumb?
2 won promotion through a pass examination?
3 got us into a nice mess by an excess of corroborative detail?
4 though well-connected was underrated?
5 was prim, trim and slim?
6 was a student of magnetism?
7 maintained that 'Man is nature's sole mistake'?
8 was ready to ill-convenience himself to save a female in distress?
9 was familiar with the frogs?
10 dealt, inter alia, in curses?

**· 5 ·** (1961, 8)

1 who said goodbye to all that?
2 who brought to light the buried day?
3 who described a sailor's odyssey?
4 who got up quite early one morning?
5 who faced the eye of the wind?
6 who noted that heaven lies about us?
7 who mingled the chime?
8 who remembered that old men forget?
9 who bade memory hold the door?
10 what midget left memoirs?

• 6 • (1961, 11) *What monster was:*

  1   a tricephalic watchdog?

  2   a Manx giant of mischief?

  3   the vastest of fowls?

  4   an insistent riddler?

  5   a feminine Hibernian ululator?

  6   lion + goat + dragon?

  7   uniquely frumious?

  8   an equine anthropod?

  9   a Jobian hippopotamus?

10   a composite heraldic beast with human head?

• 7 • (1961, 12) *Who travelled:*

  1   with a donkey?

  2   in Tartary?

  3   to and fro in the earth?

  4   with the Bible in the Peninsula?

  5   round the world, if need be?

  6   round the world in eight days?

  7   round the world in one thirty-sixth of a day?

  8   through England on a side-saddle?

  9   through England in the days of dissolution?

10   through England, shunning the great wen?

• 8 • (1961, 15)

  1   who declared what to be the root of all evil?

  2   who was accused of having an itching palm?

  3   who offered a panacea for arthritis at one shilling the box?

  4   who preferred flesh to ducats?

  5   who 'will find a tiger well repays the trouble and expense'?

  6   what cashier was engaged at enormous expense?

  7   who wisely said to whom, 'Show me first your penny'?

  8   what careful soul pulled out half a crown?

  9   who said that there are few ways in which a man can be more innocently employed than in getting money?

10   whose time was said to be worth £1000 a minute?

## • 9 • (1961, 18) *In 1961:*

1    what transporter has gone out of business?

2    what southerner sought his lady in Northumbria?

3    what well-known garden has acquired another river?

4    who, unlike Icarus, survived because he went round instead of up?

5    who, though highly valued and greatly missed, has not yet been ransomed?

6    who, being one in a hundred, was jailed notwithstanding?

7    what German successor to a useful old British prototype has proved troublesome?

8    what well-known portrait has become common currency?

9    who, except the Prince, is highest in Wales?

10    what original of a 4s. stamp is no more?

## • 10 • (1962, 1)

1    for what is St Barnabas Day 1662 memorable?

2    who pray to be a safeguard unto our most gracious sovereign?

3    which is stir-up Sunday?

4    who must be thirty years of age?

5    who must be learned in the Latin tongue?

6    what is appointed to be said on Sundays, Wednesdays and Fridays?

7    what is appointed to be said on the feast of St Andrew, but not of St Peter?

8    what days of abstinence precede the feast of the Ascension?

9    where is he that putteth his trust in man accursed?

10    for what purpose should the parish provide a decent bason?

## • 11 • 9 (1962, 6) *What county possesses:*

1    Dukeries?

2    Stannaries?

3    Eye?

4    Ruyton-Eleven-Towns?

5    Toller Porcorum?

6    Havering atte Bower?

7    Cricket Malherbe?

8    Pity Me?

9    Indian Queen?

10    Rime Intrinseca?

• 12 • (1962, 8) *Whose clothes were thus described:*

1   half of yellow and half of red?

2   to be rich, not gaudy?

3          … freely gold-laced
In a uniform handsome and chaste?

4          … nothing much before
An' rather more than 'arf o' that be'ind?

5   completed by his long red cloak, well brushed and neat?

6   enhanced by yellow stockings, cross-gartered?

7   shreds and patches?

8   unfavourably compared to a lily?

9   topped by a hat as broad as a buckler or target?

10   a new stuff suit with close knees, which becomes me most nobly?

• 13 • (1962, 9) *What pioneer aviator:*

1   first violated Britain's insularity?

2   had ticket number one?

3   made a reality of hot air?

4   crashed at Bournemouth?

5   killed himself in disgust at the use of bombers?

6   is remembered under the sign of the Southern Cross?

7   made a steam plane fly?

8   operated a Kittyhawk?

9   reversed the flight of Alcock and Brown?

10   is said to have escaped under his own steam?

## • 14 • (1962, 10)

1   whose principles were mathematical?

2   whose speculations on the divine nature were no protection in the proscriptions?

3   whose devotion to natural history brought him too close to natural eruption?

4   what royal tutor produced the *Organon*?

5   what member for Liverpool produced the *Novum Organum*?

6   who wrote of revolutions, not *urbium* but *orbium*?

7   who made practical application of the oscillator to the horologium?

8   what chymist was sceptical?

9   whose motion of the heart was not oscillatory – nor amatory?

10   whose descent might man prefer to change to ascent?

## • 15 • (1962, 11) *Elucidate the following:*

1   I will be brief: your noble son is mad.

2   Much learning doth make thee mad.

3   I inherited a vile melancholy from my father which has made me mad all my life.

4   We are all mad here. I'm mad; you're mad.

5   The dog, to gain some private ends,
Went mad and bit the man.

6   What have mad dogs and Englishmen in common?

7   Oh why am I moody and sad?
And why am I guiltily mad?

8   Mad world! Mad kings! Mad composition!

9   Be – – – – unmannerly when – – – – is mad.

10   He feigned himself mad in their hands.

## • 16 • (1962, 14) *What tree:*

1    hid the dark prince?

2    decked the Olympian victor?

3    decks the ships?

4    made pillars for the temple?

5    will 'drop a limb on the head of him that anyway trusts her shade'?

6    is the loveliest?

7    shaded the fugitive prophet?

8    blooms at Christmas?

9    gives necropolitan umbrage?

10   is a chastening influence?

## • 17 • (1962, 15) *What politician:*

1    was the apostle of preference?

2    was the apostle of passive resistance?

3    was the dockers' KC?

4    produced national insurance – and shells?

5    produced houses – and a market?

6    insured the health of the welfare state?

7    failed to pluck the flower out of the nettle?

8    propagated the Big Lie?

9    is notorious for a scrap of paper?

10   was murdered – and even the little children cried in the streets?

• 18 • (1962, 17) *What poet refers to what flower:*

1   Fair – – – –, we weep to see
    You haste away so soon?

2   A garden is a lovesome thing, God wot!
    – – – – plot, fringed pool, fern'd grot?

3   I sometimes think
        That every – – – – the Garden wears
    Dropt in its Lap from some once lovely head?

4   Odours when sweet – – – – sicken
    Live within the sense they quicken?

5   The sun on the hill forgot to die,
    And the – – – – revived, and the dragon-fly
        Came back to dream on the river?

6   Some can pot – – – – and some can bud a rose,
    And some are hardly fit to trust with anything that grows?

7   A queen in crown of rubies dress'd;
    A starvling in a scanty vest?

8   – – – –, firstborn child of Ver,
    Merry springtime's harbinger?

9   Next the – – – – seems to woo him
    Then carnations bow unto him?

10  All will be gay when noontide wakes again
    The – – – –, little children's dower?

# 1963–1964

**• 1 •** (1963, 1)

1 who brought down fire from heaven and suffered for it?

2 who was the father and prophet of fire worship?

3 what fire caused whose fiddle to become notorious?

4 where did a fire reverse whose path of conquest?

5 who recorded that what fire burned 'in a most horrid, malicious, bloody flame … it made me weep to see it?

6 whose celestial fire created 51 x 2 victims?

7 what fire kept the Turk from the Golden Horn?

8 what fire roused the burghers of Carlisle?

9 what fire consumed the City for the second time?

10 what fire gutted the building, though the Governor was Ready?

**• 2 •** (1963, 2)

1 who suffered apotomy of the right ear?

2 to whom did tonsorial ministrations prove fatal?

3 whose left hand struck a blow for freedom?

4 whose little finger threatened a crushing tyranny?

5 whose neck was broken at tidings of disaster?

6 whose head was to lose its master that very day?

7 who was caught by the beard and so slain?

8 who lost his thumbs and his great toes?

9 who declares the tongue to be full of deadly poison?

10 who is vinegar to the teeth and smoke to the eyes?

## • 3 • (1963, 3) *What monarch:*

1 sighed for more worlds to conquer?

2 died of a surfeit of peaches?

3 married the family governess?

4 tried to keep a wild boy?

5 converted the heathen of Scandinavia?

6 last 'touched' for the king's evil?

7 was shot by a subject in a cellar?

8 was called the father-in-law of Europe?

9 so reigned that men said that Christ and his saints were asleep?

10 graciously lent his name … but no more?


## • 4 • (1963, 6) *What garment would have been worn:*

1 as a skirt at the court of Queen Elizabeth I?

2 as a waistcoat by Hamlet?

3 by Robin Hood to carry his horn and sword?

4 by Hotspur over his armour?

5 as an outer vestment by Becket when celebrating mass?

6 by Crookback at Bosworth to protect his neck and shoulders?

7 and by his chaplain to keep the cold from the same?

8 by Xenophon as a mantle on his travels?

9 by Caesar as a mantle, the day he overcame the Nervii?

10 by Sir Winston in a blitz?


## • 5 • (1963, 7) *What Irish town:*

1 can listen to the bells of Shandon?

2 claims to be the most westerly town in Europe?

3 has an air of confidence, for it was never taken?

4 is otherwise known as Loch Garman?

5 appears to suffer from a severe callosity?

6 might be said to have been founded upon the rock?

7 is the birthplace of John McCormack?

8 is the grass-grown capital of ancient kings?

9 awaited in vain the arrival of the Princess Victoria?

10 like London, is overlooked by Horatio Nelson?

• 6 •   (1963, 9) *What song:*

1   laments the noselessness of Man?

2   hooted down the Penal Laws?

3   declared that 'if you hold by the right, you double your might?

4   reiterates work, 'like the engine that works by steam'?

5   wishes the disloyal 'nor yet a rope to hang himself'?

6   bids the soul be swift and the feet jubilant in their response?

7   sings of:

> 'Nightingale and babble-wren …
> And with the sound of lark and wren
> The song of mountains, moths, and men'?

8   recalls a cross-country race for

> 'We run because we must
> Through the great wide air'?

9   celebrated a decapitation, apparently with the workmen's hammer?

10   lists among its blessings 'spikenard and saffron, calamus and cinnamon?

• 7 •   (1963, 11) *Where did:*

1   the prophet take refuge from his native city?

2   Tarik disembark and leave his name?

3   the faithful feel the Hammer?

4   the Crusaders suffer their Waterloo?

5   Boabdil surrender his patrimony?

6   the Magnificent swamp the Magyar?

7   a Pole reverse the tide?

8   the Don sink the crescent?

9   Ibn Saud set up his capital?

10   Kemal drive off the islanders?

• 8 •   (1963, 13) *What animal:*

1   '... welcomes little fishes in
    With gently smiling jaws?

2   has been described as:
           'The devil's walking parody
           On all four-footed things?

3   said 'Let go! You are hurtig be!'?

4   went
           'over the hedge and into ride
           In Ghost Heath Wood for his roving bride'?

5   decided that
    'All animals are equal but some are more equal than others'?

6   whenever the Butcher was by
    '... kept looking the opposite way and appeared unaccountably shy'?

7   has
           'An indolent expression and an undulating throat,
           Like an unsuccessful literary man'?

8   has a very bad temper, all on account of the cake crumbs inside?

9   provided a caudal bell-pull?

10   even spoiled the women's chats?

• 9 • (1963, 14) *Whose demise is referred to in the following lines:*

1    But past is all his fame. The very spot
Where many a time he triumphed is forgot?

2    Nothing in his life became him like the leaving of it?

3    I go to die, you to live; but which of us goes to the better fate is veiled from all except God?

4    These to his memory, since he held them dear?

5    Thou art the ruins of the noblest man?

6    He nothing common did or mean
Upon that memorable scene?

7    Let the mournful martial music blow,
The last great Englishman is low?

8    In their death they were not divided?

9    O weep for Adonais! Though our tears
Thaw not the frost that binds so dear a head?

10    Go tell the – – – –, thou that passest by
That here obedient to her laws we lie?

• 10 • (1964, 3) *Name the well-known seven of which the following pairs*
*are two:*

1    The Pharos of Alexandria and the Colossus of Rhodes?

2    Mercia and Wessex?

3    Wrath and Gluttony?

4    Pergamos and Thyatira?

5    Solon and Periander?

6    Schoolboy and Justice?

7    Grumpy and Dopey?

8    Philip and Nicanor?

9    Numa and Tullus?

10    Mizar and Benetnasch?

**• 11 •** (1964, 4) *Who are referred to in the following:*

1    When you are a married man, – – – –, you'll understand a good many things as you don't understand now?

2    That's as much as to say they are all fools that marry. You'll bear me a bang for that?

3    O let us be married, too long we have tarried?

4    I'm to be married today, today. Yes, I'm to be married today?

5    I had rather be married to a death's head with a bone in his mouth?

6    He married Xanthippe and had but a shrewish bargain?

7    She must espouse the everlasting sea?

8    A hero who, albeit unwittingly, married his mother?

9    He's the most married man I ever saw in my life?

10    His marriage with his brother's wife has crept too near his conscience?

**• 12 •** (1964, 6) *Who:*

1    wished for bed in the bush with stars to see?

2    breakfasted at five o'clock tea, and dined on the following day?

3    awoke with a general sense that he hasn't been sleeping in clover?

4    suggested that it is nicer to stay in bed?

5    suffered from a curse that every night he should dream of the devil and wake in a fright?

6    was fated to wake when some vile thing was near?

7    sent the gentle sleep from heaven that slid into my soul?

8    comes with a tithe-pig's tail tickling a parson's nose as a' lies asleep?

9    slept for 187 years?

10    doth murder sleep?

• 13 • (1964, 7) *What queen is referred to:*

1   Q-4?

2   Queen of Queen's?

3   No Queen, no King?

4   Th' eclipse and glory of her kind?

5   I never thought to have come in here?

6   … sometimes counsel took, and sometimes tea?

7   The poor fool will never cease until she lose her head?

8   The love of all thy people comfort thee?

9   She must have been as brave as Meg Merrilies?

10  She is likely to reign between two others?


• 14 • (1964, 8) *A seventeenth-century writer attributes the following sets of products to divers counties. Name them.*

1   eels, hares, saffron and willows.

2   garlic, slate and tin.

3   lead, cheese, mastiffs and woad.

4   iron, wheaters, carps and talc.

5   pikes, wildfowl, feathers and pippins.

6   fuller's earth, walnuts and box.

7   lampreys, perry and salt.

8   red deer, honey, wax and hogs.

9   morello cherries, flaxe, saint foine, orchards and trouts.

10  nails and pots.


• 15 • (1964, 11) *Who was:*

1   the historian of Selborne?

2   the poet of Redcliffe?

3   the victim of Harmodius?

4   the victor of Lepanto?

5   the King of Bath?

6   the Carrier of Cambridge?

7   the Saviour of the Navy?

8   the founder of Leningrad?

9   the builder of the Great Eastern?

10  the last Abbot of Glastonbury?

## • 16 • (1964, 12)

1  who are said to have been provided with feather beds?
2  who serves with three feathers?
3  who was a-cold for all his feathers?
4  what feather is fatal in a crisis?
5  whose blade is feathered?
6  who wore green jacket, red cap, and white owl's feather?
7  what feathers must have been known to the Shropshire Lad?
8  who was asked if he gave feathers to the ostrich?
9  who was death to feather and fin and fur?
10  who wrote of what:

> Feather-soft creature, tail to head,
> Is golden yellow and black and red?

## • 17 • (1964, 14)

1  where is a window in Thrums?
2  who painted her face and looked out of a window?
3  who was let down through a window in a basket?
4  who fell through a window while sleeping during a long sermon?
5  what birdie hopped upon the window sill?
6  who writes of 'storied windows richly dight'?
7  what could not happen if the Lord would make windows in heaven?
8  what did happen when the windows of heaven were opened?
9  whose voice through a window asked what's in a name?
10  what county plays windows?

• 18 • (1964, 17) *Who writes, of what:*

1    Sold in the shops for the people to eat
     Sold in the shops of Stupidity Street?

2    And our sixteen waxed to thirty-two
     And they to pass three score –
     A wild, white welter of winnowing wings,
     And ever more and more?

3    [If] he and they together
     Knelt down with angry prayers
     For tamed and shabby – – – –?

4    But the – – – – thus accosted rends the peasant tooth and nail?

5    One stiff blind – – – –, his every bone a-stare; I never saw a brute I hated so?

6    The barbecu'd – – – –'s crisp'd to a turn?

7    And Bahram, that great Hunter – the – – – –
     Stamps o'er his Head, but cannot break his Sleep?

8    The wanton troopers riding by
     Have shot my – – – – and it will die?

9    In my court should – – – – flaunt
     And in my forests – – – – haunt?

10   Qui, qui, qui, kweeu quip,
     Tiurru, tiurru, chipiwi
     Too-tee, too-tee, chiu choo
     Chirri, chirri, chooee
     Quiu, qui, qui?

# 1965–1966

**• 1 •** (1965, 2)

1    what plague swept up the long walls?

2    what plague swept westwards from Cathay?

3    for rebelling against whom were 14,000 and 700 smitten by plague?

4    what plague followed batrachian footsteps?

5    who thrice vowed a double plague?

6    who cursed pickled herring with plague?

7    what French haven received a royal fugitive from an English plague?

8    what plague enabled English schoolboys to smoke with impunity?

9    who wrote a novel about a plague?

10    what decennial performance commemorates deliverance from plague?

**• 2 •** (1965, 4) *Who, of a time of crisis, said the following:*

1    For I must have the gentleman to haul and draw with the mariner and the mariner with the gentleman?

2    I think foul scorn that any Prince of Europe should dare to invade the borders of my realm?

3    The Lord made them as stubble to our swords?

4    They now ring the bells, but they will soon wring their hands?

5    Roll up that map: it will not be wanted these ten years?

6    Que Diable! Il n'a pas construit ces montagnes?

7    Russia has two generals in whom she can confide – Janvier and Février?

8    It is not best to swap horses, when crossing the river?

9    The lamps are going out all over Europe?

10    Some chicken! Some neck?

- 3 • (1965, 6) *What novel title did:*
  1 Thackeray take from *The Pilgrim's Progress*?
  2 Graham Greene take from the Lord's Prayer?
  3 Hemingway take from a sermon by Donne?
  4 H E Bates take from Michael Drayton?
  5 E M Forster take from Shelley's *Epipsychidion*?
  6 Aldous Huxley take from Miranda?
  7 Thomas Wolfe take from *Lycidas*?
  8 Thomas Hardy take from Gray's *Elegy*?
  9 Somerset Maugham take from Sir Toby Belch?
  10 Steinbeck take from Julia Ward Howe?

- 4 • (1965, 9) *What artist:*
  1 was velvet?
  2 was infernal?
  3 was a diminutive barrel?
  4 was born Michelangelo Merisi?
  5 was the Greek?
  6 was called Gellée?
  7 was the Customs Man?
  8 was dubbed 'the English Canaletto'?
  9 appeared on his canvases as a butterfly?
  10 is frequently OK?

**• 5 •** (1965, 11) *Which pass:*

1    could not now be defended by 300?
2    gave respite to the Samnites?
3    saw the massacre of a clan?
4    first saw Brownshirt meet Blackshirt?
5    observed Mackay's defeat?
6    was named after a Bishop of Hildesheim?
7    can be found in Whitby and Afghanistan?
8    was used in the trail to California?
9    suggests eminence at sea?
10   is, in the Lake District, the subject of this ditty:

> If I were a lad and loved a lass
> Who lived at the top of the – – – – Pass?

**• 6 •** (1965, 12) *Which femme fatale brought misfortune to:*

1    Hippolytus?
2    Sisera?
3    Catullus?
4    the 'Triple Pillar of the World'?
5    Edward II?
6    a corporal in the Spanish Dragoons?
7    Irish home rule?
8    Des Grieux?
9    Bossiney?
10   Oxford and presumably Cambridge?

**• 7 •** (1965, 13)

1 what Hero was mathematical?

2 which hero is Virginian?

3 whose Hero was the heroine of the two?

4 who wrote a novel without a hero?

5 which hero did deserve the fair?

6 who fed her hero on chocolate creams?

7 who wrote of a contemporary Russian hero?

8 what Hero became Dedalus?

9 for what hero's coming did trumpets sound and drums beat?

10 what self-styled hero expected the above together with cannons and the hooting of motor cars?

**• 8 •** (1965, 14) *What prison:*

1 was the heart of Midlothian?

2 was the first to be visited by a Quaker reformer?

3 was our first state penitentiary?

4 may not have seemed so holy as Bonivard?

5 saw the beginning of a pilgrimage?

6 suggests hasty unions?

7 reduced 146 to 23?

8 was not one despite stone walls and iron bars?

9 saw the birth of a Dickensian heroine?

10 is called Queen of the Sky?

**• 9 •** (1965, 15) *What mathematician:*

1 had a brainwave in the bath?

2 paradoxically recorded a defeat for Achilles?

3 believed in metempsychosis?

4 based an existential belief on a cogitative premise?

5 found a use for the Leaning Tower of Pisa?

6 produced a final, but unverifiable theorem?

7 won fame for his Mathematical Principles?

8 had no principles concerning Tartaglia's solution?

9 was apologetic?

10 entertained the dean's daughter?

## • 10 • (1966, 3) *Who lent his name to:*

1   an unintelligent person?

2   the intensity of a magnetic field?

3   bellicose jingoism?

4   a stately burial place?

5   an extract of beef?

6   a safeguard for the decanters?

7   the argument that you are rich is shown by either your opulence or your economy?

8   the principle that entities must not be unnecessarily multiplied?

9   a lack of choice, in that his customers were not allowed to hire his horses out of turn?

10   a system of algebra in which + means an alternative rather than an addition?

## • 11 • (1966, 4) *Who:*

1   produced batrachian and vespoid choruses?

2   was an emperor's *arbiter elegantiarum*?

3   hated the profane crowd and sang to maidens and boys?

4   suffered a Chelonian distraction?

5   conducted an Italian poet on a sightseeing tour through Purgatory and Hell?

6   defined happiness as an activity?

7   considered that poverty made men ridiculous?

8   mourned a fringilline fate?

9   published pathetic papers from Pontus?

10   had ideas about Ideas?

• 12 • (1966, 6) *What soldier:*

   1   Was a soldier bold and used to war's alarms;
        But a cannon-ball took off his legs so he laid down his arms?

   2   When there was peace he was for peace;
        When there was war he went?

   3   In fact in matters vegetable, animal and mineral
        He was the very model of a modern major-general?

   4   … bestrid the ocean; his rear'd arm
        Created the world?

   5   who had been wounded in the groin at the siege of Namur, devoted much of
        the rest of his life to reconstruction in miniature of that battlefield's terrain?

   6   six weeks after his wedding went off to war and was killed at the battle of
        Waterloo?

   7   Led his regiment from behind;
        He found it less exciting?

   8   because he shot a sleeping comrade was hanged in the presence of his
        regiment?

   9   attempted to persuade his bearers that they should choose
        Armed with hell-flames and fury, all at once
        O'er Heaven's high towers to force resistless way?

 10   came from Burgundy and often repeated the motto 'Courage mon ami! Le
        diable est mort'?

• 13 • (1966, 11) *What river:*

   1   flowed '… through caverns measureless to man
            Down to a sunless sea'?

   2   washed the southern walls of an infested town?

   3   was implored to run softly 'till I end my song'?

   4   was crossed 'where ford there was none'?

   5   was threatened with crossing 'land to land' by 20,000?

   6   is described as 'grey-green greasy'?

   7   was 'rolling rapidly'?

   8   'glideth of its own sweet will'?

   9   'don't say nuffin' but 'just keeps rollin' along'?

 10   is the last to be crossed?

• 14 • (1966, 12) *What lawyer:*

1     was executed for treason?

2     took refuge in the Tower of London to escape lynching, and there died?

3     was murdered in the House of Commons?

4     was impeached?

5     was a reformer of scientific method and died after an experiment in animal refrigeration?

6     taught himself law by reading a copy of *Blackstone's Commentaries* fortuitously found at the bottom of a barrel?

7     declaring that 'the schoolmaster is abroad,' helped to produce a cheap encyclopaedia and to found a university?

8     was awarded a Nobel prize?

9     was the grandson of an American merchant concerned in the Boston Tea Party and became Lord Chancellor?

10     refused a judgeship in the US Supreme Court, escaped to England as a fugitive from justice, and refused a judgeship in England?

• 15 • (1966, 13) *What British composer:*

1     died after his wife locked him out at night?

2     became Coperario?

3     had his music nailed to the door of St Paul's by Handel, who said it needed 'air'?

4     became 'Top of the Pops' on 1 August 1740?

5     held for a time an appointment at a lunatic asylum?

6     founded the Royal College of Organists?

7     produced concertos for (a) tuba and (b) harmonica?

8     was inspired by Sanskrit literature?

9     was born in Bradford?

10     was twice appointed organist of Westminster Abbey?

## • 16 • (1966, 14) *Who:*

1   claims one for white?
2   led the White Company?
3   was white, clear white, inside?
4   was lost from the White Ship?
5   wrote on the white peacock?
6   was White Surrey?
7   was the White Moon?
8   are the White Monks?
9   is a white bonnet?
10   uses white spirit?

## • 17 • (1966, 15)

1   in what year did a luciferous styloid reappear on a penny?
2   why is a pennyweight so called?
3   where and until when were fourteen pennies worth a shilling?
4   what is the significance of KN upon a penny?
5   when did the English penny become bronze?
6   over what halfpenny did the DPP take a hand?
7   what was a bawbee?
8   what was a penny-a-liner?
9   what was a penny-dog?
10   what was a penny-gaff?

• 18 • (1966, 17) *Who wrote the following:*

1    In my beginning is my end?

2    Yet for Christ's sake, whose blood hath ransomed me
Impose some end to my incessant pain?

3    His Father, who was self-controlled
Bade all the children round attend
To James's miserable end?

4    And, which is best and happiest yet, all this
With God not parted from him as was fear'd
But favouring and assisting to the end?

5    Why do sinners' ways prosper? And why must
Disappointment all I endeavour end?

6    I, like an usurpt town, to another due,
Labour to admit you, but Oh, to no end?

7    Earth's axis varies; your dark central cone
Wavers, a candle's shadow, at the end?

8    Waiting for the end, boys, waiting for the end?

9    There is now less flogging in our great schools than formerly, but then less is
learned there, so that what the boys get at one end they lose at the other?

10    This is not the end. It is not even the beginning of the end. But it is perhaps
the end of the beginning?

# 1967–1968

**• 1 •** (1967, 2) *Which saint:*

1   owned a staff which sprouted to become the Holy Thorn?

2   has a tomb near a Middle East airport, and should be of special veneration to Englishmen?

3   finds common ground in a gardener's spade and a French four-wheeler?

4   received his first challenge, 'Repair my fallen houses'?

5   translated the Bible in a grotto?

6   had sentence of death confirmed by the University of Paris?

7   crowned a King of All England in Bath Abbey?

8   welcomed, while still a pagan, a missionary and a saint to England?

9   was in the New Testament called a twin?

10  is associated with ergotism?

**• 2 •** (1967, 3) *Name:*

1   a court jester who founded a hospital.

2   a sea captain who founded a hospital.

3   the farmer credited with being the first to perform successfully cowpox vaccination on his wife and son.

4   the English Hippocrates.

5   the man who investigated the Broad Street pump.

6   the draper who was a pioneer in vital statistics.

7   the French surgeon who introduced the surgical-gauze face mask.

8   the German physician who discovered the 'islands' which produce insulin.

9   the man who used a roll of paper as an aid to diagnosis.

10  the scholar responsible for the foundation of the body which produced the first official pharmacopoeia in England.

**• 3 •** (1967, 7) *What on a wooden wall:*

1    have no bodies?

2    is not English?

3    are not plain?

4    have no criminal record?

5    are not happy?

6    is not an only child?

7    have no flowers?

8    have no wheels?

9    is not at home?

10    do not swim?

**• 4 •** (1967, 8) *Which Nell or Nelly:*

1    was surnamed Trent?

2    piped her eyes?

3    has purple flowers?

4    had a sweet named after her?

5    played hostess to the prince?

6    heard Catherine say, 'I am Heathcliff'?

7    wasn't to die?

8    was one of the ruins that Cromwell knocked about a bit?

9    sang about a fine brown frame?

10    entertained Johnny?

**• 5 •** (1967, 9) *Which Jovial inamorata:*

1    laid two eggs?

2    goes into mourning for half the year?

3    was a labourer's mother?

4    cuddled a cuckoo?

5    was showered with gold?

6    was chased by a snake?

7    gave her name to a continent?

8    was ingested?

9    became an island?

10    became a bear?

**• 6 •** (1967, 10) *What gas:*

1　is named after the sun?

2　does no work?

3　is hidden?

4　is strange?

5　is new?

6　is no longer thought acidifying?

7　is flowing?

8　is aqueous?

9　is virid?

10　may not be sent by post to the Comoro Islands?

**• 7 •** (1967, 11) *Who:*

1　'couldn't trust Mr Studd at the other end'?

2　claimed an average of 'o'wt, nowt'?

3　'… never knew till I was a first class umpire that a no-ball counted one'?

4　answered, 'Of course I was a great captain; I had great bowlers'?

5　had ten for 10?

6　weighed less than six stones 'bat and all' in the Harrow XI?

7　had a double double in a match?

8　was 'Shrimp'?

9　started with 200 in 1951?

10　were the father and son who captained England in Test matches?

**• 8 •** (1967, 13) *What mountain:*

1　has officially only 34 feet to spare?

2　made its debut on 20 February 1943?

3　descends evenly to zero?

4　is the greatest from base to summit?

5　disputed a record with Aconcagua?

6　did T E Brown thank God that blaeberries are still on?

7　overlooks the setting of *The Lady of the Lake*?

8　is described as 'dread name derived from clouds and storm'?

9　could be eaten?

10　might claim supremacy in precipitation?

• 9 • (1967, 15) *Who created the following:*

1 Grandgousier?

2 Chimène?

3 Alceste?

4 Mithridate?

5 Thunder-ten-Tronckh?

6 Vautrin?

7 Emma Roualt?

8 Cosette?

9 Mlle Fifi?

10 Meursault?


• 10 • (1968, 2)

1 what is said to have had an even chance of being named the Bunbury?

2 who was first, and the rest nowhere?

3 how far is a distance?

4 who was the Flaming Tinman?

5 when did Good Friday fall on a Boxing Day?

6 when was Sir Ivor's birthday?

7 who was the Head Waiter?

8 where is the Birdless Grove?

9 who was the Avenger of Waterloo?

10 who was the spotted wonder?


• 11 • (1968, 3) *Who or what:*

1 Peter was a red shadow?

2 was Peter's Pence?

3 Peter was besieged by Winston Churchill?

4 said 'Peter, stay at the gate'?

5 Peter was Mr Standfast?

6 investigated Black Peter?

7 Peter was whistled in a song?

8 Peter danced when given painkiller?

9 Peter forecast a great laundry loss?

10 Peter was a royal shipyard worker?

• 12 • (1968, 6) *Whose servant is or was:*

1    Bunter?

2    Abigail Hill?

3    Pigg?

4    Miggs?

5    Meadow pipit?

6    Lugg?

7    John Brown?

8    Iphigenia?

9    Blondel of Nesle?

10    Sancho Panza?


• 13 • (1968, 7) *Whose diary:*

1    dealt with madness?

2    reflected the problems of a country cleric in France?

3    is signed daily by PHS?

4    was the work of two brothers?

5    was the most voluminous ever published in English?

6    provoked its author to remark 'I never travel without it. One should always have something sensational to read on the train'?

7    was the work of a boy king?

8    frequently concluded the day's events with the words 'And so to bed'?

9    was written in a Dutch attic?

10    is no longer a diary?


• 14 • (1968, 8) *What law:*

1    is anti-feminist?

2    is concerned with Germanic phonetics?

3    refers to heredity?

4    was Great and Elizabethan?

5    is provoked in emergency?

6    is Heaven's first?

7    asserts the expulsion of the superior by the inferior?

8    is concerned with volume and pressure?

9    is ecclesiastical?

10    was concerned with summary justice?

• 15 • (1968, 9) *What philosopher:*

1    was called The Mollusc?

2    is the gourmet's patron but had ulcers?

3    preferred veined marble to white?

4    thought that philosophy is like an egg?

5    doubted in a stove?

6    lived like a dog?

7    brought space and time home to us?

8    invented a 'duck-rabbit'?

9    invented a sea monster?

10   brought Hegel down to earth?

• 16 • (1968, 13) *Which Mary:*

1    predicted the findings of a post-mortem?

2    had a peripatetic pet described by whom?

3    cometh early, the first day of the week?

4    featured prominently at the siege of Gaunt?

5    was incriminated by the casket letters?

6    was described in the marriage treaty as *nubilis et formosa*?

7    was said by whom to have been last seen on an errand in wild, rank foam?

8    was said by a contemporary diarist to have 'pleased nobody' by her birth?

9    had Whig doubts cast upon the legitimacy of her newly born prince?

10   was the grandmother of a pretending queen?

• 17 • (1968, 15) *Who:*

1 described the romance of Concordia?

2 travelled to Karameesh?

3 was expected to finance Pontevedria?

4 embezzled in Erewhon?

5 is the owner of Gabriela?

6 was king of Barataria?

7 was king of the Ochori?

8 is the gardener of Rubovia?

9 represented the United Kingdom in Gaillardia?

10 was queen of Ruritania?

• 18 • (1968, 17)

1 who was not charmed by iron?

2 who maintained that a single man in possession of a good fortune must be in want of a wife?

3 who married the alleged murderer of her father and first husband?

4 who married Tracy Draco?

5 who loved not wisely but too well?

6 whose love-making ended with 'Here comes a chopper to chop off your head'?

7 whose marriage service began 'D'b'loved we gath'd 'gether sight o' Gard 'n face this con'gation join 'gather Man Woom Ho Mat'my...'?

8 what squirrel loved what bear?

9 who cited *'per verba presenti'* as grounds for her marriage?

10 whose husband deafened her for tearing one of his books?

# 1969–1970

• 1 •  (1969, 1) *In 1869:*

1   what did Eugénie officially open?
2   what great historian was made a peer?
3   who wrote *The Subjection of Women*?
4   who met at Promontory Point?
5   what council met for the first time for over 300 years?
6   who was born at Porbandar Kathiawar?
7   who asked for and received Rouher's resignation?
8   what was disestablished?
9   who pioneered education at Hitchin?
10  what post did Fish have?

• 2 •  (1969, 2) *Who dwelt:*

1   with beauty?
2   by the brook Cherith?
3   underneath the mountain?
4   among the untrodden ways?
5   much on right and much on wrong?
6   in such a gorgeous palace?
7   in the house of the Lord for ever?
8   *sur la branche*?
9   on earth?
10  by the pleasant water-courses?

**• 3 •** (1969, 5) *What ship:*

1 should have turned from Amazon to Mary Sellars?

2 linked the Isle of Man with Gettysburg?

3 inspired Turner's *Snowstorm*?

4 preceded the Saltash over the cruel sea?

5 sailed north-west in 1969 to Seward's Folly?

6 sailed to Colchis?

7 fought fifty-three?

8 started with a larger beak than stomach?

9 was the first marine work to surpass the Ark?

10 anchored in Frenchman's Creek?

**• 4 •** (1969, 6) *Which Margaret:*

1 sponsored a baker's son?

2 lost her husband in battle with her brother's army?

3 reached the Orkneys but not the altar?

4 rose to a new peak on her marriage?

5 was described by a contemporary diarist as 'a mad, conceited, ridiculous woman'?

6 was Coward's first psychic cyclist?

7 was the 'she-wolf of France'?

8 was Merry Margaret, the mid-summer flower?

9 was the daughter of 'le Hardi'?

10 founded Wordsworth's alma mater?

**• 5 •** (1969, 7) *What month:*

1 provides 'old, old sophistries'?

2 inducts the Winter Solstice?

3 is succeeded by tempestuous breath?

4 is enriched by *Ephemera danica*?

5 is called 'the cruellest month'?

6 is fatal to abstainers?

7 provides 'no cheerfulness, no healthful ease'?

8 dements *Leporidae*?

9 celebrated another month's bank holiday?

10 hears birds exhorting regression?

• 6 • (1969, 8) *Who or what:*

1 'stole' Blue Water

2 owns the London Water Gardens?

3 said 'I don't care where the water goes if it doesn't get into the wine'?

4 gave the river at Madrid a glass of water?

5 reptile runs on water?

6 is Javel water?

7 employed Tim Linkinwater?

8 was the Water Poet?

9 is a water junket?

10 wrote of himself, 'Here lies one whose name was writ in water?

• 7 • (1969, 11) *Who or what:*

1 wrote *The Firm of Girdlestone*?

2 stone caused transmutation?

3 stone has a child called Pebbles?

4 stone married Audrey?

5 stone was David's stepfather?

6 is the Yellowstone?

7 is the Black Stone?

8 is a logan-stone?

9 stone bridged the resistance gap?

10 is a stone hatch?

• 8 • (1969, 12) *What cape:*

1 to the north-west died away?

2 is valedictory?

3 confronted *Dauntless*?

4 bade farewell to Apollo?

5 changed hands at Amiens?

6 belongs to the *Gadidae* order?

7 surveys the British Museum?

8 witnessed the triumph of Bryant and May's hero?

9 might be crystal?

10 saw the world's largest tidal wave?

**• 9 •** (1969, 14) *Who:*

1    dramatized the activities of Captain Cat?
2    possessed a runcible cat?
3    was a Cat about Town?
4    set to music *My Cat Geoffrey*?
5    wrote about the cat who walks by himself?
6    had a favourite cat which perished in fishy circumstances?
7    regarded the cat as sacred?
8    would have preferred to be a kitten than a metre-balladmonger?
9    were members of the Kit Kat Club?
10   proposed a rise in status for CATs?

**• 10 •** (1970, 4) *Who or what:*

1    rode out of the west on the best steed through the Border?
2    had a horse which was ox-headed?
3    is a Friesland Horse?
4    horse was a half-brother to Ginger?
5    surrendered on his horse Traveller?
6    horse carried me (accompanied by Dirck and Joris)?
7    horse had a talking head?
8    had a horse sewn up with laurel wood?
9    horses were white, black, red and pale?
10   horse sprang out of blood?

**• 11 •** (1970, 5) *To which sports do the following refer:*

1    Dièdre?
2    Infield fly?
3    Dead man's hole?
4    Butcher's hook?
5    Kake?
6    Wedeln?
7    Frog?
8    Toucher?
9    Spearing?
10   Barani?

• 12 • (1970, 6) *Which Henry:*

1    was given a Flanders mare?

2    has a sinister hammer?

3    joined the Roses matrimonially?

4    had a bad chewing habit?

5    used to toast his return on his departure?

6    did not object to Gladstone's ace?

7    wrote of a toxophilite's loss?

8    suggested archiepiscopal riddance?

9    would rather have been right than be president?

10    rebuilt the Abbey of St Peter?

• 13 • (1970, 7) *Identify the following:*

1    Turnbull's Blue.

2    Pearl white.

3    Scheele's green.

4    Chrome yellow.

5    Black Jack.

6    Monastral blue.

7    Mosaic gold.

8    Tyrian purple.

9    Berlin green.

10    Chinese white.

• 14 • (1970, 8) *Who referred to whom or what as:*

1    the colossus of roads?

2    the wisest fool in Christendom?

3    a cornet of horse in need of suppression?

4    the noblest Elphberg of them all?

5    clear, cold, pure and very dead?

6    the most married man I ever saw in my life?

7    having caught the Whigs bathing, he walked away with their clothes?

8    urban, squat and packed with guile?

9    believing in deities of his own invention?

10    no disgrace to a man but confoundedly inconvenient?

• 15 • (1970, 10) *What prison:*

1     saw its prisoner sacked and thrown out?
2     is known as the Tombs?
3     held the creator of St Trinian's?
4     was Black Michael's castle?
5     is by Britain's highest railway station?
6     was destroyed on 14 July?
7     has Harry Secombe come to know well?
8     is at Ossining?
9     has been replaced by the Central Criminal Court?
10    was a rock in Frisco Bay?

• 16 • (1970, 11) *With whom or what do you associate the following weapons:*

1     a Plantaganet hammer?
2     handkerchiefs?
3     'This here stick'?
4     The King's ankus?
5     a snickersee?
6     a pendant sword?
7     a crutch?
8     *baculum*?
9     a tent peg?
10    a catapult?

• 17 • (1970, 12) *How are the following first:*

1     The *Aaron Manby*?
2     Robert Edwin Peary?
3     Copper of 1797?
4     Jonas Salk?
5     Clifford Dupont?
6     John Flamstead?
7     Sopwith Pup?
8     Battle of Hampton Roads?
9     John of Newbury?
10    Edmund Hillary?

• 18 • (1970, 13) *Which Hall:*

1   is powerful?
2   offered 'no extras, no vacations, and diet unparalleled at twenty guineas a term'?
3   held the post of posts?
4   when deaspirated was annexed by Britain in 1955?
5   is a Waterhouse?
6   is backed by water and locked in by sounding keys?
7   is famous for political farces?
8   with Michaelhouse made a Trinity?
9   had an effect?
10   with a Waterhouse makes a liar?

# 1971

• 1 • *In 1871:*

  1   who was born at Pokrovskoye?

  2   who was elected MP for Limerick City?

  3   what was found at Mount Bischoff?

  4   who became minister of finance in Japan?

  5   who presumed at Ujiji?

  6   what treaty involved the cession of Alsace and Lorraine?

  7   whose birth at Dayton preluded fame at Kitty Hawk?

  8   what Act removed an Oxbridge disability?

  9   who was Chief Justice of the USA?

10   what was annexed by Sir Henry Barkly?

• 2 • *Who is otherwise known as:*

  1   Mrs J O Bayley?

  2   Lady Browning?

  3   Miss Mary Challans?

  4   Mrs Haynes Dixon?

  5   Mrs J B Priestley?

  6   Lady Mallowan?

  7   Hon. Mrs Peter Rodd?

  8   Mrs Rougier?

  9   Lady Snow?

10   Mrs Waters?

**• 3 •** *Who or what priest:*

1    was chaplain to Lord Touchwood?
2    was bishop's chaplain at St Ogg's?
3    was continually changing sovereigns?
4    tracked down the Arrow of Heaven?
5    won the Great Sermon Handicap?
6    was sure God was in his garden?
7    wrote of dissipation and Scarlett?
8    had an offending hand?
9    was opposed to Mayor Peppone?
10    died of his turbulence?

**• 4 •** *Where does she blow:*

1    Sirocco?
2    Maltemi?
3    Chinook?
4    Gibli?
5    Vardarac?
6    Maestro?
7    Mistral?
8    Chili?
9    Levanter?
10    Khamsin?

**• 5 •** *What castle:*

1    serves Derby aerially?
2    fills the Jaws?
3    is made by Wrenn?
4    is in opposition (in 1971)?
5    hindered progress?
6    starts the tour?
7    was composed by Henry Lawes?
8    preceded Dr Finlay?
9    was formerly Causewayhead?
10    was lost off Cape Town in 1901?

**• 6 •**

1   who was first over 6 feet?

2   who is remembered by over 6 feet at Wixford?

3   which four measure about 6 feet?

4   who wrote of celestial honey using 6 feet in a line?

5   what did Buntaro Adachi find equal once in every 6 feet?

6   why does the postman stand firm on 6 feet?

7   what dries 6 feet north-east of Burhou?

8   how many hands make 6 feet?

9   who set his Sixth Foot forward and swung the day at Orthez?

10  who cannot fathom at 6 feet?

**• 7 •**   *Who or what:*

1   were plucked in the temple gardens?

2   was worth 6s. 8d. in the sixteenth century?

3   was the name of Frederick's niece Ganymede?

4   is the Dean's Eye?

5   was the name of Redouté's book of paintings?

6   first appeared in Dresden in 1911?

7   is Albert Frederick Arthur George's younger?

8   did Sergeant Cuff and Mr Begbie differ over?

9   day was 26 June 1912, firstly?

10  did Gertrude Stein repeat roundly?

**• 8 •**   *Who or what:*

1   are blue buttons?

2   is studied by the Commission for Blue Oil?

3   is a blue tongue?

4   is a blue point?

5   saw nothing but blue skies?

6   is Blue John?

7   recently had a million Blue Moons?

8   were the Blue Devils?

9   are the Blue Eagles?

10  is Blue Mantle?

**• 9 •** *Who wrote the following:*

1   *Nei Ching?*
2   *De rerum natura?*
3   *Pen T'sao Kang Mu?*
4   *De humani corporis fabrica libri septem?*
5   *Exercitatio anatomica de motu cordis et sanguinis in animalibus?*
6   *De sedibus et causis morborum?*
7   *An Inquiry into the Causes and Effect of the Variolae Vaccinae?*
8   *Leçons sur les phénomènes de la vie?*
9   *Die Aetiologie, der Begriff und die Prophylaxis des Kindbettfiebers?*
10   *On the Antiseptic Principle in the Practice of Surgery?*

**• 10 •** *Who called what:*

1   Wabasso?
2   Sredni Vashtar?
3   Kebeg?
4   Mr Tod?
5   Marland Jimmy?
6   Old Deuteronomy?
7   Tito?
8   Eeyore?
9   Hathi?
10   Nana?

**• 11 •** *What wear do you associate with the following:*

1   Garland and Astaire?
2   the return of peaceful pursuits?
3   Mr Darby?
4   underwear for us but not for US?
5   Mr Pink?
6   Miss Streisand?
7   George Louis Palmella Busson du Maurier?
8   double you?
9   Diamond Lil?
10   Billy, Charlie or Colonel Prescott?

• 12 • *Who are or were known as:*

1 Tykes?

2 Yellowbellies?

3 Croweaters?

4 Loco-focos?

5 Moonrakers?

6 Sandgropers?

7 Loiners?

8 Hunkers?

9 Beanbellies?

10 Govaghs?


• 13 • *What Great:*

1 is now Greats?

2 sounds in the tower of Christ Church, Oxford?

3 is Grace at the Lord's Gate?

4 was Johnson, according to Wilkes?

5 is a Rocky Shed?

6 lasted from 28 July to 11 November?

7 is *Podiceps cristatus*?

8 escorted Christiana?

9 hovered around P Pirrip?

10 was Pitt the Elder?


• 14 • *Complete the following:*

1 A – – – – of partridge

2 A – – – – of snipe

3 A – – – – of pheasants

4 A – – – – of coots

5 A – – – – of dunlin

6 A – – – – of goldfinches

7 A – – – – of curlew

8 A – – – – of starlings

9 An – – – – of larks

10 A – – – – of rooks

## • 15 • *In song:*

1 who bought a ring for *one* shilling?
2 who had eyes like *two* holes in a blanket?
3 whence came *three* little maids?
4 what *four* and twenty were encrusted?
5 when were *five* gold rings presented?
6 what exchange had number *six* five thousand?
7 who falls in love quite madly at *seven*teen?
8 who were refused in preference to Henry *Eight*?
9 who wore size *nine* boxes?
10 who preceded one hundred and *ten* cornets?

## • 16 • *Identify the following:*

1 Old Ebor
2 Silver Billy
3 Lion of Kent
4 Old Everlasting
5 The Nonpareil
6 The Champion
7 Gubby
8 The Squire
9 Cockroach
10 The Monster

• 17 • *Which Charles:*

1 showed concern for Nellie's nourishment?

2 sang 'Glory to the new-born King'?

3 suggested an alternative to cream for disposing of a cat?

4 is in Norfolk?

5 nothing common did or mean upon that memorable scene?

6 forecast a movement of air causing the descent of a cot and its contents?

7 is an asterism?

8 was the nicest child I ever knew?

9 landed at Moidart?

10 was responsible for an auriferous onslaught in California?

• 18 • *In 1971 who or what:*

1 other famous day was recalled on 15 February?

2 was ceremonially opened on Trafalgar Day near an historic fortress?

3 spared no expense in conjuring up memories of great antiquity?

4 was the most northern of three pleased to find themselves half in and half out?

5 sport helped let in a chink of light on international affairs?

6 shook the world after an unsuccessful appeal?

7 unlike Skye, was first visited by royalty in August?

8 though it moved, instead of falling down, went up?

9 tried a quit run on Hadley Ridge?

10 may still cherish his family tree but not the other one?

# 1972

**• 1 •** *In 1872 who or what:*

1    opened his innings on 10 September at Sarodar?
2    'pleasing ground for the benefit of the people' was opened?
3    aggression was assessed at $15,500,000?
4    introduced a Republican motion in the Commons?
5    painted *Snap-the-Whip*?
6    measure provided polling privacy?
7    launched his agricultural trade union movement?
8    ship lost Captain Briggs?
9    presidential aspirant was known as Madam Satan?
10   'second Barrow' was born?

**• 2 •** *Where could one sit in:*

1    Knesset?
2    Sejm?
3    Sobranje?
4    Storting?
5    Eduskunta?
6    Tynwald?
7    Riksdag?
8    Althing?
9    Panchayat?
10   Eerste Kamer?

• 3 • *Who or what:*

1   is a long-plumed type of heron?
2   will prevent you remaining in Thermopylae?
3   requires inversion for effectiveness?
4   resembled kissing an unwaxed moustache?
5   joins fraternity and liberty?
6   is partly good?
7   is a tremulous resonance heard in auscultation in cases of pleurisy?
8   means neediness?
9   should not be put in one vessel of interwoven twigs?
10  is singularly vain?

• 4 • *What bird does Linnaeus describe as:*

1   whistler?
2   watchman?
3   kernel-remover?
4   berry-breaker?
5   cave-dweller?
6   goat-milker?
7   nanny goat?
8   little brother?
9   little king?
10  wingless?

• 5 • *Who lastly said these words?*

1   '… my design is to make what haste I can to be gone'
2   'Display my head to the people. It is worth your trouble'
3   'How is the Empire?'
4   'Kiss me, sweet wife and I will try to sleep a little'
5   'Ah a German, and a genius, a prodigy, admit him'
6   'Die, my dear doctor? That's the last thing I shall do'
7   'That is impossible on grounds of general policy. Forward'
8   'Pity this beard should be cut which has never committed treason'
9   'I feel very ill. Send for the apothecary!'
10  'I think I could eat one of Bellamy's veal pies'

## • 6 • *In 1972 who or what:*

1   disease allegedly afflicted Headingley?
2   was the first Brazilian champion in his sport?
3   became *Sportsworld*?
4   banned the press from the Olympics?
5   planned another victory, this time at Strady Park?
6   made a timely confession at Augsburg and had the course drained?
7   was the first Irish double centenarian?
8   became Bradsen?
9   struck gold unprecedently?
10  were *Daffodil* and *Golden Eagle*?

## • 7 • *What type is suggested by:*

1   a modish pugilist?
2   Corporal John's victory?
3   the investigations of Major Ronald Ross?
4   feline damnation?
5   John of Gaunt?
6   a cruiser of Barbary?
7   the Flickertail State?
8   the cart before the horse?
9   inflammable expectoration?
10  the Iron Duke?

## • 8 • *What novel title might have been taken by:*

1   F Scott Fitzgerald from *Ode to a Nightingale*?
2   André Gide from St Luke?
3   Aldous Huxley from Marlow?
4   Alexander Solzhenitsyn from Dante's *Inferno*?
5   John Steinbeck from *Richard III*?
6   E M Forster from Pope's *Essay on Criticism*?
7   Howard Spring from Shirley's *The Contention of Ajax and Ulysses*?
8   Nicholas Monserrat from *Othello*?
9   James Hilton from Daniel Webster?
10  Mary Renault from Campion's *Third Book of Airs*?

**• 9 •**  *What ship or ships:*

1  had one brand of Cain for mate and a human mistake for cook?

2  went rolling down to Rio?

3  was idle as a painted ship upon a painted ocean?

4  was rat-ridden, bilge bestank?

5  had her bowsprit mixed up with her rudder sometimes?

6  was 300 cubits on the water-line with a beam of 50 cubits?

7  had a boy stand on her burning deck?

8  was just a pack of rotten plates puttied up with tar?

9  was a beautiful pea-green boat?

10  went down by the island crags to be lost evermore in the main?

**• 10 •**  *Who was opposed to or by:*

1  Saknussem?

2  Mr Monks?

3  Mr Meers?

4  Blofeld?

5  Massala?

6  Mr Medina?

7  Twala?

8  Carl Peterson?

9  Chauvelin?

10  Rev John Laputa?

**• 11 •**  *What Edward:*

1  was impersonated by a baker's son?

2  wrote of Pobbles and Jumblies?

3  first had three feathers for his badge?

4  wrote of a feather called Macaroni?

5  suggested that a fool at forty is a fool indeed?

6  conducts and sails the ship of state?

7  was born Jones, became German, but was English?

8  had middle age foretold for him by Girolamo Cardano?

9  was referred to in *The Times* as 'omnium consensu capax imperii nisi imperasset'?

10  was buried at Wareham?

## • 12 • *What:*

1  was B W Procter's pseudonym?
2  fourth of three was Miss Holtby's?
3  series was introduced by the warden?
4  tales came in 1888 between *The Woodlanders* and *Tess?*
5  borders on both Cornwall and Surrey?
6  house is the home of the revenue men?
7  author was caricatured by Sheridan as Sir Fretful Plagiary?
8  has a fringe on top?
9  came between musket and drum?
10  can you get from both an elephant and a duck?

## • 13 • *Who were the masters of the following:*

1  Flush?
2  Asta?
3  Pedro?
4  Bullseye?
5  The Bluidy Mackenzie?
6  Bobby of Greyfriars?
7  Turk and Bill?
8  Muttley?
9  Crab?
10  Montmorency?

## • 14 • *Who:*

1  made a sword blade in Italy, or was it in Scotland?
2  resigned as a president to become Secretary of the Treasury?
3  was cricket (in imitation of Emerson)?
4  spills the beans, but not at nine?
5  was known as Banjo?
6  was a man of steel and changed the Music Hall?
7  wrote an ode to stormy waters?
8  practised in Callander?
9  makes sport for others?
10  succeeded Dudley Pound?

**• 15 •** *Who was assassinated, and where, by the following:*

1   Charles Guiteau?
2   Morville de Breton?
3   Bonnier la Chapelle?
4   Ravaillac?
5   Gavrilo Princip?
6   Bellingham?
7   Czolgosz?
8   Lee Oswald?
9   Charlotte Corday?
10   Prince Felix Yusupov?

**• 16 •** *Quintuplicate the following:*

1   Tunstall, Burslem, Hanley, Longton – – – –
2   Emilie, Cecile, Marie, Annette – – – –
3   Hastings, Sandwich, Romney, Hythe – – – –
4   Utah, Sword, Juno, Gold – – – –
5   Hampden, Hazelrig, Holles, Strode – – – –
6   Bryher, Tresco, St Martin's, St Agnes – – – –
7   Derby, Lincoln, Leicester, Nottingham – – – –
8   Jhelum, Chenab, Ravi, Beas – – – –
9   Cervical, Thoracic, Sacral, Coccyx – – – –
10   Common Sense, Imagination, Fantasy, Estimation – – – –

**• 17 •** *Where and when:*

1   do the Tutti Men run with the Orangeman?
2   are the fenny poppers fired?
3   is the Furry danced?
4   do the Uppards meet the Downards?
5   is the champion tolley flicked?
6   does Boggins catch the Hood?
7   is the Grovely Procession?
8   is the Millenary horn blown?
9   do hot pennies follow the glove up?
10   does King William perform with Tenpenny Nit?

• 18 • *In 1972 who or what:*

1    arrived unshrouded by Manannan but left the fish behind?

2    took fifty years to reach the land of the discoverer?

3    celebrated half a century of sound endeavour?

4    celebrated its centenary though only ninety-one?

5    caused trouble by substituting half a hundred for a dozen?

6    celebrated a quarter of a century with partial repetition?

7    through weakening power won a high reward?

8    is a lover of Mann, old places and fun and surprised at the honour he found he had won?

9    arrived late, but quickly moved up to pass the holder?

10    applied but then withdrew?

# 1973

**• 1 •** *In 1873:*

1    whose Royal progress ended at Chislehurst?

2    what nobleman travelled westward on the footplate?

3    who started upon the even teno(u)r of his ways?

4    who started to get their men?

5    whose fairy godmother must have presented a pair of 'silver shoon'?

6    what master of song saw the light at Novgorod?

7    whose centenary reminded the Victorians of light interference?

8    what insular colony joined the Dominion?

9    who breathed his last, but not beneath the ashes of Vesuvius?

10    who started his liberal course to Number 11?


**• 2 •** *Whose scale:*

1    registers terrestrial convulsions?

2    is also known as dyadic?

3    assesses hardness?

4    records the reading of an anemometer?

5    is piscine and membranous?

6    controls nurses' salaries?

7    proceeds by semitones?

8    is a sign of the Zodiac?

9    is a pedagogic regulator?

10    enables fractional adjustments?

QUESTIONS

## • 3 •  *Which Richard:*
1   was the beau ideal of the pump room?
2   was mistaken on the Nile?
3   drank a health to the thrifty housewife?
4   rose from a Gloucestershire lad to a cockney lord?
5   loved honour more?
6   enumerated the Laws of Ecclesiastical Polity?
7   missed the support of a King of Mann?
8   might be called a master of song and son-in-law of rhapsody?
9   hailed from Bordeaux but hardly had a summer of roses and wine?
10  is being weighed in the balances?

## • 4 •  *What is, or was, the surname of:*
1   Lenin?
2   Lord Tweedsmuir?
3   Earl of Bothwell?
4   Gerald Londin?
5   Stella?
6   Gustav VI of Sweden?
7   Adrian IV?
8   George Eliot?
9   Donald Ebor?
10  Duke of Rutland?

## • 5 •  *Who in Greek Mythology:*
1   won the gold award in the first beauty contest?
2   depicted a world within a circle of a targe?
3   was stranded at Naxos?
4   purchased a wind with his daughter's life?
5   had a grandson who, it seems, fought at long range?
6   hibernated in Hades?
7   like a good motorist watched his mirror, and scored with a backhander?
8   eloped with a witch and murderess to boot?
9   was the victim of the original Oedipus complex?
10  succeeded where Eurydice failed?

• 6 • *What and where in the British Isles are the following:*

1    Heathery Coming Home?
2    The Postage Stamp?
3    The Suez Canal?
4    Calamity Corner?
5    South America?
6    The Dowie?
7    Gumbleys?
8    The Race Course?
9    Risk-an'-hope?
10   The Cardinal's Back?

• 7 • *Who described what botanically as:*

1    full of dewy wine, the murmurous haunt of flies?
2    wearing of time, seeking after that sweet golden clime?
3    firstborn of Ver, merry springtime's harbinger?
4    drenched with dews of summer eves?
5    a modest crimson-tipped flower?
6    shrinking, like many more, from cold and rain?
7    a little Cyclops with one eye staring to threaten and defy?
8    being a year and a day away, by sail?
9    nothing but a cabbage with a college education?
10   having to 'skip like a calf'?

• 8 • *What bird is suggested by:*

1    a sailor's progress?
2    the Gael's wood horse?
3    a day's work?
4    a set of three?
5    a plasterer's slab?
6    a trump?
7    a flannel scarf with sleeves?
8    erstwhile judgment on the murderer?
9    a third degree of excellence?
10   an island currency?

**• 9 •** *Explain the following:*

1. Askival and Hallival
2. Guron and Scynthius
3. Urim and Thummim
4. Epimetheus and Prometheus
5. Fetlar and Foula
6. Snout and Starveling
7. Trotternish and Vaternish
8. Lethe and Acheron
9. Erebus and Terror
10. Muppim and Huppim

**• 10 •** *What count:*

1. was the 'quack of quacks'?
2. introduced the broom to England?
3. chopped wood on Sparrow Hill?
4. fathered the Bohemian Girl?
5. had an appetite for blood but a dislike for stakes?
6. sang of smiling Irish eyes?
7. assisted a great Russian woman to remove a great Russian man?
8. designed LZ4?
9. employed a musical barber in southern Spain?
10. took his name from his treasure island?

**• 11 •** *What composite creature consists of:*

1. lion-goat-serpent?
2. snaky tresses upon a winged woman?
3. three heads, with a dog attached?
4. a human head with wings upon a lion's body?
5. a winged dragon with eagle's talons?
6. the head and wings of an eagle on the body of a lion?
7. an hirsute man with the hindquarters of a goat?
8. nine heads, one immortal, upon a writhing serpent?
9. bust human, rest equine?
10. songster, part nymph, part bird?

**• 12 •** *Explain the following:*

1   Black damp
2   Black velvet
3   Black Rod
4   His black diaries
5   Black Pope
6   Land of the Blacks
7   Black Bradman
8   All Blacks
9   Black Sluggard
10  Black Assize

**• 13 •** *Which political philosopher:*

1   tutored a world-beater?
2   though a monarchist, seemed more at home in the infernal regions?
3   fell foul of the Medici?
4   doubled his republic with demonology?
5   found the sheep so carnivorous that 'They doe eate up man'?
6   though a friend of the Merry Monarch, prescribed autocracy as the cure for brutish nature?
7   though a Somerset youth, had more to do with Shaftesbury?
8   graduated from the son of a watchmaker to the father of revolution?
9   was most unwelcome to the impeached governor?
10  wrote his *magnum opus* after an apology?

**• 14 •**

1   what is the Gabba?
2   what club played on Broad Halfpenny Down?
3   who was the Emperor of Bowlers?
4   from which county came the Band of Brothers?
5   who was Benjamin Aislabie?
6   under what name did Nicholas Wanostrocht play?
7   where is Parr's Tree?
8   for whom did King Cole and Dick-a-Dick play?
9   who described what as the Woolsack of Cricket?
10  for what was Dorset Fields famous?

• 15 • *What is a:*

1    fanion?

2    gabion?

3    cation?

4    terpodion?

5    gemellion?

6    trunnion?

7    mercerization?

8    collodion?

9    trituration?

10    tintinnabulation?

• 16 • *Which river:*

1    is all set about with fever trees?

2    washes its walls on the southern side?

3    is held up by the Fort Peck Dam?

4    left Achilles' heel uninsured?

5    stages the Fairbairns?

6    falls over the Salta das Sece Quedas?

7    is crossed by the Pontcysyllte?

8    saw Ajax and Achilles together again?

9    suggests a sea eagle?

10    is crossed by steps of tar?

**• 17 •** *Who said, wrote, or sang the following?*

1 God loveth a cheerful giver
2 Though God cannot alter the past, historians can
3 Youth shows but half: trust God; see all, nor be afraid
4 Justfy the waves of God to man
5 God's soldier be he!
6 Had I but served God …
7 Stern daughter of the voice of God
8 A neck God made for other use
9 God Almighty first planted a garden
10 The hope of the City of God at the other end of the road

**• 18 •** *In 1973, who or what:*

1 spiritual exile made his first visit to England?
2 gained a tenth from All Fools' Day?
3 brought no rest on the seventh day this time?
4 took this jump together instead of in competition?
5 travelled far to play unseasonably but won in the end?
6 was royally visited three times in forty-eight hours?
7 were fined for pleasing thousands?
8 tried to get everything taped but lost his job?
9 has the ladies sharing the floor?
10 is rather wider than its twelfth-century predecessor?

# 1974

**• 1 •**   *In 1874:*

1   what followed a range of exhausted volcanoes?
2   what claimant received fourteen years?
3   what were annexed from King Thakombau?
4   how did Mrs Weiss start an escapee on his way?
5   what premises were opened at Stepney Causeway?
6   who first left the colliery for the Commons?
7   how did the planets start their musical orbit?
8   how did the girdling of the earth become a possibility?
9   who submitted after Coomassie?
10  how did Parliament try to reduce pollution?

**• 2 •**   *Who or what:*

1   is the west wind?
2   rock is exposed and resistant?
3   is well-mixed egg yolk, honey and sherry?
4   is galvanizing metal?
5   springs about with Dougal?
6   artist carves wood?
7   is orange peel?
8   is the wheel of life?
9   is a Sumerian temple-tower?
10  is a Russian unit of weight?

• 3 • *With which rivers are the following associated:*

1 Pouilly Fuissé?

2 Fino San Patricio?

3 Chante-Alouette?

4 Château Pichon-Longueville-Lalande?

5 Schloss Böckelheim?

6 Veuve Cliquot?

7 Wachauer Schluck?

8 Quinta da Foz?

9 Piesporter Michelsberg?

10 Pouilly Fumé?


• 4 • *Who is indicated by:*

1 dotty writing?

2 treating cotton with caustic soda?

3 empty barometric space?

4 a sleeve starting at the neck?

5 a terpsichorean suit of clothes?

6 a vesicant gas?

7 a black profile?

8 a well-scrubbed *Shakespeare*?

9 Liffey water?

10 a newsreel?


• 5 • *What oleaginous area recalls:*

1 a Scottish order of knighthood?

2 a voracious seabird?

3 the assertion of the plutonic origin of granite?

4 *Alca impennis*?

5 a two-edged broadsword?

6 the eldest daughter of M. Tascher de la Pagerie?

7 a miner's sledge?

8 a husk, or the bearings of an axle, or a fish?

9 the saintly founder of a church at Whithorn?

10 the intermediary of Golders Green and Hendon?

**• 6 •** *Whose last command was:*

1   *Defiance?*

2   *Ellan Vannin?*

3   *Monarque?*

4   *Titanic?*

5   *Rawalpindi?*

6   *Graf Spee?*

7   *Marie Celeste?*

8   *Trinidad?*

9   *Lusitania?*

10   *Revenge?*


**• 7 •** *Whose signature tune might be called:*

1   'Lightin-up Time'?

2   'Under One's Breath'?

3   'Castro's Serenade'?

4   'Wells Fargo'?

5   'Transmitting'?

6   'Oglethorpe's Philanthropy'?

7   'Stale Chocolates'?

8   'A bientôt'?

9   'Comatose Lake'?

10   'Prandial Starters'?


**• 8 •** *Who created the following:*

1   Van der Valk?

2   C Auguste Dupin?

3   Miss Maud Silver?

4   Philip Marlowe?

5   Ironside?

6   Mr Campion?

7   Harry Palmer?

8   Sir John Appleby?

9   Martin Hewitt?

10   Lestrade?

**• 9 •** *Who advised whom to:*

1 try sparrow-hawks, Ma'am?

2 change England confides to England expects?

3 use a little wine for thy stomach's sake?

4 attempt self-decapitation?

5 remember time is money?

6 take the cylinder out of my kidney?

7 leave the Saxons alone?

8 try rum punch as a prophylactic against rheumatism?

9 fire when you are ready?

10 be off or I'll kick you downstairs?

**• 10 •** *Who was number two for:*

1 J S Bach?

2 Catherine of Aragon?

3 Nero?

4 Paderewski?

5 Frances Nisbet?

6 Mary Queen of Scots?

7 Dorothy Payne Todd?

8 Percy Bysshe Shelley?

9 Euphemia Ruskin?

10 Mme Antoine Lavoisier?

**• 11 •** *Who:*

1 experimented at Blackstone Gaol?

2 followed Sir Francis Hinsley at Megalopolitan Pictures?

3 moved from 14 Blight Street, HQ?

4 was the first lady embalmer of Whispering Glades?

5 was the founder and editor of *Survival*?

6 did Bill's wife follow at the Malt House, Grantley Green?

7 was junior Dean at Scone College?

8 was the diplomatic adviser to HOO HQ?

9 had his thunder-box put out of bounds by Brigadier Ritchie-Hooke?

10 was bigamously united with Captain Grimes?

- 12 • *How are they better known:*
  1 Paolo Caliari?
  2 Domenico Theotocopoulos?
  3 Raffaello Santi?
  4 Michel Angelo Merisi?
  5 Zorgo da Castelfranco?
  6 Alessandro di Mariano Filipepi?
  7 Jacopo Robusti?
  8 Tiziano Vecelli?
  9 Antonio Allegri?
  10 Pieter van der Faes?

- 13 • *Identify these firsts:*
  1 Bull's eyes
  2 Cotton reels
  3 Sydney Views
  4 Lady McLeods
  5 Scinde Dawks
  6 Double Genevas
  7 Basle Doves
  8 Montevideo Suns
  9 Missionaries
  10 Cameos

• 14 • *Who parodied whom in these lines:*

1 I'll tell thee everything I can;
   There's little to relate?

2 One, who is not, we see; but one whom we see not, is;
   Surely, this is not that; but that is assuredly this?

3 Wot, 'e would, would 'e? Well,
   Then you've got ter give 'im 'Ell,
   And it's trunch, trunch, truncheon does the trick?

4 I cannot chew my peanuts
   Or drink my lemonade:
   Good God, I am afraid?

5 As we get older we do not get any younger.
   Seasons return, and today I am fifty-five,
   And this time last year I was fifty-four?

6 O suitably attired in leather boots
   Head of traveller, wherefore seeking whom
   Whence by what way how purposed art thou come?

7 With a rumour of ghostly things that pass
   With a thunderous pennon of pain,
   To a land where the sky is as red as the grass,
   And the sun as green as the rain?

8 Gin a body meet a body
   Flyin' through the air.
   Gin a body hit a body;
   Will it fly? And where?

9 Look in my face. My name is Used-to was;
   I am also called Played-out and Done-to-death,
   And It-will-wash-no-more?

10 From the depth of the dreamy decline of the dawn
   Through a notable nimbus of nebulous noonshine?

**• 15 •** *Which William:*

1    was florid and met with toxophilitic misfortune?
2    was Thomas Clarkson's associate?
3    is Just?
4    was the bastard son of Robert the Devil and Arletta?
5    gave his name to Isaac Barrow's?
6    dedicated Karlotis to Pierre Charlot?
7    wrote *The Idiot Boy*?
8    was shot by Balthazar Gerard?
9    congratulated Kruger?
10   wrote a *Book of Snobs*?

**• 16 •** *Which:*

1    Alva switched on New York?
2    Langhorne loved the Mississippi?
3    Schwenk objected to a Savoy carpet?
4    Branwell was a brother to Bells?
5    Lutwidge was a friend of Miss Liddell?
6    Wadsworth knew he was ill when his sister came?
7    Makepeace described vanity and the Virginians?
8    Klapka was a third boater and bummeller?
9    Sorrell essayed in biology?
10   Brinsley had rivals and scandal?

## • 17 • *Which books by whom begin thus?*

1 It is a truth universally acknowledged, that a single man in possession of a good fortune must be in want of a wife.

2 He sat in defiance of municipal orders, astride the gun Zam-Zammah …

3 Old Deemster Christian of Ballawhaine was a hard man …

4 The education bestowed on Flora Poste by her parents had been too expensive, athletic and prolonged.

5 My father had a small estate in Nottinghamshire; I was the third of five sons.

6 This is the saddest story I have ever heard.

7 Stately, plump Buck Mulligan came from the stairhead …

8 It was the best of times, it was the worst of times …

9 The Schoolmaster was leaving the village, and everybody seemed sorry.

10 Call me Ishmael.

## • 18 • *In 1974 who or what:*

1 enigmatic lady made her first flight?

2 bird has proved to be the fastest so far?

3 was finally included out?

4 was in charge of the seventieth birthday celebration in the hall, although second fiddle in the House?

5 airport reached a million?

6 uniquely arrived unballoted?

7 won when they first mixed it, with a champion third?

8 has died, once called a fool and then an eagle?

9 made his debut on sport and leisure?

10 rosebuds celebrated their diamond jubilee?

# 1975

**• 1 •** *In 1875:*
1   what captain matched his strength against the waves?
2   how was slum clearance facilitated?
3   whose nun took the veil?
4   how did Edwin first escape Angelina?
5   who began his travels to Lambaréné?
6   how did Ismail Pasha ease his burdens?
7   whose westward journey ended at Eversley?
8   who established a new Sinking Fund?
9   what discovery filled the first periodic gap?
10   whose advent anticipated Sir Edward Leithen and Sandy Clanroyden?

**• 2 •** *Who or what:*
1   is Ko-Ko?
2   is pit-pit?
3   is a yo-yo?
4   is poi-poi?
5   is Xai-Xai?
6   is an aye-aye?
7   is ylang-ylang?
8   is ju-ju?
9   is peque-peque?
10   is Katikati?

• 3 • *What invention is associated with:*

1 an attack with pitchforks at Gonesse?

2 'Mr Watson, come here, I want you'?

3 a thin man and a fat man?

4 the letter S, repeatedly?

5 *teredo navalis*?

6 'Kruesi, make this'?

7 a mysterious disappearance off the steamer *Dresden*?

8 a courtyard at Châlon-sur- Saône?

9 perversely, a peace prize?

10 Fred Ott's sneeze?


• 4 • *What island:*

1 has great Liberty in Stone?

2 sheltered the Wake?

3 is the home for the Lord of the Isles?

4 saw the death of Israel Hands?

5 was Aemonia?

6 was the home of King Kong?

7 saw a colossal fall?

8 witnessed Raleigh's failure?

9 has a rocky Old Man?

10 saw the defeat of Flatbush?

## • 5 • *Indicate the deceased:*

1 Suddenly – – – –, a dramatist, victim of an airborne carapace

2 Tragically, at Inverness – – – –, beloved father of the Prince of Cumberland

3 – – – – – – – –, killed by a passerine toxophilite

4 At Newgate, his former place of employment, while participating in a public function. July 1780, – – – –.

5 Religiously sacrificed in a toolshed, – – – –, cousin and guardian of Conradin

6 From a head injury, while camping at Harosheth, – – – –.

7 – – – –, debtor of Aesculapius, by poison

8 – – – –, beloved wife of Canio, during a theatre production

9 In affectionate remembrance of – – – – – – – –, which died 29 August 1882. NB the body will be cremated and the ashes taken to Australia

10 Died 14 September as a result of wounds received at the Pan American Exposition in Buffalo, – – – –, beloved husband of Ida

## • 6 • *Who wrote the following:*

1 *Sinister Street?*

2 *On the Road?*

3 *Ten Rillington Place?*

4 *Washington Square?*

5 *Sunset Boulevard?*

6 *Slaughter on Tenth Avenue?*

7 *Swann's Way?*

8 *Desolation Row?*

9 *The Bloodhounds of Broadway?*

10 *Up the Junction?*

• 7 • *Whose slogan?*

1 An amicable twice two bonus
2 A lusty survival from George IV's accession
3 A limit of 2½p
4 A prophylactic for the sensation of falling slowly down
5 Judges 14: 14
6 A personal arrest for a single purchase
7 Valued at £1.05 per container
8 The retention of the skin texture of an adolescent female
9 Negative − − − − ... − − − −
10 A remedy for nocturnal vitamin deficiency

• 8 • *What New:*

1 was St Mary's College, Winchester?
2 was Rhosyr?
3 replaced Exning market?
4 houses the Metropolitan Water Board?
5 was Panjim?
6 is the site of Old Eli?
7 was composed by Friml?
8 is Salisbury?
9 was also Gregorian?
10 ended with the loss of Montreal?

• 9 • *Who or what:*

1 died on the screen saying Rosebud?
2 Rose sailed round the world?
3 rose is won internationally at bridge?
4 were wooed by Tokyo Rose?
5 Rose described Towers of Trebizond?
6 said a rose is a rose is a rose?
7 rose is also St John's Wort?
8 state has a tuneful yellow rose?
9 rose was medievally spent?
10 created *Le Spectre de la Rose?*

- 10 • *Identify the following:*

  1  Tom o'Ten Thousand
  2  Old Dreadnought
  3  Vinegar
  4  Old Grog
  5  Billy Blue
  6  Black Dick
  7  Cuddy
  8  Foul Weather Jack
  9  Dismal Jimmy
  10  Stiffo Rumpo

- 11 • *Complete the following:*

  1  Earth, air, water, – – – –
  2  Ulster, Munster, Leinster, – – – –
  3  Eurus, Boreas, Auster, – – – –
  4  Chlorine, Bromine, Fluorine, – – – –
  5  Arithmetic, Astronomy, Geometry, – – – –
  6  Intake, ignition, compression, – – – –
  7  Sanguine, phlegmatic, choleric, – – – –
  8  Circle, parabola, ellipse, – – – –
  9  Barbara, Celarent, Darii, – – – –
  10  Io, Europa, Ganymede, – – – –

- 12 • *What region of what country produces:*

  1  Port Salut?
  2  Dolcelatte?
  3  Vacherin du Mont D'Or?
  4  Sardo?
  5  Münster?
  6  Caerphilly?
  7  Nokkelost?
  8  Feta?
  9  Limburger?
  10  Blue Vinney?

# 1975

## • 13 • *Where in the United States:*

1   is Parkland hospital?
2   is the Rosebowl?
3   are Hoosiers found?
4   did a golden spike link east and west?
5   does John Brown's body lie a-moulding?
6   did Key observe the flag was still there?
7   was sued by McCulloch?
8   did 50,000 sing?
9   was Ricardo stabbed at a masked ball?
10   did the 'Lady in Red' betray at the Biograph?

## • 14 • *What Peter:*

1   was removed from German woods and entrusted to Dr Arbuthnot?
2   was that peerless paper peer?
3   was the pupil of Nikita Zotov?
4   launched Lemmy Caution?
5   founded the Premonstratensian Abbey of Titchfield?
6   is the signal of immediate departure?
7   joined Walter the Penniless at Constantinople?
8   picked a peck of pickled pepper?
9   was born in Pallet and married the niece of Canon Fulbert?
10   was victim of arrested development?

## • 15 • *Who or what:*

1   is required to knock three times?
2   is a sanguinary comestible?
3   asks for aces?
4   was 14 April 1360?
5   suffocated all but twenty-three?
6   is a noxious subterranean exhalation?
7   is *vingt-et-un*?
8   is invisible, ineluctable and collapsed?
9   suffragistically excludes?
10   allegedly manifests itself in Peel Castle?

## • 16 • *Who, in what work, is mine host at:*

1   the Potwell Inn?

2   the Boar's Head, Eastcheap?

3   the Admiral Benbow?

4   the Three (Jolly) Pigeons?

5   the Marquis of Granby, Dorking?

6   the Prancing Pony?

7   the Polka Saloon, Cloudy Mountain?

8   Antoine's?

9   the Café Momus?

10   the Maypole Inn, Chigwell?

## • 17 • *Whose invective, in what work?*

1   'I give thee sixpence! I will see thee damn'd first – Wretch! Whom no sense of wrongs can rouse to vengeance – sordid, unfeeling, reprobate, degraded, spiritless outcast!'

2   'Jounce ye, an' strip ye an' trip ye! A livin' gale – a livin' gale. Yah! ... You won't see Gloucester no more, no more!'

3   I quite lost my temper ... and pointed out to him what a drivelling maniac of an imbecile he was; but he only roared the louder

4   'The devil damned thee black, thou cream-fac'd loon!'

5   ' You have ... the privilege of being the world's most incompetent, drivelling, snivelling, jibbering, jabbering, idiot of a steward in France'

6   He cursed him in eating, he cursed him in drinking, he cursed him in coughing, in sneezing, in winking

7   – – – – got to cussing, and cussed everything and everybody he could think of, and then cussed them all over again to make sure he hadn't skipped any

8   'Back ye cowardly dogs ... Back t' the lines, ye goddam lily-livered cattle!'

9   ' – a gang of ignorant, pot-bellied, sacrilegious, money-scooping robbers ... hop-off-my-thumbs from God-forsaken places like Carlow or County Leitrim'

10   'Get packing, you hypocrites! To your sheep, you dogs! Clear out of here, you canting cheats! ... Gzz, gzzz, gzzzz! ... Are they not gone yet?'

• 18 • *In 1975 who or what:*

1    was publicly accolade for all-round achievements?

2    belied his name in the premier chase?

3    produced new signs of cumulo-nimbus?

4    went to the Bourne from which no Hollingsworth returns?

5    King queened it for the sixth time?

6    fell on his ninth anniversary?

7    internationally reached the highest points?

8    approved a German tea party?

9    March finished at Los Angeles?

10   was six miles unlucky on the third lap?

# 1976–1977

**• 1 •** (1976, 3) *In which musical:*

1 was the quest impossible?

2 did Ferenc Molnar's 'Liliom' finish up in Maine?

3 was Mrs Levi greeted?

4 was the music borrowed for an Arabian night?

5 was the astronomical title intended to be of a nautical nature?

6 did the Philadelphia Story get a boost?

7 did Fred occasionally become Petruchio?

8 did Fleming's creation take flight?

9 did the old man say nothing?

10 did 'Green grow the Lilacs' get state recognition?

**• 2 •** (1976, 4) *What brothers:*

1 were Leonard, Adolph and Julius?

2 harnessed levity at Annonay?

3 amassed an anatomical museum?

4 introduced Vitaphone?

5 diarized Nobody?

6 used 'no musical instruments other than one guitar'?

7 discovered the brachistochrone to be cycloid?

8 are known for folklore and consonantal law?

9 became elevated at Kitty Hawk?

10 won gold at adjoining weights?

• 3 •   (1976, 5) *Identify the following:*

  1   The Boston Tar-Baby.

  2   The Benicia Boy.

  3   The Brown Bomber.

  4   The Gas Man.

  5   Gentleman Jim.

  6   The Cinderella Man.

  7   Bendigo.

  8   Homicide Hank.

  9   The Game Chicken.

 10   The Ghost with a Hammer in his Hand.

• 4 •   (1976, 6) *Who chose the title and who:*

  1   speaks the line, '*Perchance to dream*'?

  2   sings the line, '*Under the greenwood tree*'?

  3   speaks the line, 'My *salad days* when I was green'?

  4   wrote the line, '*the darling buds of May*'?

  5   speaks the line, 'And *kiss me Kate*'?

  6   speaks the line, 'There shall be no more *cakes and ale*'?

  7   speaks the line, '*Bell, book and candle* shall not drive'?

  8   speaks the line, '*Old men forget*'?

  9   wrote the line, 'To thee *blythe spirit*'?

 10   wrote the line, '*The lonely sea and the sky*'?

• 5 •   (1976, 7) *What bridge:*

  1   was Saint Benezet divinely inspired to build?

  2   was Galloping Gertie?

  3   links palace and prison?

  4   had boiling wine prescribed as an anticorrosive?

  5   is the fifth proposition of the first book?

  6   was posthumously completed at Giant's Hole?

  7   was invented by Harold A Vanderbilt in 1925?

  8   is featured in *Rain, Steam and Speed*?

  9   has a view as fair as anything earth can show?

 10   saw the end of Billy Joe McAllister?

**• 6 •** (1976, 10) *What Walter:*

1  founded the Daily Universal Register?

2  was accused of regicide with Ralph of Aix?

3  was advised to be wise, avoid the wild and new?

4  had his secret life portrayed by Daniel Kominski?

5  according to Riemann first advocated the consonance of thirds?

6  described a fish that talks in the frying pan?

7  was the mother of James Scott or Crofts?

8  fired St Mary-at-Bow and had William Fitzosbert hanged?

9  was an impecunious Crusader?

10  introduced *Nicotiana tabacum* and *Solanum tuberosum*?


**• 7 •** (1976, 12) *What:*

1  lies between Musca and Centaurus?

2  marks the penultimate resting place of Eleanor?

3  is paramount in the Pennines?

4  precipitates a quarrel?

5  arose from the experience of Dunant at Solferino?

6  was first cast from a gun captured at Sebastopol?

7  links piston rod and connecting rod?

8  bears the boast that its maker 'made this and all in Man'?

9  divides output between tweeter and woofer?

10  appeared first in the *New York World* in December 1913?


**• 8 •** (1976, 13) *Identify the state:*

1  lower portion of the face-guard of a helmet.

2  companionless celestial body.

3  a pouch-billed waterfowl.

4  a reddish-brown horse.

5  a treeless tract of grassland.

6  sky-coloured herbage.

7  a free-will military entrant.

8  Paris underworld hooligans.

9  to cadge.

10  Brigham Young's.

• 9 • (1976, 15) *What schoolmaster:*

1    played the flute at Salem House?

2    fatally wounded Lord Tangent with a starting-pistol?

3    taught Laughing and Grief?

4    by 'bread and butter' meant oyster-patties and apple tart?

5    was rocked by Rabbits-Eggs?

6    had lived long in the alms-basket of words?

7    went upon the practical mode of teaching?

8    studied *Lives of the Great Poisoners*?

9    missed Lord Saltire from the Priory School?

10    ran Narkover?

• 10 • (1976, 16) *What was the aim of:*

1    Avalanche?

2    Baytown?

3    Cobra?

4    Dracula?

5    Galvanic?

6    Husky?

7    Iceberg?

8    Olive?

9    Shingle?

10    Slapstick?

• 11 • (1977, 3) *Who:*

1 said, 'The subjects that made me educated were never taught at school'?

2 said, 'Educate men without religion and you make them but clever devils'?

3 had the epitaph, 'Taught us how to live ... taught us how to die,' though the price was high?

4 wrote, 'He who can does, he who cannot teaches'?

5 wrote, 'Let not England forget her precedence of teaching nations how to live'?

6 sings, 'Education should be scientific play, boys'?

7 wrote *L'Education Sentimentale?*

8 said, 'Soap and education are not as sudden as a massacre but they are more deadly in the long run'?

9 wrote, 'To make your children capable of honesty is the beginning of education'?

10 wrote, 'Education makes people easy to lead but difficult to drive'?

• 12 • (1977, 5) *Identify the following:*

1 the knee-straightener.

2 the residence of Misses Throssel.

3 a large wedge of French bread.

4 non-alcoholic black Eastern beer.

5 the extra ancient element.

6 Bunter's academic cross.

7 apparatus for grinding corn.

8 a campanologist on the Seine.

9 geometry, arithmetic, astronomy and music.

10 the daily fever.

• 13 • (1977, 6) *Which Benjamin (or diminutive thereof):*

1   borrowed a cigar box and the fire-irons to explain his case?

2   was rare?

3   wrote of Coningsby and Sybil?

4   wore clogs and a tam-o-shanter?

5   preceded Bosanquet and Sissons?

6   dreamed of cheese … toasted mostly?

7   received a quintuple portion at a fraternal reunion dinner?

8   appeared as a ghost and recommended neat grog?

9   offered on approval?

10   transformed the Maltings?

• 14 • (1977, 7) *Whose salutary invention:*

1   enforced maximum draught in an Act of 1876?

2   provided pneumatic railroad arrest in 1872?

3   involved painting amorphous phosphorus into a striking surface in 1855?

4   provided nocturnal reflection en route in 1934?

5   was a converted coble for Archdeacon Sharp in 1876?

6   harnessed *fulmen* to *terra* in 1753?

7   facilitated pulmonary auscultation in 1819?

8   was filed as US Patent No. 775134 in 1904?

9   illuminated subterranean extraction in 1815?

10   secured a crossing between amber orbs in 1934?

• 15 • (1977, 9) *Which Philip:*

1   was fair, except to the Templars?

2   sired a knot-cutter?

3   suffered hirsutical defacement by fire?

4   came from Oldenburg by the Sonderburg-Glücksburg line?

5   assisted his grandfather to abolish the Pyrenees?

6   claimed that his sun had not yet set?

7   engineered the removal of the third Marcus Antonius Gordianus?

8   was wounded at Zutphen and died at Arnhem?

9   had a fearless father and a rash son?

10   was equality?

## • 16 • (1977, 10) *Who or what:*

1 appeared first in *Master Humphrey's Clock*?
2 was formerly the Coburg Theatre?
3 begins with discarding a queen?
4 did public penance for incontinence when over 100?
5 having no inhabitants, returned two?
6 was said to have slipped into bed in a warming-pan?
7 was en route from Lynchburg to Danville?
8 was in fact the husband of her daughter?
9 became Falstaff?
10 ain't what she used to be?

## • 17 • (1977, 13) *Locate the following:*

1 an Alafin.
2 a Zamorin.
3 a Yang di-Pertuan Agong.
4 an Ard-ri.
5 a Dogaressa.
6 a Suffette.
7 a Pfalzgraf.
8 a Mehtar.
9 a Negus.
10 a Monomopata.

## • 18 • (1977, 15) *Who lived at:*

1 The Laurels, Brickfield Terrace?
2 Bay View, Llaregyb?
3 Pondicherry Lodge, Upper Norwood?
4 The Admiral Benbow, Black Hill Cove?
5 7 Eccles Street?
6 70 St Mary Axe?
7 The Rookery, Blunderstone?
8 The Rectory, Battersby-on-the-Hill?
9 The Cedars, Muswell Hill?
10 Draynflete Abbey?

# 1978

• 1 • *In 1878 who or what:*

1 became Leo XIII?

2 were nationalized on 1 April?

3 was murdered in St Petersburg by Kravchinsky?

4 ended the Cuban rising at El Zanjon?

5 stationed the original project of Thotmes on 13 September?

6 succeeded Victor Emmanuel II?

7 received one farthing from John Ruskin?

8 was stopped by Afghans at Ali Masjid?

9 married Mercedes, daughter of the Duke of Montpensier?

10 became Grand Master of the Knights of Labour?


• 2 • *What are or were separated by:*

1 the Curzon line?

2 the Mason-Dixon line?

3 the Radcliffe line?

4 the Beloe line?

5 the Bidasson line?

6 the Hornbeam line?

7 the lines of Torres Vedras?

8 the Mannerheim line?

9 the Attila line?

10 the McMahon line?

**· 3 ·** *Who:*

1 admired family photographs in the Malayan jungle?
2 stole a fire shovel at Calais?
3 purchased a tombstone at Casterbridge?
4 had a wayward daughter in Panglin?
5 was drunk while on duty in Cyprus?
6 called for beer in Half Moon Street?
7 with his wife was not invited to the ball at Brussels?
8 put money in a hollow tree near Mile End?
9 lost his ear in Venice?
10 was thought to have murdered his wife at the Abbey?

**· 4 ·** *Give the name or names of the following:*

1 Emil Jellinek's daughter
2 The Birmingham 'Sheep Shearing Company'
3 the twins from the photographic business in Massachusetts
4 The Three Ps
5 639,000 wartime spam cans
6 the Tea and Bread Vans
7 the cars made in Springfield, Massachusetts between 1920 and 1931
8 the mosquito which came of age in 1970
9 'Le camion le plus vite du monde'
10 the third son of Lord Llangattock

**· 5 ·** *Where:*

1 in the First World War was a 500-year-old defeat avenged?
2 were five Richmonds slain?
3 did victory follow arrival and observation?
4 did a king ask his men whether they wished to live for ever?
5 was victory gained by a future president two weeks after peace had been signed?
6 did Miloš Obilić assassinate the winner?
7 might the war have been 'lost in an afternoon'?
8 was the remark made, *'Marmont est perdu'*?
9 was the tide turned at Tsaritsyn?
10 did four sultans of the Deccan chain their guns together and break an empire?

• 6 • *What line is (or was) known as:*

1    the Drain?

2    God's wonderful railway?

3    the languisher and yawner?

4    the late and never early?

5    the London, smashem and turnover?

6    the muck sludge and lightning?

7    the old worser and worser?

8    the muddle and go nowhere?

9    the slow and dirty?

10    the slow, easy and comfortable?

• 7 • *Who or what:*

1    tries for ever to make Table Bay?

2    was the invention of Leotard?

3    was Pacific 4472?

4    introduces Lionel Hampton?

5    was reputedly the fastest racehorse ever bred?

6    was patented by John Kay in 1733?

7    was known also as Sky Louse?

8    won five golds in 1924?

9    was B-17?

10    was paradoxically claimed to be at rest?

• 8 • *What are the following:*

1    $78 \times 36$?

2    $9 \times 4\frac{3}{8} \times 2\frac{5}{8}$?

3    0–12 at 33?

4    2–8–2?

5    $66 \times 8\frac{2}{3}$?

6    $2\frac{1}{4} \times \frac{13}{16}$?

7    $8\frac{13}{16} - 9$ and $5\frac{1}{2} - 5\frac{3}{4}$?

8    $56\frac{1}{2}$ (Man 36)?

9    $841 \times 594$?

10    $8\frac{1}{2} \times 4\frac{1}{2}$?

### • 9 • *Who in what work described these:*

1   a little dragon who might scratch and spit but couldn't do anything really?

2   a courteous and considerate dragon … he kept one of his forepaws near his nose?

3   the dragon of 'Just now land'?

4   a dragon which became a god in asbestos boots?

5   one who thinks trains are dragons which smoke once they've swallowed people?

6   a dragonized boy?

7   a dragon, that serpent of old, chained for a thousand years?

8   a dragon as the chiefest and greatest of all calamities?

9   a dragon called Kishdo?

10   a dragon from Smoke Hill joining Mr Jones?

### • 10 • *In which Ford vehicle did:*

1   Cheyenne Harry kill 'Placer' Freemont?

2   Captain Nathan Bristles reach retiring age?

3   The Ringo Kid kill the Plummer brothers?

4   Robert Marmaduke Sangster Hightower reach New Jerusalem?

5   Martin Pawley kill Chief Scar?

6   Sean Thornton fight Red Will Danaher?

7   Guthrie McCabe kill Stone Calf?

8   John Brickley and Rusty Ryan not prove to be expendable?

9   Tom Doniphon kill Liberty Valance?

10   'Guns' Donovan do battle with 'Boats' Gilhooley?

### • 11 • *What father and son:*

1   won Oscars at Sierra Madre?

2   descended in *Trieste*?

3   presided at the Astronomical Society?

4   triumphed at Rainhill?

5   tunnelled from Rotherhithe?

6   came from Braintree to the Presidency?

7   took the name of their transport from Maeterlinck?

8   lit the Bishop Rock?

9   were awarded for what they saw in the crystal?

10   were 'Father and Son'?

- 12 • *What mathematician or scientist:*
  1  has a sieve for prime numbers?
  2  died after increasing his sleeping time by fifteen minutes a day until it reached twenty-four hours?
  3  recognized 'God Save the Queen' because people stood up?
  4  had his condemnation commuted by Pericles?
  5  said that God made the integers; all the rest is the work of man?
  6  saved his mother from the witches' stake?
  7  discovered a 'bottle'?
  8  said, 'Science is nothing but trained and organized common sense'?
  9  invented matrix?
  10  set a problem which Newton solved in twelve hours?

- 13 • *Complete the following:*
  1  Mayis, Haziran, Temmuz, – – – –
  2  Dek sep, Dek ok, Dek nau, – – – –
  3  E Dielle, E Hene, E Marte, – – – –
  4  Syyskuu, Lokakuu, Marraskuu, – – – –
  5  Hetven, Nyolcvan, Kilencven, – – – –
  6  Fyre, Halvtredsinstyve, Tredsinstyve, – – – –
  7  Maggio, Giugno, Luglio, – – – –
  8  Onze, Treze, Quinze, – – – –
  9  Zuid, Oost, Noord, – – – –
  10  Prvi, Drugi, Treci, – – – –

- 14 • *Whose motto is:*
  1  'Per Ardua Ad Astra'?
  2  'E Pluribus Unum'?
  3  'Curae Genus Omne Animantium'?
  4  'Luck to Loyne'?
  5  'Boreas Domus, Mare Amicus'?
  6  'Ars Gratia Artis'?
  7  'Après Nous le Déluge'?
  8  'Ubique'?
  9  'Eureka'?
  10  'All the news that's fit to print'?

**• 15 •** *Who was Marshal Duke of:*

1   Abrantes?

2   Albufera?

3   Belluno?

4   Dalmatia?

5   Istria?

6   Montebello?

7   Ragusa?

8   Reggio?

9   Taranto?

10   Treviso?

**• 16 •** *What land:*

1   viewed embezzlement as an illness?

2   saw Rassendyll crowned as substitute?

3   got the wrong Boot?

4   saw sailors turned to swine?

5   was supported by a loadstone?

6   was visited by Raphael Hythloday?

7   was ruled by an enchantress and her eight sisters?

8   is ruled by Hel?

9   had a horse of a different colour?

10   had Firefly for President?

• 17 • *What collectively are:*

1   a murder?

2   a murmuration?

3   a rafter?

4   a dopping?

5   an exaltation?

6   an unkindness?

7   a tiding?

8   a charm?

9   a wisp?

10  a convocation?


• 18 • *In 1978 who or what:*

1   record-breaker was eleven minutes late?

2   had a rocky road to Rio?

3   shrank in more than value?

4   achieved male and female dominance?

5   died and left 212,000?

6   provided an immediate solution to Number 15,070?

7   celebrated his jubilee with a cartoon?

8   repeatedly warned about changing stations?

9   achieved three times three consecutively?

10  switched on the lights as a birthday treat?

# 1979–1980

- 1 • (1979, 2) *What work by whom is alternatively:*
  1  *A Tragedy Rehearsed?*
  2  *The Naval Officer?*
  3  *Episode in the Life of the Artist?*
  4  *First Impressions?*
  5  *The Parish Boy's Progress?*
  6  *The World Well Lost?*
  7  *The Two Nations?*
  8  *The Newgate Festival?*
  9  *The Second Play for Puritans?*
  10  *The Pot of Basil?*

- 2 • (1979, 3) *Which Peter:*
  1  conspired against Paul and thus fatally delayed Barbarossa?
  2  marched with Sans Avoir?
  3  sewed up the problem of the nine tailors?
  4  married a determined young lady from Zerbst?
  5  acquired a couple of gallons of preserved spice?
  6  sacked Alexandria?
  7  proved a destructive guest for Admiral Evelyn?
  8  is Great?
  9  held out at Sidney Street?
  10  yielded an empire to his son and set out to regain a kingdom for his daughter?

• 3 •   (1979, 5) *What:*

1   rebuked a prophet in Moab?

2   carried a bailiff from Norfolk?

3   pursued a Sicilian in Bohemia?

4   submerged fatally at Twickenham?

5   succumbed to an arbalest in the Antarctic?

6   inspired a dresser at Hampstead?

7   remained forever faithful by the Shannon?

8   escaped excommunication at Rheims?

9   accompanied an advocate through Cheylard?

10  engaged a taxidermist in Muscovy?

• 4 •   (1979, 11) *Identify the month:*

1   and the singer of 'Don't talk at all, show me'.

2   and the famous northern races on the ninth.

3   and the roundabout when the girls were contrary.

4   and the location where 'I was taken by surprise'.

5   and the author, when branches of a 'too happy, happy tree, ne'er remember the green felicity'.

6   and who wrote, 'The sun is set, the spring is gone … we frolic'.

7   and the work in which Byron ends the English winter.

8   and the author when 'The steamers sidle up to meet the effusive welcome of the pier.

9   and what was carried 'butting through the channel in the mad March days.

10  and the author when 'The beef-red bricks and the sky-green stones are buried in the jungle leaf'.

• 5 • (1979, 13) *Identify the character and author whom the following inspired:*

1 Josiah Henson.
2 Leigh Hunt.
3 Alexander Selkirk.
4 William Brodie.
5 Claire Clairmont.
6 Mary Cecilia Rogers.
7 Delphin Delamare.
8 Marie Duplessis.
9 Dr Joseph Bell.
10 Chester Gillette.


• 6 • (1979, 14) *Give the first lines of these second lines:*

1 Ring ye Bells at Whitechapel.
2 Ni sit bisextus, februus minor est duobus.
3 Have you any feathers loose.
4 Barcelona, bona, strike.
5 I says the Quarterly.
6 A popingo-eye.
7 Your mamie's gone to Seaton.
8 Had once a doubtful strife, Sir.
9 Die ist zerbrochen.
10 Am now in my Castle.


• 7 • (1979, 15) *In what:*

1 did he board a carriage carrying a double bass?
2 was he annoyed by a small boy on the Underground?
3 was he a press photographer outside the court?
4 did he pose in *Reduca* newspaper advertisements?
5 was he a silhouette on the door of the Registrar of Deaths?
6 did he nurse a damp baby at Grand Central Station?
7 did he leave a pet store with his own two Sealyhams?
8 did he appear in a Gaudy photograph?
9 did he wait to use the public telephone?
10 who?

• 8 •  (1979, 16) *Who:*

1    ran the society paper, *Truth*?

2    did doubt 'truth to be a liar'?

3    said, 'Truth is the glue that holds government together'?

4    reckoned, 'There's more things told than are true and more things true than are told'?

5    said 'Truth does not cease because people give up believing it'?

6    wrote, 'Long years must pass before the truths we have made for ourselves become our very flesh'?

7    wrote, 'Convictions are more dangerous foes of truth than lies'?

8    placed Truth 'on a huge hill, cragged and steep'?

9    had 'an instinct for loving the truth; but only an instinct'?

10    wrote, 'When you have eliminated the impossible, whatever remains, however improbable, must be the truth'?

• 9 •  (1979, 17) *Identify the following:*

1    The Clutching Hand.

2    Tripe Hound.

3    The Tea Tray.

4    The Elephant.

5    Long Horn.

6    Harry Tate.

7    Jenny.

8    The Double-dirty.

9    Sparrow.

10    The Field Kitchen.

• 10 • (1980, 2) *Who or what:*

1 marked a Roman lucky day?

2 was known formerly as York Place?

3 was derived by York from Mortimer?

4 denotes a clerical worker?

5 struck a rock of Barfleur?

6 was a ruinous gift from a king?

7 was eaten by cabinet ministers on Trinity Monday?

8 gave his horse anklets against the bites of sharks?

9 do stars become before they die?

10 concealed the bones of Edward V?

• 11 • (1980, 4) *What pair:*

1 supplied Dr Knox with beef?

2 are commemorated by the sons of the desert?

3 successfully crash-landed in a bog in the west of Ireland?

4 had their door kept by Cat Morgan?

5 wrote of the Knight of the Burning Pestle?

6 were suckled by a she-wolf?

7 introduced the separate condenser?

8 created Railway Cuttings, East Cheam?

9 won the Great Paris–Bordeaux Race of 1895?

10 took the surname Bunker having none of their own?

• 12 • (1980, 6) *Who, by whom, were these:*

1 Prince Leo Nikolayevich Myshkin?

2 Septimus Harding?

3 John Wellington Wells?

4 Philip Christian?

5 Leonard Charteris?

6 John Loveday?

7 Sir William Patterne?

8 Lem Putt?

9 Subtle?

10 Mac Davies, alias Bernard Jenkins?

• 13 • (1980, 7) *What:*

1    provided for temporary discharge in 1913?

2    is a Scottish monolith?

3    gem possesses chatoyancy?

4    expresses displeasure or impatience?

5    fine wire made contact with the crystal?

6    was purchased for a vast sum by the King of Barbary?

7    is a cacophony?

8    is a formation of sandstone veined with chalk?

9    is the second highest English inn?

10    is a subterranean gallery for the dead?


• 14 • (1980, 9) *Which monarch died:*

1    in the Calycadnus?

2    of a fall from the Column of Theodosius?

3    shot in the back at a masked ball?

4    despite a roomful of gold as ransom?

5    asserting his artistic qualities?

6    from a bump on the head at Amboise?

7    having stepped backwards through a window?

8    when a cannon exploded at Roxburgh?

9    stunned by an Argive roof tile?

10    from toxophily amid venery?


• 15 • (1980, 10) *Whence:*

1    Minas?

2    Tia Juana?

3    Dukhan?

4    Zakum?

5    Zuetina?

6    Hassi Messaoud?

7    Kirkuk?

8    Forcados?

9    Mandji?

10    Fateh?

• 16 • (1980, 13) *What name unites:*

1   a Scottish philosopher and a Scottish mathematician?

2   the third of three astronauts and an Irish patriot?

3   a lord chancellor and a modern painter?

4   a satirical poet and a satirical novelist?

5   a winner of the US Open and a comedian?

6   a party leader and a band leader?

7   the Nonpareil and the long count?

8   the founders of a 'firm' and a car factory?

9   a singer and an eponymous hero?

10   'Qualtrough' and a Scottish patriot?

• 17 • (1980, 14) *Who:*

1   exercised independent jurisdiction in Nevada?

2   experienced matrimonial misunderstandings in Milan?

3   corporately exemplified monomachy in Paris?

4   inaugurated an anti-extradition campaign in Cadiz?

5   represented their unions on the road to Canterbury?

6   evoked queenly compassion at Calais?

7   were supernaturally anaesthetised near Ephesus?

8   escaped diluvian catastrophe in Mesopotamia?

9   comprised a heroic pageant in Navarre?

10   exerted plenipotentiary public protection in Venice?

• 18 • (1980, 16) *Who or what:*

1   is a semi-precious fluorite?

2   receives letters of termination from females?

3   was landlord of the Spy-glass?

4   is large, with a bulging body and a narrow neck?

5   wrote 'Leaf by Niggle'?

6   was warned that the Devil was loose?

7   is a geographical extremity?

8   was larger than his name suggests?

9   was nonexistent in a series of twenty-three?

10   is a personification of malt liquor?

# Answers

# 1920–1928

**• 1 •**  (1920, 12)

1 Tennyson, Browning and Fitzgerald!
2 Coleridge
3 Keats (*Lamia*)
4 Wordsworth
5 R L Stevenson
6 Alfred Austin
7 Tennyson
8 Crabbe (*The Elder Brother's Tale*)
9 Cowper
10 Hood (*Faithless Nelly Gray*)

**• 2 •**  (1920, 17)

1 Fear of the Lord
2 Lying lips
3 Mercy
4 Hypocrisy
5 Patriotism
6 A loan
7 Something
8 Gratitude
9 Words
10 Women

**• 3 •**  (1922, 12)

1 Good currency drives out bad
2 Hang first, try afterwards
3 *re* English railways in the Argentine
4 Customary as opposed to Statute Law
5 Prohibition in America
6 Taking the law into your own hands
7 Law of consonantal change (Philology)
8 A woman cannot inherit
9 A man may marry his brother's widow
10 A hill

**• 4 •**  (1923, 8)

1 Mr Asquith
2 Mr Lloyd-George
3 Mr Bonar Law
4 Mr Winston Churchill
5 Lord Haldane
6 Sir John Simon
7 Mr Baldwin
8 Mr Ramsay Macdonald
9 Protégé of Mr Lloyd-George and Mr Churchill
10 Capital Levy in instalments

**• 5 •**  (1924, 7)

1 *Agamemnon* (Aeschylus)
2 *Merry Wives of Windsor* (Shakespeare)
3 *Peter Pan* (Barrie)
4 *Becket* (Tennyson)
5 *Hassan* (Flecker)
6 *Ruddigore* (Gilbert)
7 *Yeomen of the Guard* (Gilbert)
8 *School for Scandal* (Sheridan)
9 *Macbeth* (Shakespeare)
10 *The Private Secretary* (Hawtrey)

**• 6 •**  (1924, 9)

1 Eve
2 Atalanta
3 Paris
4 George III
5 William Tell
6 Adam's apple
7 Snowdrop
8 Gravitation
9 The Mackintosh Red
10 Duke Senior in *As You Like It*

**• 7 •**  (1925, 16)

1 Corbies (Old English ballad)
2 Albatross (Coleridge – *The Rime of the Ancient Mariner*)
3 Cow (R L Stevenson – *A Child's Garden of Verses*)
4 Lion, Tiger (Gilbert – *The Mikado*)
5 Bear (Longfellow – *The Song of Hiawatha*)
6 Leopard, Buffalo (Kipling – *The Jungle Book*)

7 Horse (Shakespeare – *King Richard III*. I, i)

8 Lion (Shakespeare– *Julius Caesar*. I, iii)

9 Butterfly (Kipling – *Just So Stories*)

10 Lark, Snail (Browning – *Pippa Passes*)

• 8 • (1926, 8)

1 *The Laughing Cavalier* (Frans Hals)

2 *Si probitatis impendio constat* (Quintilian)

3 At the Second Council of Carthage

4 'The vacant mind' (Goldsmith – *The Deserted Village*)

5 Strange fellows (Shakespeare – *The Merchant of Venice*. I, i)

6 Democritus

7 Jean qui rit

8 He who laughs last

9 Mother 'when Father laid the carpet on the stairs'

10 To laugh the wrong side of your face

• 9 • (1927, 6)

1 Hooking off with a fishing rod the Bishop's handkerchief while asleep under a tree – *Just William* (Richmal Crompton)

2 'Spell it with a "we" – Sammy' – *Pickwick Papers* (Dickens)

3 When they told her to liberate Iliam Dhone, she had already shot him – *Peveril of the Peak* (Scott)

4 Because he was not alive – *Uncle Remus*

5 She was in Looking Glass Land – *Alice Through the Looking Glass* (Lewis Carroll)

6 Because he made a long nose at the fairy Blackstick – *The Rose and the Ring* (Thackeray)

7 Irene – *The Forsyte Saga* (Galsworthy)

8 Selling the colt – *The Vicar of Wakefield* (Goldsmith)

9 Made pussy return it (Tartar emetic) – *Cranford* (Elizabeth Gaskell)

10 Mary kissed him – *Stalky and Co.* (Kipling)

• 10 • (1927, 8)

1 Bishop Barnes

2 Lord Haldane

3 The voyagers in *The Voyage of Maeldune* (Tennyson)

4 Childe Roland (Browning)

5 Vision in Rugby Chapel – Matthew Arnold

6 Jehovah (*Isaiah* 63, 1)

7 The Pilot of the Galilean Lake – *Lycidas* (Milton)

8 Heifer to the sacrifice – *Ode on a Grecian Urn* (Keats)

9 Themistocles

10 Mother of second Lord Lytton

• 11 • (1927, 9)

1 Lovelace (*Lucasta*)

2 Shylock (Shakespeare – *The Merchant of Venice*)

3 Lucifer (Milton – *Paradise Lost*)

4 T O Mordaunt (*The Call*)

5 Major General James Wolfe – *Gray's Elegy* – Quebec

6 Shelley

7 Achilles (Homer – *The Odyssey*, XI, 489)

8 The writer of *Proverbs*

9 Tennyson (*Locksley Hall*)

10 Andrew Selkirk (Cowper)

• 12 • (1928, 1)

1 St Simon Stylites

2 Jonah

3 Ariel

4 W B Yeats (*The Lake Isle of Innisfree*)

5 Diogenes

6 An old woman

7 Mr Darling (J M Barrie – *Peter Pan*)

8 Wayland Smith (Scott – *Kenilworth* and in Norse mythology)

9 Elsie, Lacie and Tillie (Lewis Carroll – *Alice's Adventure in Wonderland*)

10 Asher

• 13 • (1928, 3)

1 The *Dimbula* (Kipling)

2 The *White Ship*

3 The *Dulcibella* (Erskine Childers – *The Riddle of the Sands*)

4 A tin paddle steamer (Kipling – *The Brushwood Boy*)

5 The Flettner Rotor ship (*Buckau* was the first)

6 The *Bolivar* (Kipling)

7 The *Ark* (*Genesis*)

8 The *Snark* (Jack London's Yacht – see Lewis Carroll's *Hunting of the Snark*)

9 SMS *Königsburg* Battle of the Rufiji Delta (1914–15)

10 The ship in *The Tempest*

• 14 • (1928, 4)

1 Greedy man taken to task for eating too much spinach

2 Cain when asked where Abel was

3 Oscar Wilde answering an invitation to dinner

4 Charles Lamb taken to task for being late

5 Friedrich Staps (attempted assassination of Napoleon)

6 Sir Launcelot to himself

7 Charles II (who never said a foolish thing and never did a wise one)

8 Nelson at Copenhagen

9 Earl of Kildare taken to task by Henry VII for burning the Cathedral at Cashel (1495)

10 Australian private summoned before Orderly Room for not shaving (seven men at one mirror)

• 15 • (1928, 5)

1 Clarence (*King Richard III*)

2 Ghost (*Hamlet*)

3 The Private of the Buffs (Sir Francis Doyle)

4 She, i.e., Rosalind (*As You Like It*)

5 Macbeth

6 Lives there a man ... (Scott – *The Lay of the Last Minstrel*)

7 The Traveller (Goldsmith)

8 Beastie, i.e., mouse (Robert Burns)

9 The Aesthete (Gilbert – *Patience*)

10 The Schooner (T E Brown)

• 16 • (1928, 6)

1 Archbishop Temple to Curate

2 Wolsey to Cromwell

3 Polonius to Laertes (*Hamlet*)

4 St Paul (*1 Timothy* 5, 23)

5 St Peter (*1 Peter* 3, 8)

6 St Peter (*1 Peter* 2, 17)

7 Sergeant to recruit (Kipling – *The 'Eathen*)

8 Quaker in *Northern Farmer: Old Style* (Tennyson)

9 Tony Weller to his son (Dickens – *Pickwick Papers*)

10 Mr Punch to those about to marry (*Mr Punch's Book of Love*)

• 17 • (1928, 9)

1 Thomas Hardy

2 Lord Haig

3 Cecil Rhodes

4 R L Stevenson (*Requiem*)

5 W E Henley (*The Full Sea Rolls and Thunders*)

6 John Masefield

7 St Swithin

8 Omar Khayam

9 Christina Rossetti (*Let Me Go*)

10 Feste (*Twelfth Night*)

• 18 • (1928, 12)

1 Old men

2 Kubla Khan

3 Erther (Masefield)

4 The Lotus Eaters (Tennyson)

5 Aeneas (*Aeneid 2*)

6 Xanthias (Aristophanes – *The Wasps*)

7 Joseph

8 Broken Men (Kipling)

9 Tennyson (just before he was made Poet Laureate)

10 Charles Lutwidge Dodgson (Lewis Carroll)

# 1930–1933

### • 1 •   (1930, 11)

1 Annexation of Sindh.

2 Queen Victoria after a doubtful story told in her presence.

3 Messenger of fall of Ratisbon to Napoleon who asked if he was hurt (Browning).

4 Queen of Sheba, having viewed all Solomon's glory.

5 William of Orange to Buckingham, explaining how to avoid seeing the ruin of his country.

6 Clive during his impeachment for doing so well in India.

7 The Curate asked by his Bishop at breakfast if his egg was good.

8 Oliver Cromwell to painter, insisting on correction of a flattering likeness of himself.

9 Dean Inge to a garrulous diner who asked him what the Church was coming to.

10 Browning, after explaining to lady inquirer that when he wrote *Sordello* only two people knew what it meant, God and himself.

### • 2 •   (1930, 13)

1 The Grammarian (Browning)

2 Duke of Wellington (Tennyson)

3 a favourite cat (Gray)

4 Sir John Moore (Wolfe)

5 Heraclitus (William Cory)

6 Keats (Shelley – *Adonais*)

7 Dr Robert Levet (Samuel Johnson)

8 William Hervey (Cowley)

9 Mistress Anne Killigrew (Dryden)

10 Lucy (Wordsworth)

### • 3 •   (1930, 14)

1 Balak

2 Jeremiah

3 Zedekiah

4 Amos

5 Isaiah

6 Elisha

7 John the Baptist

8 Elijah

9 Deborah

10 Job

### • 4 •   (1930, 18)

1 London from Westminster Bridge (Wordsworth)

2 Cadiz Bay (Browning – *Home Thoughts from the Sea*)

3 Ithaca (Tennyson – *Ulysses*)

4 Isle of Man (Eliza Craven Green – *Ellan Vannin*)

5 Lake Isle of Innisfree (Yeats)

6 Melrose Abbey (Scott – *The Lay of the Last Minstrel*)

7 Shropshire Hills (Housman)

8 Scotland /Caledonia (Scott – *The Lay of the Last Minstrel*)

9 Aegean Islands (Arnold – *The Scholar Gipsy*)

10 Paris (Dickens – *Bleak House*)

### • 5 •   (1931, 7)

1 Stanley and Livingstone

2 Edward I and infant Prince of Wales

3 Charles I to Laud

4 The White Queen and Alice

5 'Old lady' to Henry VIII about Elizabeth

6 Gladiators to Caesar

7 American to the King at Wembley

8 Mrs Gamp introducing herself

9 Titania introducing Bottom to the Fairies

10 Jingle and the Pickwickians

• 6 •   (1931, 8)

1  Robert Bacon
2  Thomas Aquinas
3  Antonio Andreas
4  St Bernard
5  Raymond Lully
6  Wycliffe
7  Alexander Hales
8  Richard Middleton
9  John Duns Scotus
10  Character in Richard Dehan's novel

• 7 •   (1931, 18)

1  Venus and Adonis (Shakespeare)
2  Paolo and Francesca
3  Anthony and Cleopatra (Shakespeare)
4  Romeo and Juliet (Shakespeare)
5  Menelaus and Helen (Rupert Brooke)
6  Aucassin and Nicolette (old French)
7  Abelard and Heloïse (Alexander Pope)
8  Robert and Elizabeth Browning
9  Dante Gabriel Rossetti and Elizabeth Siddal
10  Orlando and Rosalind (Shakespeare – *As You Like It*)

• 8 •   (1932, 1)

1  Aphrodite with Psyche, who had stolen Proserpina's cosmetics for her
2  Helen – the face that launched a thousand ships
3  Penelope – *Song of the Shirt*
4  Hercules, diverting the river Alpheus to cleanse the Augean stables
5  Proserpina, because she had eaten a pomegranate in Hades
6  Perseus, beheading Medusa
7  Narcissus, contemplating his own beauty
8  Pyramus and Thisbe
9  Orpheus, who made stones and trees move at his music
10  Achilles, whose heel alone was vulnerable

• 9 •   (1932, 5)

1  Ganges
2  Abana and Pharpar than all the rivers of Israel
3  Iser (Bennett – *Hohenlinden*)
4  Danube
5  Seine
6  Rhine (Loreley)
7  Nile (Tennyson – *A Dream of Fair Women*)
8  Scheldt
9  Ebro
10  The River in *Pilgrim's Progress*

• 10 •   (1932, 7)

1  Mrs Nickleby's version of Ann Moore, fasting imposter c. 1800
2  Pretended Ghost in 1762
3  Daniel Lambert
4  Mohammed Abdullah Hassan
5  Joan (Jeanne) of Burgundy
6  Unidentified French prisoner of State
7  Bank of England
8  One of the claimants in Partition Treaty
9  Elizabeth Barton (executed Tyburn 1534)
10  Pilate's doorkeeper

• 11 •   (1932, 16)

1  *Seaweed* (Longfellow)
2  *Martin Chuzzlewit* (Dickens)
3  *Three Fishers* (Kingsley)
4  *The Tempest* (Shakespeare)
5  *Barnaby Rudge* (Dickens)
6  *Typhoon* (Conrad)
7  Motley's *Dutch Republic*
8  *Ballad of Sir Patrick Spens* (Anon)
9  *The Revenge* (Tennyson)
10  Hymn by Reginald Heber

• 12 •   (1932, 17)

1  Eleven
2  Seventy
3  Forty-two
4  'Nigh on ninety-seven'

5 'Seven, seven , seventeen'
6 One hundred and twelve
7 '… not seventeen'
8 'Twelve months'
9 Four hundred and thirty-three
10 Three

• 13 • (1933, 1)

1 Queen Anne
2 Mrs Gamp
3 Falstaff
4 Hansel
5 Fat Boy (*Pickwick Papers*)
6 William I (joke by Philip I of France)
7 George IV
8 Schubert
9 Edward IV
10 Charles I

• 14 • (1933, 7)

1 Elizabeth Woodville (Southey)
2 St Elizabeth
3 St Elizabeth of Hungary
4 Elizabeth of Bohemia
5 Elizabeth of Wied, Queen of Roumania
6 Elizabeth of York, eldest daughter of Edward IV
7 Elizabeth Barrett Browning
8 Elizabeth Bennet (*Pride and Prejudice*)
9 Elizabeth of Russia
10 Elizabeth Schumann

• 15 • (1933, 13)

1 Disraeli
2 Menasseh ben Israel
3 Ben Hur
4 Lord Reading/Rufus Isaacs (Viceroy of India)
5 Moses Mendelssohn
6 Fagin
7 Spinoza
8 Isaac of York (*Ivanhoe*)
9 Shylock
10 Jocen of York (temp. Richard I)

• 16 • (1933, 14)

1 St Geneviève
2 St Denis
3 St Patrick
4 St Ursula
5 St Dunstan
6 St Christopher
7 St Catherine
8 St Anastasia
9 St James the Great
10 Jem Crow of Rheims (R H Barham)

• 17 • (1933, 15)

1 Amsterdam
2 Belgrade
3 Escorial
4 Marlborough House (Sarah Churchill)
5 Tuileries
6 Fotheringay (Katherine of Aragon)
7 Kremlin
8 Kenilworth (George Gascoigne)
9 Holyrood
10 Solomon's

• 18 • (1933, 17)

1 Charles I – Marvell
2 Mr Valiant-for-Truth – Bunyan
3 Mary Queen of Scots – Glassford Bell
4 St Stephen – St Luke
5 Sir Richard Grenville – Tennyson
6 Cawdor – Shakespeare
7 Ophelia – Shakespeare
8 Steerforth – Dickens
9 Victoria – W E Henley
10 Sydney Carton – Dickens

# 1934–1935

• 1 • (1934, 1)

1 Richard Rice (Cardinal Fisher's cook, 1530)
2 Boadicea
3 Rosamond, Eleanor

4 Socrates
5 Yolande de Bourgogne
6 Cleopatra, Caesar
7 Alexander's butler
8 Marchioness de Brinvilliers
9 Lakmé
10 Palmerston (Rugeley – William Palmer)

• 2 •   (1934, 3)

1 Edward III
2 Henry III
3 Edward VI
4 Elizabeth
5 Charles I's Silver Pound minted from silver of Oxford colleges
6 Henry VIII's sovereigns
7 Charles II
8 stamped with Michael and Dragon
9 half gold – 'merk' of James VI
10 'Traitor Scot sold his king for a groat'. Betrayal of Charles I by Scots

• 3 •   (1934, 4)

1 a weed
2 a scolder
3 bad writing
4 courage born of drink
5 ethylene dichloride
6 horsetail for polishing
7 price lowered instead of being raised
8 one concluded by drinking
9 cacophony
10 a frog

• 4 •   (1934, 8)

1 The Suspenders (*How the Whale Got His Throat*)
2 Puck (*Puck of Pook's Hill*)
3 Red Dogs (*The Dholes of the Deccan*)
4 Danny's Soul (*Danny Deever*)
5 Mule-train drawing the Screw Guns (*Barrack Room Ballads*)
6 A ham (*Their Lawful Occasions, Traffic and Discoveries*)

7 King (by Rabbit's Eggs – *Stalky and Co*)
8 The Starboard of Greenside (*The Horse Marines*)
9 A spur (*The End of the Passage, Life's Handicap*)
10 A man (*If*)

• 5 •   (1934, 14)

1 Edward II
2 Thomas More
3 Katherine of Aragon, Francis I
4 the guillotine
5 Alexander the Great
6 Scipio Africanus
7 Nero to Jupiter Capitolinus
8 'By the beard of the Prophet', Mahomet
9 Henry VIII and Elizabeth, who taxed beards
10 barbé

• 6 •   (1934, 16)

1 'Glorious First of June'/Third Battle of Ushant
2 Agincourt and Balaclava
3 Trafalgar
4 Blenheim
5 Bannockburn and Sluis
6 Zeebrugge
7 Plassey
8 Naseby
9 Quatre Bras
10 Barnet

• 7 •   (1934, 17)

1 Helen, Tennyson (*A Dream of Fair Women*)
2 Anne Boleyn, Francis I
3 Alexandra, Tennyson
4 Elizabeth, Shakespeare
5 Marie Antoinette, André Chénier
6 Henrietta Maria, Edmund Waller
7 Anne, Pope (*The Rape of the Lock*)
8 Katharine Howard, George Cavendish

9 Prithvi, Sarojini Naidu (*Harvest Hymn*)
10 Bombay, Kipling (*The Song of the Cities*)

• 8 •  (1935, 3)

1 Ely (temp. Elizabeth)
2 Courtenay, of London
3 Latimer
4 Father O'Flynn's
5 Sir Henry Rowley Bishop (composer)
6 Hatto
7 Barrow
8 Absalon
9 Sodor and Man
10 drink

• 9 •  (1935, 5)

1 Monks in *The Jackdaw of Rheims*
2 Alice
3 Miss Miggs (*Barnaby Rudge*)
4 Greta Garbo
5 Frau Kilmansegge
6 Mrs Prig (*Martin Chuzzlewit*)
7 Ramsay MacDonald
8 Toddie (John Habberton – *Helen's Babies*)
9 George II
10 Topsy (Harriet Beecher Stowe – *Uncle Tom's Cabin*)

• 10 •  (1935, 6)

1 Derby and Chester
2 James III of Scotland
3 Ashbourne
4 England *v.* Wales, 1910
5 Eton Wall Game
6 H W Day
7 England *v.* France, Price of Bishop's Stortford College
8 W J A Davies
9 William Webb Ellis
10 Auxerre

• 11 •  (1935, 7)

1 Stheno, Euryale (Gorgons)
2 Regan, Goneril (*King Lear*)
3 Thalia, Aglaia (Graces)
4 Emily, Anne (Brontës)
5 Dagmar, Thyra (daughters of Christian IX of Denmark)
6 Athene, Aphrodite (Judgement of Paris)
7 Mary Seton, Mary Carmichael (Virginia Woolf)
8 Constance, Natalie (Talmadge – silent movies)
9 Olga/Olya, Irene/Irina (Chekhov – *The Three Sisters*)
10 Peep Bo, Pitti Sing (*The Mikado*)

• 12 •  (1935, 8)

1 George IV
2 Henry VIII (Anne of Cleves)
3 George III
4 Cophetua
5 Sam Weller
6 Boaz (*Ruth* 2, 5)
7 Henry V
8 Ferdinand (*The Tempest*)
9 Darcy (*Pride and Prejudice*)
10 Mrs Nickleby's neighbour

• 13 •  (1935, 10)

1 Dick Whittington's
2 Felix
3 Cat and Fiddle
4 the dog, the ass and the cock
5 Cheshire
6 Binkie
7 Selina (Gray)
8 The Owl
9 Chat d'Or
10 to see the Queen

• 14 •  (1935, 11)

1 A E Housman
2 Mourne
3 Donegal
4 Pisgah (*Deuteronomy* 3, 27)

5 Great Gable (Moses Rigg, a Honister quarryman)
6 Mönch (between Jungfrau and Eiger)
7 Dom (4545m)
8 Popocatepetl
9 Blaven
10 Cronk ny Arrey Laa

• 15 • (1935, 12)

1 Anne of Cleves
2 Anne of Geierstein (Scott)
3 Anne Askew (1546)
4 Anne Page (*The Merry Wives of Windsor*)
5 Anne Hyde
6 Anne (Neville) of Warwick
7 Queen Anne
8 Anne of Austria
9 Fatima's sister
10 Anne, Duc de Montmorency (battles)

• 16 • (1935, 14)

1 Lerwick
2 Leicester
3 Minehead, also Padstow
4 Helston
5 Dublin
6 Whitby
7 St Ives, Hunts
8 Ambleside
9 Isle of Man
10 Nottingham

• 17 • (1935, 15)

1 Mary in *Up from Somerset* (Frederick Weatherly)
2 John the Baptist
3 the baker in *The Hunting of the Snark*
4 big bell of Ghent
5 Mrs Harris in Martin Chuzzlewit
6 Olivia in *The Vicar of Wakefield*
7 David Copperfield
8 Queen Victoria
9 Rosalind (*As You Like It*)
10 Haigha in *Alice in Wonderland*

• 18 • (1935, 16)

1 a full bus
2 distance between buses
3 drive
4 the bus
5 loitering to prevent arriving too early
6 an accident
7 plain clothes inspector
8 free pass
9 inspector of bus crews
10 holiday spent on a bus

# 1936–1938

• 1 • (1936, 1)

1 Richard I
2 William I
3 Edward III (at Calais)
4 Henry I
5 Empress Matilda
6 Margaret and the Robber
7 Eleanor of Aquitaine
8 Clarence
9 John
10 Mary I

• 2 • (1936, 5)

1 Kekule (the carbon ring)
2 the rattlesnake
3 *Murex*, a sea snail (Tyrian Purple, used in the byzantine Court)
4 the dodo (dead as a dodo)
5 the leech
6 the scarab beetle
7 the eel (lays its eggs and dies in the Sargasso Sea)
8 the camel
9 the kiwi
10 a benevolent reformer in *Erewhon* (Samuel Butler)

• 3 • (1936, 8)

1 mediaeval catapult
2 large shield with prop

3  neck mail
4  narrow mail shoe
5  part of trigger mechanism
6  small cannon
7  small flag or pennon
8  a shafted weapon resembling a bill
9  arquebus or early musket
10  early wheel-lock musket

• 4 •   (1936, 9)

1  14 miles
2  three score and ten, sir
3  15 furlongs (*St John* 11, 18 – King James Bible)
4  about three score furlongs (*St Luke* 24, 13)
5  'An hour out of Guildford town' (Kipling)
6  within a mile
7  more than 70 miles
8  about 3,500 miles
9  about 12 miles (*Barnaby Rudge*)
10  one step

• 5 •   (1936, 14)

1  Horlicks
2  Three Nuns
3  Persil
4  Hoover
5  De Reszke Minors
6  'Did you Maclean your teeth?'
7  Players
8  Shell
9  Guinness
10  Churchman's No. 1

• 6 •   (1936, 17)

1  Longfellow – *Hymn to the Night*
2  Charles Towne – *A Lover in Damascus*
3  Tennyson – *Crossing the Bar*
4  David – Psalm 104
5  Edward Teschemacher – *Summertime*
6  Shakespeare – *Macbeth*
7  Gilbert – *The Yeomen of the Guard*
8  Dickens – *A Tale of Two Cities*

9  Scott – *The Lay of the Last Minstrel*
10  Sarojini Naidu – *Nightfall in Hyderabad*

• 7 •   (1937, 1)

1  George IV (Queen Caroline)
2  Elizabeth
3  John
4  Edward II
5  William I
6  Victoria
7  Edward VII
8  Anne
9  William and Mary
10  James II

• 8 •   (1937, 4)

1  aposiopesis
2  litotes
3  tmesis
4  oxymoron
5  onomatapeia
6  hyperbole
7  metonymy
8  syllepsis
9  chiasmus
10  zeugma

• 9 •   (1937, 5)

1  Alice
2  Pilate (*St John* 18, 38)
3  Jezebel (*2 Kings* 9, 31)
4  Witches in *Macbeth*
5  Alfred Austin
6  Mr Justice Darling
7  John Ball
8  George III
9  Essex in *Merrie England*
10  Lady Jane Grey

• 10 •   (1937, 7)

1  Erysipelas
2  Pig-nut
3  Yellow Rocket (flower)
4  Quinsy
5  Flag of British Navy
6  Carob bean

7 Mediaeval public preaching place
8 Virgin's Well at Nazareth
9 Drunkenness
10 John Dory

• 11 • (1937, 14)

1 Charles Peace (Karlsruhe)
2 Crippen
3 Rudge, father of Barnaby
4 Dr Roylott (Conan Doyle – *The Speckled Band*)
5 Landru
6 Eugene Aram (in the stocks)
7 First Murderer in *Macbeth*
8 murderer in *The Tell-tale Heart* (Edgar Allan Poe)
9 Cain
10 Bill Sikes

• 12 • (1937, 15)

1 *O God our Help*
2 *When I Survey*
3 *O Worship the King*
4 *City of God*
5 *The Church's One Foundation*
6 *Abide With Me*
7 *Eternal Father*
8 *Lo! He comes*
9 *Holy, Holy, Holy*
10 *All People that on Earth do Dwell*

• 13 • (1937, 17)

1 Victoria – Tennyson
2 Elizabeth – Spenser
3 Henry of Navarre – Macaulay
4 King Olaf – Longfellow
5 Cleopatra – Tennyson
6 Charlemagne – Scott
7 Henry VI to Richard III – Shakespeare
8 Saul and Jonathan – David
9 Anne Boleyn – herself
10 Queen Mary – F E Weatherley

• 14 • (1938, 1)

1 Macaulay's
2 Shakespeare's

3 Head boy at Dotheboys Hall
4 The schoolmaster's pupils in *The Deserted Village* (Goldsmith)
5 Eric (F W Farrar)
6 Clive
7 Alexander of Battenberg
8 William
9 'A young Lucas' (*Pride and Prejudice*)
10 Midshipman Easy (Marryat)

• 15 • (1938, 7)

1 Part of the mine from which ore is being extracted
2 Internal connection between two levels. Always sunk downwards
3 Exactly the same as Winze, but upwards
4 Connection from shaft to reef
5 Shaft headgear
6 Windlass operated by man or animal power (never mechanical power) when prospecting
7 A simple steam pump for removing water
8 The bucket in the shaft of a mine
9 A platform in the shaft
10 A passage to bring water to the surface

• 16 • (1938, 8)

1 Bray
2 Wakefield
3 George Robey (Vicar of Mirth)
4 Sir Francis Bryan (Vicar of Hell – early 16th century)
5 The village preacher at Auburn (Goldsmith – *The Deserted Village*)
6 Clergyman of Dingley Dell (*Pickwick Papers*)
7 Mr Quiverful (Trollope – *Barchester Towers*)
8 Mr Collins (*Pride and Prejudice*)
9 'The Pazon' (T E Brown)
10 Vicar General

(1938, 12)

1  Red Riding Hood
2  Fatima
3  Snow White
4  Cinderella
5  Jack the Giant Killer
6  Sleeping Beauty
7  Rapunzel
8  Goldilocks
9  Gretel
10 Rumpelstiltskin

• 18 •  (1938, 17)

1  *Evangeline* – Longfellow
2  *Love's Labours Lost* – Shakespeare
3  *St Joan* – G B Shaw
4  *The Faerie Queen* – Spenser
5  *Pride and Prejudice* – Jane Austen
6  *Of Truth* – Bacon
7  *The Canterbury Tales* – Chaucer
8  *Robinson Crusoe* – Defoe
9  *The Task* – Cowper
10 *Concerning the Service of the Church in the Book of Common Prayer* – Cranmer et al. (1549)

# 1939

• 1 •

1  Austrian Succession
2  Spanish Succession
3  Thirty Years'
4  Seven Years'
5  Napoleonic
6  Franco-Prussian
7  Civil War
8  American Civil
9  Boer
10 Armageddon

• 2 •

1  10d.
2  'for so much'
3  13s. 4d.
4  144 green spectacles

5  £12 a year
6  'a threepence bowed'
7  18s.
8  'above rubies'
9  100 pence
10 6d.

• 3 •

1  Hotspur in *Henry IV*
2  Michael Hunter, Sheffield, 1875
3  Humphry Davy
4  George Stephenson
5  off French Guiana
6  Benedictus in France
7  Rupert Brooke
8  Once during each performance
9  MG Car Company
10 Harold Lloyd

• 4 •

1  Reynaud
2  Sikorski
3  Newall
4  Kalinin
5  Von Brauchitsch
6  Raeder
7  Molotov
8  Dudley Pound
9  Zaleski
10 Gamelin

• 5 •

1  The Line
2  southern boundary of Pennsylvania
3  Northern Line
4  Marriage Lines
5  Thin Red Line
6  Apollo Line in palmistry
7  'Orient, Anchor, Bibby, Hall'
8  Torres Vedras
9  the dotted line
10 Siegfried

• 6 •

1  composer, 1650
2  opera by Puccini
3  song composer, 19th century

4 Non-Coll. Student
5 town in Turkey
6 Harold's brother
7 village in Scotland
8 town in Argentina
9 composer
10 Italian conductor

• 7 •

1 Medusa
2 Python
3 Cobra
4 Hercules
5 Kaa
6 Speckled Band
7 Boa
8 Snakes and Ladders
9 Ye spotted snakes
10 Garden of Eden

• 8 •

1 Schubert
2 Mrs Skewton
3 Mary Queen of Scots
4 Peter Magnus
5 Richard II or III
6 William III
7 Coutts
8 George IV
9 Halifax (temp. Charles II)
10 Baker, *Hunting of the Snark*

• 9 •

1 Elizabeth
2 Dunbar
3 Culloden
4 Queen Victoria's profile is on them
5 Jellalabad
6 Edward Medal
7 Military Medal
8 Naval General Service
9 Volunteer Long Service
10 VC

• 10 •

1 Robert Taylor
2 Mary Pickford

3 Boris Karloff
4 George Arliss
5 Eddie Cantor
6 Loretta Young
7 Ginger Rogers
8 Fred Astaire
9 Mickey Rooney
10 Greta Garbo

• 11 •

1 The father in the *Erl-King*
   (Goethe)
2 Joris and Dirck
3 Louis XVI at Varennes
4 The Brushwood Boy
5 Paul Revere (Longfellow)
6 Death – Light Brigade
7 Roushan Beg (Longfellow)
8 Mazeppa
9 The Moorish King (Byron –
   *The Siege and Conquest of Alhama*)
10 El Dorado

• 12 •

1 circus
2 waxworks
3 freaks
4 magic
5 horsemanship
6 gardens
7 tea gardens
8 dinner
9 polo
10 boxing

• 13 •

1 Master Henry (temp. Henry III)
2 John Kaye (temp. Edward IV)
3 Skelton (temp. Henry VIII)
4 Ben Jonson
5 Southey
6 Dryden
7 Tennyson
8 Wordsworth
9 Masefield
10 Austin

• 14 •

1 Red Riding Hood's
2 Nelson
3 Tennyson's Grandmother's Apology
4 Eleanor of Aquitaine
5 Mrs Wardle
6 Naomi
7 Mrs Smallweed
8 Lois
9 Mme Mère, Napoleon's mother
10 sucking eggs

• 15 •

1 Carr's Biscuits
2 Morris Cars
3 HMV Gramophone
4 Pears' Soap
5 Pullar's Dye Works
6 Lever's Soaps
7 Huntley and Palmer Biscuits *or* Sutton's Seeds
8 Fry's Chocolate
9 Ford Cars
10 Tynwald Woollen Mills

• 16 •

1 Hanway
2 Maratha Princes
3 Gaza
4 PM
5 Mrs Bagnet
6 *Magnolia umbrella*
7 Burma
8 Umbrella Man
9 Duke of Cambridge
10 Mrs Gamp

• 17 •

1 Wellington – Tennyson
2 Cromwell – Milton
3 Napoleon – Byron
4 Henry of Navarre – Macaulay
5 Henry V – Shakespeare
6 John Moore – Wolfe
7 The Private of the Buffs – Doyle
8 Kamal – Kipling

9 Richard III – Shakespeare
10 Marlborough – Samuel Garth

• 18 •

1 caricature of *Le Chat*
2 Aden
3 Hugh Rotherham died (inventor of the bogey)
4 *L'Indifférent*
5 Dutch Princess Irene
6 King and Queen in Canada
7 President Lebrun
8 IRA
9 *Ark Royal*
10 Hitler

# 1940–1941

• 1 •   (1940, 1)

1 Sir Richard Grenville
2 Haig
3 Foch
4 Henry V
5 Nurse Cavell
6 Napoleon
7 Sir Charles Napier
8 Elizabeth
9 George V
10 George VI

• 2 •   (1940, 3)

1 Missouri
2 Abana
3 Seine
4 Sambre et Meuse
5 Danube
6 Jordan
7 Nile – Cleopatra's
8 Amazon
9 Isis
10 Pison

• 3 •   (1940, 6)

1 Creakle
2 Schoolmaster in *The Deserted Village*

3 Dr Busby
4 Dr Arnold
5 T E Brown
6 Mr Bonnycastle (Capt Marryat, *Mr Midshipman Easy*)
7 Gordon (F W Farrar, *Eric*)
8 Ascham of Elizabeth
9 Nicholas Udall
10 Squeers

• 4 •   (1940, 7)

1 wind in the beam
2 the galley funnel
3 the inboard end of a hemp cable, secured round the 'bitts'
4 swinging the lead (malingering)
5 The Devil was a large, very difficult, seam in the planking and took a whole bucket of pitch to 'pay'
6 the 'docked' or short watch
7 a warrant officer
8 the purser
9 boots issued by the 'pusser' (purser)
10 a bogus seaman

• 5 •   (1940, 10)

1 Victoria
2 Captain of *Pinafore*
3 Henry VIII
4 *The Mystery of Edwin Drood*
5 *Eric*
6 William the Silent
7 *As You Like It*
8 Henry I
9 Duchess of Marlborough
10 Royal Air Force

• 6 •   (1940, 12)

1 'When the night wind howls' etc.
2 Herne the Hunter
3 Banquo
4 Marley (*A Christmas Carol*)
5 Molly Malone – a barrow
6 Hamlet's father
7 The White Lady (Scott, *The Monastery*)

8 by going west
9 Tom Pearce's mare
10 Ghost in *Barnaby Rudge*

• 7 •   (1940, 16)

1 Eliza in *Uncle Tom's Cabin*
2 Za Za
3 Blondin
4 Catharine Douglas
5 Judith
6 Phileas Fogg
7 Jael
8 Charlotte Corday
9 Samson
10 Atlas

• 8 •   (1940, 17)

1 Browning – *Home Thoughts from the Sea*
2 Basil Hood – *Merrie England*
3 Kipling – *The Flag of England*
4 Macaulay – *The Armada*
5 Campbell – *Battle of the Baltic*
6 Doyle – *The Red Thread of Honour*
7 Kingsley – *A Welcome*
8 Swinburne – *England*
9 Harold Begbie – *A Song of England*
10 Shakespeare – *Richard II*

• 9 •   (1940, 18)

1 Ribbentrop
2 Pétain
3 Naval bases to America
4 Admiral Jervis
5 Leopold
6 'Random'
7 Vichy
8 *When It Was Dark*
9 the Greeks
10 BBC

• 10 •   (1941, 1)

1 Napoleon
2 Druid to Boadicea
3 Nelson
4 Philip Faulconbridge
5 Henry V

6 George II
7 Elizabeth
8 Harold
9 Victoria
10 Wellington

• 11 • (1941, 3)

1 Bulle
2 Jack Ketch
3 Samson – French Revolution
4 Bluebeard
5 M de Calais, Executioner of Anne
Boleyn
6 Lord High Executioner in *The
Mikado*
7 Dennis in *Barnaby Rudge*
8 Executioner in *The Yeomen of the
Guard*
9 Executioner of Lille in *The Three
Musketeers*
10 Joab

• 12 • (1941, 5)

1 Sir Walter Scott
2 William IV
3 Caroline, wife of George II
4 Irish Rebellion – Charles I
5 Charles II
6 Victoria
7 Henry VIII
8 George II
9 William III
10 Elizabeth

• 13 • (1941, 7)

1 90
2 17
3 43
4 21
5 50
6 365
7 16
8 7, 10
9 80
10 three score years and ten

• 14 • (1941, 8)

1 The Lizard in *Alice*
2 Sam Weller
3 Anne Boleyn
4 Jane Austen
5 Mr Pickwick
6 Paston Letters
7 Darcy (*Pride and Prejudice*)
8 Elizabeth
9 Wemmick (*Great Expectations*)
10 St Paul to Timothy

• 15 • (1941, 9)

1 £20
2 £67
3 £40
4 £115
5 'Very little less than £1,000'
6 £5
7 20,000 measures of wheat
8 £400
9 Many a sorrow, many a labour,
many a tear
10 £930,935,000

• 16 • (1941, 11)

1 BE 1 (1912)
2 Super Handley Page
3 Sopwith Camel
4 Sopwith Pup
5 Aeronautical Scholarships
6 Kronfeld
7 Wallace – towing drogues
8 Wolfenden – Headmaster of
Uppingham
9 226
10 Capt. Pixon

• 17 • (1941, 14)

1 Clarinet
2 String bass
3 Wing fan
4 Swing hater
5 Old-fashioned jazz
6 Impromptu swing music
7 Trombone
8 Female vocalist

9 Drummer
10 Sweet Rhythm Band

• 18 • (1941, 18)

1 Baden Powell's
2 Metaxas
3 *Punch*
4 The Kaiser
5 Bismarck
6 Atlantic Meeting
7 1812
8 BBC Interlude
9 Hess
10 Emperor of Abyssinia

# 1942–1943

• 1 • (1942, 1)

1 Elizabeth of Philip III
2 Caesar, the Belgians
3 The Kaiser
4 Mazzini, Italy
5 Motley of William the Silent
6 Bismarck
7 Henry V before Harfleur
8 Lannes at Ulm
9 Sydney Carton of France
10 the bell, Roland (at Ghent. Longfellow – *The Belfry of Bruges*)

• 2 • (1942, 2)

1 John Harmon
2 Anne Catherick
3 Richard
4 Thorkell Mylrea
5 Mrs Graham
6 the March family
7 Percy Blakeney
8 Gaston de Bonne (Sieur de Marsac)
9 the Warringtons
10 Not named

• 3 • (1942, 4)

1 Alice
2 Wise Men of Gotham

3 Mr Stiggins (*The Pickwick Papers*)
4 The owl and the pussy-cat
5 Cinderella
6 St Paul
7 Mrs Bagnet (*Bleak House*)
8 Europa
9 husband of rump-fed ronyon (*Macbeth*)
10 Young Lady of Riga

• 4 • (1942, 5)

1 Pear Tree
2 Cherry
3 Beechy
4 Chestnut
5 Palm and Pine
6 Sycamore
7 Ash
8 Yggdrasil
9 Oak
10 Oak, Ash and Ivy

• 5 • (1942, 8)

1 Du Guesclin
2 Lytton
3 Balzac
4 Kipling
5 Pope
6 Tennyson
7 Shakespeare
8 Byron
9 Dickens
10 Solomon

• 6 • (1942, 11)

1 Leiden
2 Uppsala
3 Wittenberg
4 Oxford
5 Louvain
6 Dublin
7 Cambridge
8 St Andrews
9 Göttingen
10 London

# ANSWERS

**• 7 •**  (1942, 13)

1 *Peggy's Wedding* – T E Brown
2 *Westward Ho!* – Charles Kingsley
3 *Armadale* – Wilkie Collins
4 *Tynwald Hill* – Wordsworth
5 *The Good Companions* –
 J B Priestley
6 *Godred Crovan* (1768) – Thomas
 Chatterton
7 *Eric, or Little by Little* – F W Farrar
8 The Lay of the Last Minstrel – Sir
 Walter Scott
9 *The Deemster* – Hall Caine
10 *The Raiders* – S R Crockett

**• 8 •**  (1942, 14)

1 Boyle
2 Cavendish
3 Paracelsus
4 Bragg
5 Soddy
6 Mendeleev
7 Newton
8 Van 't Hoff
9 Joule
10 Priestley

**• 9 •**  (1942, 17)

1 *Twelfth Night* – Shakespeare
2 *Ode on a Grecian Urn* – Keats
3 *Princess Ida* – W S Gilbert
4 *Maud* – Tennyson
5 *My love she's but a lassie yet* – Burns
6 *The Ballad of Reading Gaol* – Oscar
 Wilde
7 Psalm 85 – David
8 *Tom Jones* – Charles Taylor
 (operetta, music Edward German)
9 *Love's Philosophy* – Shelley
10 *King Henry V* – Shakespeare

**• 10 •**  (1943, 1)

1 The Kaiser
2 Napoleon
3 Tacitus
4 Queen Victoria of Mr Gladstone
5 Lord Chesterfield

6 King John in Magna Carta
7 Elizabeth
8 Thirty-seventh Article
9 George V
10 James II

**• 11 •**  (1943, 2)

1 Asoka
2 Vishnu
3 Delhi, in honour of Shahab-ud-din
4 Bombay, Parsee place of disposal of
 the dead
5 Kaisar-i-Hind
6 Nizam of Hyderabad
7 Mother Ganges
8 Mumtaz Mahal, wife of Shah
 Jehan
9 Bombay – dowry of Catherine of
 Braganza
10 The Jhelum

**• 12 •**  (1943, 5)

1 Saturday (Solomon Grundy)
2 Wednesday
3 Friday
4 Thursday
5 Monday
6 Sunday
7 Monday
8 Sunday
9 Friday
10 Every day

**• 13 •**  (1943, 6)

1 Matilda's house
2 Fire of London: Solomon Eagle
3 Bishop Hatto's burning of
 peasants
4 Paris bazaar: sister of Empress of
 Austria
5 Augusta's house: Augusta
6 Chicago Fire, 1871
7 Shadrach, Meshach and Abednego
8 Newgate
9 Moscow
10 Krook's

• 14 • (1943, 8)

1 'Sherman'
2 Machine gun co-axially mounted with heavy gun in turret of tank
3 derived from 'Vickers Armstrong Ltd, Elswick, Newcastle-upon-Tyne'
4 Voroshilov
5 My Boy Billy
6 'Covenanter'
7 in the use of the 'Crusader'
8 'The Priest' – mobile heavy gun
9 the 'Grant'
10 Major-General Swindon

• 15 • (1943, 9)

1 Charlie Chaplin
2 Zaza
3 Grimaldi
4 Jacob Hall
5 Chevalier
6 Blondin
7 Nijinsky
8 Cinquevalli
9 Sandow
10 George Robey

• 16 • (1943, 12)

1 Rugby
2 Marlborough
3 Eton
4 Wellington
5 King William's
6 Westminster
7 Merchant Taylors'
8 Charterhouse
9 Harrow
10 Clifton

• 17 • (1943, 13)

1 Old Scarlet
2 Gabriel Grub (*The Pickwick Papers*)
3 Antigone
4 Trappist
5 Sexton Beetle
6 Sexton Blake
7 Miss Blimber (*Dombey and Son*)
8 Matthew Malmain
9 The Owl
10 Sexton in *Hamlet*

• 18 • (1943, 18)

1 Princess Juliana's child (Margriet) born in Canada
2 Unconditional surrender at Casablanca
3 Rachmaninov
4 Fourth French Republic
5 Regency during the King's absence
6 'General Chase', Bay of Biscay
7 Flying death of Leslie Howard
8 Russian Patriarch
9 Azores Treaty
10 Hitler

# 1944

• 1 •

1 Charles II
2 Edward VI
3 James II
4 George II
5 William III
6 Elizabeth
7 Mary I
8 Victoria
9 Anne
10 William IV

• 2 •

1 Heartbreak House
2 A Doll's House
3 The Small House at Arlington
4 The Fall of the House of Usher
5 The House where I was born
6 The House of the Arrow
7 The House of the Wolf
8 The Deserted House (Tennyson)
9 Danesbury House
10 Bleak House

ANSWERS

### • 3 •

1 *1812* – Meissonier
2 *The Fighting Téméraire* – Turner
3 *Shoeing the Bay Mare* – Landseer
4 *Anne of Cleves* – Holbein
5 *The School of Anatomy* – Rembrandt
(See also *The Judgment of Sisamnes* –
Gerard David)
6 *I dreamt that I dwelt* – Belcher
7 *Cromwell* – Lely
8 *Delft* – Vermeer
9 *The Gleaners* – Millet
10 *The Angelus* – Millet

### • 4 •

1 Californian Redwood (363 feet)
2 Alpine Willow (one inch)
3 Bald Cypress, Mexico
(4,000–6,000 years)
4 Jamaica
5 Finland
6 Persia
7 Hickory
8 Chestnut
9 Oak
10 Lignum Vitae

### • 5 •

1 Mercutio – *Romeo and Juliet*
2 Third Witch – *Macbeth*
3 Petruchio – *The Taming of the Shrew*
4 Clown – *Twelfth Night*
5 Gratiano – *The Merchant of Venice*
6 Hamlet – *Hamlet*
7 Fluellan – *King Henry V*
8 Falstaff – *King Henry IV* Part 1
9 Maria – *Twelfth Night*
10 Iago – *Othello*

### • 6 •

1 Euston
2 St Pancras
3 King's Cross
4 Liverpool
5 Cannon Street
6 Charing Cross
7 Waterloo
8 Paddington
9 Marylebone
10 Fenchurch Street

### • 7 •

1 *Vanity Fair* – W M Thackeray
2 *The Ordeal of Richard Feverel* –
George Meredith
3 *Waverley* – Sir Walter Scott
4 *Tess of the d'Urbervilles* – Thomas
Hardy
5 *Twelfth Night* – Shakespeare
6 *Mary Barton* – Mrs Gaskell
7 *Back to Methuselah* – George
Bernard Shaw
8 *St Winifred's* – F W Farrar
9 *Kipps* – H G Wells
10 *Oliver Twist* – Charles Dickens

### • 8 •

1 Second Witch in *Macbeth*
2 Alfred
3 James Douglas (1307)
4 Arctic Explorer Frederick Cook
5 Mrs Glass
6 Thomas Cook
7 Queen of Hearts
8 Witch in *Hansel and Gretel*
9 Rouse (cook to Cardinal Fisher)
10 James Cook (explorer)

### • 9 •

1 La Pallice
2 Rio
3 Adelaide
4 Le Havre
5 Port of London
6 Piraeus
7 The Haven under the Hill
8 Walmer Castle
9 Ijmuiden
10 any port

### • 10 •

1 Dr Johnson
2 Charlotte Brontë
3 Dickens

4 Scott
5 The Queen of England
6 Victoria
7 Cromwell *or* Montrose
8 Marlborough
9 Frederick the Great
10 Grimaldi

• 11 •

1 Boadicea
2 Saul
3 The Little Tom-Tit
4 Lady Macbeth
5 Merdle (*Little Dorrit*)
6 Madame Butterfly
7 Suffragette at the Derby (Emily Wilding Davison)
8 Tosca
9 Don Bolero Fizzgig (*The Pickwick Papers*)
10 Brutus

• 12 •

1 Hellevoetsluis
2 Gorinchem
3 Delft
4 Zaandam
5 Leiden
6 Kampen
7 Utrecht
8 Rotterdam
9 Arnhem
10 The Hague

• 13 •

1 Moses
2 Esau
3 Achilles
4 The Old Pretender
5 The Duchess's baby in *Alice in Wonderland*
6 Hercules
7 Elizabeth
8 The 'Bavarian baby'
9 'Ma curly-headed babby'
10 Helen's baby

• 14 •

1 De Valera
2 Gen. O'Connor
3 Dean Swift
4 Phil the Flute
5 Vincent Wallace in *Maritana*
6 Mr Dillon
7 Tim Finnegan
8 Jimmy O'Dea
9 Cannon Hannay (George Birmingham)
10 Father O'Flynn

• 15 •

1 William Webb Ellis
2 Jingle
3 Polo (Pulu)
4 Drake
5 Lacrosse
6 Charles I (golf)
7 Alice (croquet)
8 the billiard sharpener
9 Hockey
10 Third Estate in Estates General (1789)

• 16 •

1 Oliver Twist
2 Humpty Dumpty
3 Mrs Bagnet (*Bleak House*)
4 Frederic (*Pirates of Penzance*)
5 Duchess of Kent, mother of Queen Victoria
6 Queen Victoria
7 Princess Alice, Duchess of Gloucester (1901, as was Princess Alexandra in 1936)
8 Charles II
9 Pepys
10 Shakespeare

• 17 •

1 Henry VIII
2 Mary, Queen of Scots
3 Anne Boleyn
4 Francis I
5 James I

6 Marguérite of Alençon
7 James I of Scotland
8 Edward of York (temp. Henry IV)
9 Charles of Orléans (Father of Louis XII)
10 Elizabeth

• 18 •

1 50,000 (no. of *The Times* issues)
2 Montagu Norman
3 The Budget
4 Princess Elizabeth did not become Princess of Wales
5 Sir Henry Wood
6 *Te Deum* in Notre Dame
7 Caen to Paris
8 Isle of Wight – death of Princess Beatrice
9 The Crossing of the Rubicon
10 D-Day

# 1945

• 1 •

1 Utrecht
2 Versailles
3 Cambrai
4 Pretoria
5 Berlin
6 Cateau Cambrésis
7 Vienna
8 Amiens
9 Étaples
10 Charles

• 2 •

1 Jenkins
2 Cyrano de Bergerac *or* Durante
3 Carker *or* Wolf in *Red Riding Hood*
4 Adam
5 Miss Sarah Biffin
6 Katisha (*The Mikado*)
7 Justice in *As You Like It*

8 Cripple at the Gate called Beautiful (*Acts* 3, 7)
9 Anne Boleyn
10 Churchill

• 3 •

1 Wellington
2 Lloyd George
3 Palmerston
4 Asquith
5 Melbourne
6 Gladstone
7 Walpole
8 Chatham
9 Disraeli
10 Churchill

• 4 •

1 Oxford and Cambridge
2 Foreign Secretary and Minister of Health
3 Sovereign and Wench
4 Village and River
5 Riding School and Household
6 Master and Pupil
7 MP and Song by Stephen Adams
8 French Revolutionary and French Poet
9 Male and Female
10 Fourteen miles

• 5 •

1 Hanging Gardens of Babylon
2 Alice's Garden
3 Eden
4 Mary, Mary's
5 Kirk O'Field
6 Shalimar
7 High Hall Garden
8 Epicurus
9 Hesperides
10 Jerusalem

• 6 •

1 to boast
2 CB
3 AC2

4 bombed or crashed
5 in the sea
6 tea
7 beer
8 failure of parachute to open
9 tank on fire
10 a Wellington

• 7 •

1 Stanley and Livingstone in Africa
2 George IV on meeting Caroline
3 Henry VIII and Anne Boleyn
4 Mrs Gamp to Mercy Chuzzlewit
5 Charles I to Laud
6 Artful Dodger and Oliver Twist
7 The Amalekite to David
8 Rosamond in *The Dream of Fair Women*
9 Louis XIV to his Court
10 Red Queen and Alice

• 8 •

1 Mrs Ronnback of Stockholm
2 Florence Nightingale
3 Ellen Douglas
4 Empress Matilda
5 Thye Virgin
6 Elaine
7 Violetta
8 Canada
9 Pauline
10 The Queen

• 9 •

1 Olivia – *Twelfth Night*
2 Theseus – *A Midsummer Night's Dream*
3 Bastard (Philip Falconbridge) – *King John*
4 Sir Toby Belch – *Twelfth Night*
5 Ariel – *The Tempest*
6 King Richard – *King Richard III*
7 Touchstone – *As You Like It*
8 Nym – *King Henry V*
9 First Clown (Gravedigger) – *Hamlet*
10 Bassanio – *The Merchant of Venice*

• 10 •

1 Rev. Blank-Blank (*Our Mutual Friend*)
2 Mr Elton (*Emma*)
3 The Doge
4 Friar Tuck
5 Benevolent old clergyman of Dingley Dell (*The Pickwick Papers*)
6 Archdeacon Grantley (*Barchester Towers*)
7 Bishop of Orkney
8 Archbishop Howley (Victoria and Albert)
9 Gardiner (Mary I and Philip II of Spain)
10 Cranmer

• 11 •

1 Spode
2 Chelsea
3 Sèvres
4 Dresden
5 Wedgwood
6 Delft
7 Cologne
8 Ming
9 The Potter's Field
10 North Staffs Railway

• 12 •

1 Hades
2 a halo; a (rain) cloud
3 a blood clot
4 New Testament Prophet
5 a crush hat
6 a roundabout method
7 the Sun God
8 early gun
9 Place of Darkness
10 Greek game

• 13 •

1 A shop. The Prince
2 Haig Whisky *or* Hovis
3 Gibbs
4 Pears

5 Gillette
6 Heinz's
7 Maclean your teeth
8 Bird's Custard
9 Bovril
10 Guinness

• 14 •

1 Coronets
2 St Augustine
3 Midlothian
4 Melrose
5 Jerusalem
6 Rouen
7 Hearts' Content, Newfoundland
8 Heartsease
9 Piccadilly Circus
10 Love

• 15 •

1 Bredon
2 Bow Bells
3 Roland, Roland – at Ghent
   (Longfellow)
4 St Clement's
5 Cloches de Corneville
6 Shandon
7 The Chimes (Dickens)
8 Münster (Schaffhausen)
9 Clermont Town (Hilaire Belloc)
10 'Quit you like men'

• 16 •

1 Marat's
2 Nancy's (*Oliver Twist*)
3 Cock Robin's
4 Daniel Clark (Eugene Aram)
5 Abel's
6 Zimri's master's (*2 Kings* 9)
7 Belle Elmore's (Crippen)
8 Archduke Ferdinand's
9 Princes in the Tower
10 Edwin Drood's

• 17 •

1 *The Battle of the Baltic* – Campbell
2 *Horatius* – Macaulay

3 *Now thank we all our God*
   – Winkworth
4 *In Memoriam* – Tennyson
5 *Epistle to the Romans* – Paul
6 *Peace, perfect peace* – Bickersteth
7 *In Memoriam* – Scott
8 *My Garden* – T E Brown
9 *To the Lord General* – Milton
10 *A Psalm of Life* – Longfellow

• 18 •

1 President Roosevelt
2 Dr McIntyre
3 General Election
4 Barham
5 Miss Campbell (first London
   woman magistrate)
6 *Queen Mary* and *Queen Elizabeth*
7 Fido and Pluto
8 Dr Barnardo
9 Royal Tynwald
10 The Mighty Atom

# 1946–1947

• 1 •   (1946, 1)

1 Empress Matilda
2 Richard I's
3 Bruce
4 Edward I
5 Henry VIII
6 Mary Queen of Scots
7 Queen Anne – Duchess of
   Marlborough
8 George II at Dettingen
9 William IV
10 Queen Victoria

• 2 •   (1946, 2)

1 Medina
2 Heliopolis
3 Limerick
4 Montreal *or* Salt Lake City
5 Caerleon on Usk
6 Philadelphia

7 The World of the Unconverted (*The
   Pilgrim's Progress*)
8 Galway
9 Novel by Temple Thurston
10 Florence

• 3 •   (1946, 7)

1 Blenheim orange
2 Strawberries – Lord Hastings
3 Pomegranate – Persephone
4 Cherries – Julia
5 Grapes – Ezekiel
6 Apricot – Dr Grant (*Mansfield Park*)
7 Pineapple – William IV
8 Greengage – Queen Claude
9 Apple – Prince Ahmed
10 Bananas

• 4 •   (1946, 8)

1 Mrs Varden's (*Barnaby Rudge*)
2 Mary's (the mother of Mark)
3 Elisha's
4 Carlyle's
5 Miss Matty's (*Cranford*)
6 Don Quixote's
7 The Brass's
8 Mr B's *or* Mr Rochester's
9 The King who delivered the talents
10 Queen Anne's

• 5 •   (1946, 9)

1 Zeno
2 Kitcat
3 Carlton
4 Smithfield
5 Almack
6 For Japanese Members
7 Bankers
8 Portland
9 White's
10 House of Commons

• 6 •   (1946, 13)

1 The Bed of Ware
2 Red Riding Hood's Grandmother's
3 Looking-Glass House Garden
4 Taffy

5 The French 'Lit de justice'
6 Pierrot – a pen *or* Man in Parable –
   three loaves
7 Macbeth's Castle
8 Sleepy Head
9 Roker (*The Pickwick Papers*)
10 Wilkie Collins

• 7 •   (1946, 15)

1 Eve
2 Mrs Proudie *(Barchester Towers)*
3 Anne Boleyn
4 Anne Catherick (Wilkie Collins)
5 Mrs Arbuthnot (Oscar Wilde)
6 Mona Craine (Hall Caine)
7 Ruth
8 Babylon
9 Mrs Raddle (*The Pickwick Papers*)
10 March sisters

• 8 •   (1946, 16)

1 Sister Anne (*Bluebeard*)
2 Cassandra
3 Medusa
4 Charlotte Brontë
5 Euphrosyne
6 Marie Antoinette
7 Victoria Cross
8 Lady Dedlock (*Bleak House*)
9 Katharine (*The Taming of the Shrew*)
10 Anne Boleyn

• 9 •   (1946, 17)

1 The Massacre in Piedmont –
   Milton
2 The Royal George – Cowper
3 Cassabianca – Hemans
4 Boadicea – Cowper
5 Murder of Edward II – Gray
6 Execution of Charles I – Marvell
7 Death of Saul – David
8 Attack on Maud's brother
   – Tennyson
9 Wreck of the Hesperus
   – Longfellow
10 Revolt of the Northern Earls
   – Wordsworth

**• 10 •** (1947, 1)

1 Cophetua and the Beggar Maid
2 Louis XVI and Marie Antoinette
3 Edward IV and Elizabeth Woodville
4 Henry VIII and Jane Seymour
5 Henry II and Eleanor of Aquitaine
6 George IV and Caroline of Brunswick
7 Richard II and Isabel of France
8 Herod and Herodias
9 William I and Matilda of Flanders
10 Edward VII and Alexandra

**• 11 •** (1947, 3)

1 Dr Fell
2 Lady Macbeth's
3 Henry King – chewing string
4 St Bonaventura
5 Lancet Fish
6 Sherry
7 Duchess of Marlborough
8 Mr Slasher's (*The Pickwick Papers*)
9 Dr Perry to Mr Woodhouse (*Emma*)
10 Dr Parker Peps (*Dombey and Son*)

**• 12 •** (1947, 4)

1 Queen Alexandra's
2 George V
3 St Stephen
4 Saxony
5 Henry III
6 her hair
7 Antioch
8 for the first Roman to scale an enemy wall
9 Miss Snevellicci (*Nicholas Nickleby*)
10 The Lass of Richmond Hill

**• 13 •** (1947, 6)

1 Deacons at Ordination
2 Taking the baby
3 To make them attend Sunday School
4 The Navy
5 Forbidding the Banns

6 Commination Service
7 In Lent *or* after First Lesson (The *Benedicite* is the only Canticle, so called)
8 Hierome
9 Just before the Psalms (*The Pickwick Papers*)
10 A woman may not marry her husband's sister's son

**• 14 •** (1947, 8)

1 Mr Dick (*David Copperfield*)
2 George III
3 Juana (La Loca) of Castile
4 Ophelia
5 The gentleman next door (*Nicholas Nickleby*)
6 Don Carlos
7 Mrs Rochester (*Jane Eyre*)
8 Henry V
9 Louis of Bavaria
10 Schumann

**• 15 •** (1947, 9)

1 Frederick Barbarossa
2 The Ancient Mariner
3 Henry VIII and Francis I
4 Socrates
5 cut off one side of their beards
6 Alexander the Great
7 Nero
8 Leo III
9 Landru
10 Bottom

**• 16 •** (1947, 10)

1 Emperor Henry IV
2 Saul
3 Our King (Henry V)
4 Philip (*Acts*, 8)
5 the Gallant Knight (Poe)
6 Paul Revere (Longfellow)
7 Joseph's brethren (*Genesis*, 37)
8 Chamberlain
9 Mrs Gilpin
10 I

• 17 • (1947, 11)

1 Sir Eric Geddes
2 Disraeli
3 Ellen Wilkinson
4 Burke
5 John Bright
6 Sir Edward Grey
7 Lloyd George
8 Clive
9 Churchill
10 Edward VII

• 18 • (1947, 17)

1 The Squire's son and the Bailiff's daughter of Islington – Traditional
2 Priscilla and John Alden – Longfellow (*The Courtship of Miles Standish*)
3 Robin Hood and Marion – Basil Hood
4 Annie Lee and Philip Ray – Tennyson (*Enoch Arden*)
5 Princess Louise and Duke of Argyle – Mrs Gurney
6 Colonel Fairfax and Elsie Maynard – Gilbert (*The Yeomen of the Guard*)
7 Solomon and the Shulamite Maiden – Solomon
8 Venice and The Adriatic – Wordsworth
9 Ellen of Netherby Hall and 'A laggard in love' – Scott (*Lochinvar*)
10 The Bullet and her love – Bret Harte

# 1948–1949

• 1 • (1948, 1)

1 Victoria (eldest daughter of Queen Victoria)
2 William I
3 Edward V
4 Elizabeth
5 Solomon
6 Prince Arthur (son of Henry VII)

7 Edward II
8 Mary, Queen of Scots
9 The Old Pretender (the warming pan child)
10 Edward VII

• 2 • (1948, 2)

1 Henry VI
2 Philippa of Hainault
3 Margaret of Anjou and Elizabeth Woodville
4 Thomas Lord
5 Duke of Devonshire
6 Earl of Oxford
7 Prince Regent
8 William, Bishop of London
9 Black Prince
10 Canons of St Bartholomew, Smithfield

• 3 • (1948, 3)

1 a window in Thrums
2 window at Carisbrooke
3 window in the house where I was born
4 Rapunzel's
5 The Guillotine
6 Jezebel's
7 window with a twenty years' unobstructed view
8 The Lady of Shalott's
9 The White Rabbit's
10 window at Dotheboy's Hall

• 4 • (1948, 4)

1 an apothecary
2 Ralph (Beaumont and Fletcher)
3 Member of a USA Trade Union Organization
4 footpad, thief or sharper
5 a shoemaker
6 Lohengrin
7 a civil as opposed to a military knight
8 a tapster, publican
9 a compositor
10 Don Quixote

• 5 •   (1948, 7)

1 Rosemary
2 Marybuds (*Cymbeline*)
3 Violets
4 Passion Flower (*Maud* – Tennyson)
5 Lily (*Now Sleeps the Crimson Petal* – Tennyson)
6 Wild Thyme (*A Midsummer Night's Dream*)
7 Ladies fair – Lavender
8 Rose
9 Hemlocks (*Evangeline* – Longfellow)
10 The flower of all the world

• 6 •   (1948, 10)

1 Sam Weller
2 Samuel Langhorne Clemens (Mark Twain)
3 Samuel Pepys
4 Samuel Rutter (Bishop of Sodor and Man – inscription on his tomb in St German's Cathedral, Peel Castle)
5 Sam Costa (*Much Binding in the Marsh*)
6 Samuel Johnson
7 Samuel Taylor Coleridge
8 Samuel Butler (*Hudibras*)
9 Samuel Pickwick
10 Samuel the prophet

• 7 •   (1948, 12)

1 Minerva
2 Brer Rabbit
3 New Hebridean infants
4 Venus
5 Castor and Pollux
6 David Copperfield
7 Marina's (*Pericles*)
8 Zeus
9 Kaiser Wilhelm II's
10 Topsy (*Uncle Tom's Cabin*)

• 8 •   (1948, 15)

1 Podsnap to Mrs Veneering (*Our Mutual Friend*)
2 The Kaiser's to Kruger

3 Alfred Austin's
4 *The Daily Telegraph*
5 Queen Victoria's telegram to Gladstone on the murder of Gordon
6 The Ems Telegram
7 'Peccavi'
8 ships' semaphore and railway signals
9 Crippen
10 Mr Platt Mills's

• 9 •   (1949, 1)

1 David Copperfield
2 George Knightley, Emma, daughter of Mr Henry Woodhouse
3 Anne Boleyn, Henry VIII
4 Elizabeth, Edward IV
5 Alfred Lammle, Spohronia
6 Matilda
7 Franz Schubert
8 Fairfax, Elsie Maynard
9 Amy, Lord Robert Dudley
10 Fred (son of George II)

• 10 •   (1949, 2)

1 'Place-makers' misprinted for Peace-makers
2 Malachi
3 Psalms 120–134, Pilgrim Psalms sung on the way to Jerusalem
4 The Pentateuch, enlarged to include *Joshua*
5 Ezekiel
6 The Bride (or Gentile Church) in *The Song of Solomon or* the Rose of Sharon
7 *Philemon*
8 'Vinegar' misprinted for Vineyard
9 Pre-Reformation 'Poor Man's Bible' consisting of pictures
10 A document, drawn on the first three Evangelists

• 11 •   (1949, 4)

1 Charivaria
2 Général Février
3 Saxpence

4 'I used your soap two years ago, since then I have used no other.'
5 'Feed the Brute.'
6 The Kaiser – Bismarck (*Dropping the Pilot*)
7 Harry Furniss
8 The curate and the egg
9 King Albert and the Kaiser
10 Don't

• 12 • (1949, 5)

1 Mrs Raddle
2 Alice
3 William III
4 Scotch scarecrow
5 Mrs Nickleby's neighbour
6 Mrs Rice wrote *Mrs Wiggs of the Cabbage Patch*
7 The Prodigal Son – the swine
8 A 'big noise'
9 Sam Weller, pot-boy of the Blue Boar
10 Townshend – Minister of George I ( known as Turnip Townshend)

• 13 • (1949, 6)

1 South Sea Bubble
2 Mississippi Bubble
3 Mark Tapley at Eden City of Scadder's Swindle
4 Chatterton's spurious poems
5 Dr Dee (1527) *or* Snow White's mirror – pig's heart substituted for Snow White's
6 Ananias and Sapphira
7 Van Meegeren counterfeiting Vermeer's style
8 The Great Merdle Swindle (*Little Dorrit*)
9 Coining
10 Jacob's impersonation of Esau

• 14 • (1949, 9)

1 Throwing of stool by Jenny Geddes at Introduction of English Liturgy at St Giles, Edinburgh
2 Whitefield

3 Farm Street, Father Bernard Vaughan
4 Knox at Perth
5 Florence Dombey's wedding, Toots' face
6 Henry VIII on his second marriage
7 Thanksgiving after relief of Leiden
8 Queen Caroline (George IV's wife)
9 Elizabeth
10 Maud

• 15 • (1949, 10)

1 Mary, daughter of Charles I
2 *Princess of Kensington* (Edward German – produced at the Savoy Theatre)
3 Ex-Queen Wilhelmina
4 Joan (Fair Maid) of Kent
5 Princess de Lamballe
6 Tennyson's *Princess*
7 Princess Margaret Rose
8 Augusta Princess of Wales
9 Princess Clementina
10 Elizabeth

• 16 • (1949, 11)

1 The Pied Piper and the rats
2 £1,527 owed by Madame Mantalini
3 Joseph's
4 Charles I
5 The tin gee-gee
6 The closing of St James' Park (temp. George II)
7 Wood's Irish Half-pence (1725)
8 Henry VIII to Anne of Cleves
9 Elizabeth's fine for non-conformity
10 Micawber

• 17 • (1949, 14)

1 the poet Cowper
2 White gloves
3 Crockett, *The Raiders*
4 Dr Johnson
5 When the gentlemen go by
6 The De'il
7 Cranmer
8 Tony Weller, Mr Pickwick

9 Dirk Hatteraick (*Guy Mannering*)
10 Queen Caroline (wife of George II)

• 18 • (1949, 16)

1 Sir Lancelot (Tennyson)
2 Feste (*O Mistress Mine*)
3 Gipsies at the Castle gate (*Wraggle Taggle Gipsies*)
4 The maid who wandered down the mountain-side
5 The Nightingale
6 The Psalmist
7 the village blacksmith's daughter (Longfellow)
8 Chibiabos (Longfellow – *Hiawatha*)
9 Taillefer (Roland's song)
10 Prince Henry (Longfellow – *The Golden Legend*)

# 1950

• 1 •

1 Jethro's
2 Edward the Martyr's
3 Cornelia
4 Mrs Hominy (*Martin Chuzzlewit*)
5 Hamlet's
6 James I
7 Har Dyal's (Kipling)
8 Caspar's
9 Ruth's
10 The Kaiser, *or* other grandchildren of Queen Victoria

• 2 •

1 Richard III
2 King John
3 Alexander Borgia
4 Toby Crackit, Bill Sikes
5 Christopher Columbus
6 Guy Fawkes
7 Dr Watson, Holmes
8 Macbeth, *or* Malcolm
9 Jack Ketch, Tyburn Tree
10 Robinson Crusoe

• 3 •

1 Cesarewitch
2 Derby (1913 – Suffragette death)
3 Warrig-a-borrig aroma
4 Victory of Witch of the Air at Kempton Park (Edward VII)
5 Drouet
6 Prince William in the White Ship
7 Everybody
8 Doncaster
9 Helter-Skelter Plate (*The Old Curiosity Shop*)
10 To the swift

• 4 •

1 Provence *or* Troubadours
2 Dacotahs (Longfellow – *Hiawatha*)
3 Shropshire (Housman)
4 The Silent Land (Longfellow)
5 Arcady
6 Land of Nod (*Genesis*)
7 Connecticut (home of rigid Puritanical laws)
8 Heaven
9 Canaan *or* play by Somerset Maugham
10 Land of the Lotus-eaters (Tennyson)

• 5 •

1 one third
2 eight
3 twenty-three
4 two
5 twenty-four
6 thirty-two
7 nine
8 three
9 two
10 seventy-five

• 6 •

1 Henry VI
2 Elizabeth
3 Veneering (*Our Mutual Friend*)
4 Horatio Fizkin (*The Pickwick Papers*)

5 Wilkes
6 Mr MacManaway
7 Barchester
8 Old Sarum
9 Adullam
10 Zinoviev

• 7 •

1 Menelaus *or* Romeo
2 Winchelsea
3 Canning
4 Winkle (*The Pickwick Papers*)
5 Little John
6 Hamlet
7 M'Intyre (Scott – *The Antiquary*)
8 Sohrab
9 Mme Defarge (*A Tale of Two Cities*)
10 The White Knight *or* Gareth

• 8 •

1 Job
2 Richard I, *or* John
3 The Three Grey Sisters of the Gorgons
4 Simon Tappertit in the Gordon Riots
5 Dent du Midi in Switzerland
6 Elizabeth
7 Dog-tooth
8 The Winter Wind's
9 Harald Bluetooth, father of Sweyn Forkbeard
10 Mr Gamp (*Martin Chuzzlewit*)

• 9 •

1 Charles I
2 Bismarck
3 Talus – a production of Vulcan
4 Napoleon III
5 Napoleon I
6 a man of no substance or means
7 Antichrist *or* the Pope *or* Cromwell
8 Mr Weller Senior (*The Pickwick Papers*)
9 John Kyrle (philanthropist)
10 Character in *Tom Jones*

• 10 •

1 Mr Pickwick
2 Romeo
3 Queen Victoria
4 John the Baptist
5 Mary in *Up from Somerset*
6 Miss Gibbs
7 The Vicar of Wakefield's
8 The Sleeping Beauty's
9 Marina (*Pericles*)
10 Oliver Twist

• 11 •

1 Anne, Duc de Montmorenci became Constable of France
2 Queen Anne in Mrs Morley and Mrs Freeman correspondence
3 Sister Anne in *Bluebeard*
4 Anne Boleyn in Shakespeare's *Henry VIII*
5 Anne of Austria in *The Three Musketeers*
6 Greedy Nan
7 Anne Hathaway
8 Annie Laurie
9 St Anne
10 Princess Anne

• 12 •

1 Charles I's
2 Nanki Poo's (*The Mikado*)
3 Athaliah's (*II Kings* 11, 14)
4 Cheshire Cat's
5 Robespierre's
6 MacHeath's (*The Beggar's Opera*)
7 Thomas More's
8 Haman's (*Esther* 7, 9)
9 a peer's
10 Dennis (*Barnaby Rudge*)

• 13 •

1 Jehu
2 Eric
3 Cape St Vincent
4 to call on Baal
5 Sir John Moore
6 The Red Queen

7 Penelope
8 Wind of the Western Sea
9 Ariel
10 Maud

• 14 •

1 Conjunction of two heavenly bodies
2 Holst
3 Sisera (*Judges* 5, 20)
4 St Dominic
5 Star of Bethlehem (*Ornithogalum umbellatum*)
6 Stripes represent the original thirteen states, stars those admitted later to the Union
7 Star of Eve (*Tannhauser*)
8 Arc de Triomphe
9 Lottie Collins
10 Stella Maris *or* The Red Planet

• 15 •

1 Ceylon
2 Damascus
3 Kedar's tents
4 Macedon
5 Canaan
6 Bethlehem
7 Sinai
8 Tyburn's
9 Jordan
10 Tyre's

• 16 •

1 Holman Hunt
2 Edwin Arnold
3 Oxford
4 Paris
5 Rabbi Moses ben Maimon of Cordoba
6 the eyesight of Dick Helder (Kipling) *or* Maisie
7 5,876,068,880,000 miles
8 a claim made in connection with Ancient Lights
9 Goethe
10 Jo (*Bleak House*)

• 17 •

1 Goldsmith of Wolfe
2 Dibdin of Tom Bowling
3 Burns of Mary Morison
4 Scott of Bonny Dundee (Claverhouse)
5 Campbell of Prince Christian (VIII) of Denmark
6 Byron of Sennacherib
7 Macaulay of Horatio, Spurious Lartius and Herminius
8 Tennyson of the Prince consort
9 Ingoldsby (Barham) of Jem Crow
10 F E Weatherly of Douglas Gordon

• 18 •

1 Mr Profumo – Mr Morrison
2 Holy Year
3 Nina Boucicault
4 Queen Mary's Carpet
5 Strangers at Prayers in new House of Commons
6 Death of Gustavus V
7 Harry Lauder
8 King Leopold
9 Dewey's – offence taken by Vyshinsky
10 Priestley

# 1951

• 1 •

1 Napoleon III's seizure of power
2 Palmerston
3 Ernest (son of George III) of Hanover
4 *Bleak House* (Jarndyce)
5 Duke of Mantua (La donna e mobile – *Rigoletto*)
6 Shoreditch
7 St John's, Leatherhead
8 Foch
9 Da Costa
10 Longfellow (*The Golden Legend*)

• 2 •

1 The Franco-British, Edward VII
2 Buffalo, President McKinley
3 Eiffel Tower, Paris (1889)
4 Jarley's Waxworks
5 Paris (1867), La Grande Duchesse
6 Crystal Palace, Paxton, Duke of Devonshire's gardener
7 Queen of Sheba, Solomon's glory
8 Wembley
9 Motor Exhibition, Olympia
10 Ideal Home

• 3 •

1 Animal magnetism
2 Waterfall at Ullswater
3 Archimedian screws and bullocks
4 Royal Irish Constabulary
5 Gravity
6 of habit
7 a screw-back
8 Destiny
9 House of Correction
10 breakfast food

• 4 •

1 The Medway
2 Kentish Sir Byng
3 Wat Tyler, Joan of Kent
4 Edward, father of Queen Victoria
5 Ramsgate, Frith
6 Shakespeare's Cliff
7 Bertha
8 rapturous applause
9 London, Chatham and Dover Railway
10 Apples, cherries, hops and women

• 5 •

1 *The Listener*
2 *Punch*
3 *The Times*
4 *Daily Graphic*
5 *Daily Mail*
6 *Sunday Express*
7 *The Spectator*

8 *Sunday Times*
9 *Observer*
10 *Green Final*

• 6 •

1 Mausolus
2 Sir John Moore
3 Norwich
4 Eleanor of Aquitaine
5 Shah Jehan and Nour Mahal (Taj Mahal)
6 Napoleon
7 Dickens
8 The Capulets'
9 Abraham and Sarah
10 'Jacques' (*A Tale of Two Cities*)

• 7 •

1 Becket
2 The Rhymer
3 Fool in *King Lear*
4 Great Bell at Oxford
5 Peeping Tom
6 the piper's son
7 Saint Thomas
8 Gun in Boar War
9 Ingoldsby ('As I laye a-thynkiynge')

• 8 •

1 Tom Pinch (*Martin Chuzzlewit*)
2 The damp
3 Trilby
4 Mrs Perker (*The Pickwick Papers*)
5 The lute player
6 We hanged them up
7 Orpheus with his lute
8 Carmen
9 Yippy-i-addy-i-ay
10 Cecilia

• 9 •

1 Society figure in *The School for Scandal*
2 Itinerant preacher in *Old Mortality*
3 Doctor in *Barchester Towers*
4 Ranting Minister in *Dombey and Son*

5 Sailor in *Ruddigore*
6 Barrister in *The Pickwick Papers*
7 Character in *The Pilgrim's Progress*
8 Justice in *The Merry Wives of Windsor*
9 Butcher in card game 'Happy Families'
10 'Foolish gentleman' in *Measure for Measure*

• 10 •

1 Patrick O'Connor (Marie Manning for her execution, 1850)
2 Marat *or* Agamemnon
3 Lord Randall
4 Naboth
5 Tulkinghorn (*Bleak House*)
6 Sisera
7 D'Aubray
8 Young Jemmy Groves
9 Mme Defarge (*A Tale of Two Cities*)
10 Mary Hamilton's baby

• 11 •

1 Grand Old Man (Gladstone)
2 Very Important Person
3 Perpetual Vice-President Member of the Pickwick Club (Joseph Smiggers)
4 Displaced Person
5 Amelia Lehman (composer)
6 W G Grace
7 British Public *or* Baden Powell
8 Robert Louis Stevenson
9 Kitchener of Khartoum
10 Bach, Beethoven, Brahms

• 12 •

1 Mimi's (*La Bohème*)
2 Marguerite (*Faust*)
3 The Toreador (*Carmen*)
4 Pagliacci
5 The Factotum (*The Barber of Seville*)
6 Manrico *or* The Troubador (*Il Trovatore*)

7 A thread of smoke (*Madame Butterfly*)
8 Lohengrin and Elsa
9 Delilah (*Samson and Delilah*)
10 The rich attorney's daughter (*Trial by Jury*)

• 13 •

1 Saint Paul
2 Kempenfeld
3 William the Conqueror
4 Crippen
5 Martin Chuzzlewit
6 Drake
7 Kitchener
8 Princess Elizabeth
9 George V
10 Jack Bunsby (*Dombey and Son*)

• 14 •

1 the cow
2 Bo-peep's sheep
3 Mother Hubbard
4 Jack (and Jill)
5 Jack Sprat
6 four and twenty blackbirds
7 Miss Muffet
8 a frog who would a-wooing go
9 The Man in the Moon
10 Dick Whittington

• 15 •

1 loss of *Princess Alice*
2 murder of Austrian Crown Prince
3 explosion in chemical factory
4 railway disaster (1879)
5 massacre of British garrison
6 loss of *Birkenhead*
7 Paris underground railway disaster
8 loss of *Forfarshire* (Grace Darling)
9 death of King Albert of Belgium
10 murder of Lord Frederick Cavendish and Thomas Henry Burke

# 1952–1953

• 16 •

1 Children, Elisha (*II Kings* 2)
2 Macbeth, servant
3 Buckingham, Wolsey
4 Mrs Gamp, Mrs Prig (*Martin Chuzzlewit*)
5 St Paul, Elymas (*Acts* 13, 8)
6 Elizabeth, Bishop of Ely
7 Walpole, Pitt
8 Arthur, Bedivere (Tennyson)
9 Pooh Bah, Nanki Poo (*The Mikado*)
10 Bevan, Tories

• 17 •

1 Waterloo Ball, Byron
2 Macbeth's feast, Shakespeare
3 Christmas at Dingley Dell, Dickens (*The Pickwick Papers*)
4 Alice's banquet, Lewis Carroll
5 Feast at Branksome, Scott (*The Lay of the Last Minstrel*)
6 Banquet at Rheims, Ingoldsby (*Jackdaw*)
7 Alexander's feast, Dryden
8 Dance of the flowers, Tennyson (*Maud*)
9 Hiawatha's Wedding Feast, Longfellow
10 Manx Wedding, W H Gill

• 18 •

1 The census
2 The Scotch stone
3 The Abbey Theatre, Dublin
4 Voronoff
5 Boscobel and Worcester tercentenary
6 Elleano (crossed the Thames on a tightrope)
7 Princess Elizabeth and Indian chief
8 Queen Amélie of Portugal
9 Persia
10 The Lord Warden became prime Minister on 25 October

• 1 • (1952, 1)

1 Anne
2 Queen of Sheba
3 Kristina of Sweden
4 Mary Queen of Scots
5 Mary I (Bloody)
6 Cleopatra of Egypt
7 Margaret of Scotland (The Maid of Norway)
8 Victoria
9 Candace of Ethiopia
10 Elizabeth I

• 2 • (1952, 2)

1 Edward VII
2 Charles II
3 George III
4 George II
5 Henry VII
6 Napoleon III
7 Rehoboam (*I Kings* 12)
8 Anne
9 Victoria
10 Elizabeth I

• 3 • (1952, 3)

1 Alice
2 Drake
3 Archbishop Parker
4 Charles I to Laud
5 Saul
6 James I (Sir-loin)
7 'Old Lady' in Shakespeare's *Henry VIII*
8 Asquith
9 Macbeth
10 Princes and lords (Goldsmith – *The Deserted Village*)

• 4 • (1952, 4)

1 Sir Geoffrey Boleyn (of London)
2 Mayor of Hamelin

3 Mayor of Eatanswill (*The Pickwick Papers*)
4 Dorchester (Casterbridge)
5 Mayor of Leiden
6 Walworth (of London) to Richard II
7 Bow Bells to Dick Whittington
8 Lord Mayor = large Jemmy
9 Prime Minister of Frankish Kings
10 De la Bère (Lord Mayor of London, 1952)

**• 5 •**  (1952, 6)

1 Childe Roland (Browning)
2 Siloam
3 Camelot
4 Dr Manette (*A Tale of Two Cities*)
5 Babel
6 Pisa
7 Eiffel
8 The Parsees
9 Bruges belfry
10 Tomb (*The Yeomen of the Guard*)

**• 6 •**  (1952, 8)

1 Deborah in 'Song of Deborah' (*Judges*, 5)
2 Blondel 'O Richard, O mon Roi'
3 Bill Primrose (*Vicar of Wakefield*) – 'Elegy on the death of a mad dog'
4 Maud, a 'chivalrous battle song' (Tennyson)
5 Chibiabos, 'Onaway! Awake, beloved!' (Longfellow – *The Song of Hiawatha*)
6 Thurio (and musician), 'Who is Silvia' (*The Two Gentlemen of Verona*)
7 Miriam, 'Song of Miriam' (*Exodus*, 15)
8 Mad Hatter, 'Twinkle, twinkle, little bat'
9 The Gleeman, 'The Song of the Bow' (Conan Doyle – *The White Company*)
10 Canio, 'On with the Motley' (*Pagliacci*)

**• 7 •**  (1952, 12)

1 That of the Ancient Mariner
2 The *Mayflower*
3 the voyage of the *Hesperus* (Longfellow)
4 Drake's voyage around the world
5 Lycidas's return from Ireland
6 Humphrey Gilbert's return from Newfoundland
7 Anson's voyage
8 That of the White Ship
9 Saint Paul's journey to Rome
10 The Hunting of the Snark

**• 8 •**  (1952, 15)

1 Tom Bowling's (Dibdin)
2 Ruben Ranzo
3 King Charles
4 Jack Briton
5 John Peel
6 Danny Boy
7 Christopher Robin's
8 Charlie
9 Father O'Flynn
10 Old Father Thames

**• 9 •**  (1952, 17)

1 Shakespeare, Ophelia
2 Scott, Duncan (*The Lady of the Lake*)
3 Longfellow, Burial of the Minisink
4 Housman, 'My Love'
5 Gray, Edward III
6 F H Doyle, 'Eleven Men of England'
7 David, Saul and Jonathan
8 Southey, Elizabeth Woodville
9 Wolfe, Sir John Moore
10 Tennyson, Arthur

**• 10 •**  (1953, 1)

1 Prince Charles
2 The Prime Minister
3 The Moderator of the Church of Scotland
4 sweepers of the aisle
5 Sir W McKie conducted, Messrs Peasgood and Gabb played

6 Setting of Psalm 122 ('I was glad')
7 Curtana
8 St James's Street
9 Australia
10 Queen Salote of Tonga

• 11 • (1953, 3)

1 Boadicea
2 Cophetua's
3 Tony Weller (*The Pickwick Papers*)
4 Anna in the Temple
5 Lord Glenmire's (*Cranford*)
6 The Widowbird
7 Dean Arabin (Trollope)
8 Elijah (widow of Zarephath, *I Kings*, 17)
9 Owen Tudor
10 Queen Victoria – the Widow of Windsor

• 12 • (1953, 6)

1 Canute
2 William I, Pevensey
3 The Carpenter (*Alice in Wonderland*)
4 Take hands
5 Saint Paul (Melita/Malta, *Acts* 28)
6 Weymouth
7 Monmouth
8 India's Coral Strand
9 Beachy Head
10 Normandy *or* Gallipolli

• 13 • (1953, 7)

1 The Temple
2 Hesperides
3 Shalimar
4 Maud
5 Letchworth
6 The Hanging Gardens of Babylon
7 Kirk O'Field (Darnley)
8 Bishop of Ely, Elizabeth I's
9 The desert (Hichens)
10 Dan Cupid

• 14 • (1953, 10)

1 Mrs Nickleby
2 Alice's

3 Naaman's leprosy (*II Kings*, 5)
4 Lady Macbeth
5 Mr Woodhouse (*Emma*)
6 Eleanor (wife of Edward I)
7 The guillotine
8 Saint Paul (*I Timothy* 5, 23)
9 Effects of eating string (Henry King)
10 It keeps the doctor away

• 15 • (1953, 12)

1 The schooner *Ben-my-Chree*
2 *Arethusa*
3 *Royal George* (Cowper)
4 *Old Superb* (Newbolt)
5 *Don* and *Magdalena* (Kipling – *Just So Stories*, *The Beginning of the Armadilloes*)
6 The Lady of Shalott
7 *San Philip* (Tennyson, *The Revenge*)
8 *Golden Vanity*
9 *Pinafore*
10 Big Steamers (Kipling)

• 16 • (1953, 14)

1 Suez and Panama Canals – De Lesseps
2 Languedoc
3 North Sea
4 Caledonian
5 Grand Junction
6 Canaletto
7 Kiel
8 navvies
9 Dortmund-Ems
10 Miss Hook of Holland

• 17 • (1953, 16)

1 Alfred Jingle's (*The Pickwick Papers*)
2 Robinson Crusoe's
3 Sahib's (Kipling, *Gunga Din*)
4 Prospero's
5 Eva's (Harriet Beecher Stowe, *Uncle Tom's Cabin*)
6 Naaman's wife's
7 Bella Donna's
8 Mary Queen of Scots' (Rizzio)

9 Mary de Medici's
10 Lady Dedlock's (*Bleak House*)

• 18 • (1953, 17)

1 Cleopatra
2 Titania
3 Mary Queen of Scots
4 Katherine of Valois (wife of Henry V)
5 Lady Macbeth
6 Elizabeth Woodville (wife of Edward IV)
7 Katharine of Aragon
8 Gertrude, Queen of Denmark
9 Eleanor of Aquitaine (wife of Henry II)
10 Elizabeth I

# 1954–1955

• 1 • (1954, 1)

1 That through Georgia
2 The Entente Cordiale
3 Ottawa
4 Jubilee instituted by Pope Boniface in 1300
5 Queen Victoria's Diamond Jubilee
6 Mrs Pipchin's (*Dombey and Son*)
7 George V's Silver Jubilee
8 Edward III (Gray)
9 Opening of the Coliseum, 1904
10 The Israelites' 'jubilee' after their sabbatical year

• 2 • (1954, 3)

1 Otto of Roses
2 Lavender water and Eau de Cologne
3 O'er Ceylon's isle
4 The king in *Psalm* 45
5 The bergamot
6 A rosy wreath
7 Perfumes of Arabia
8 Woodbines

9 The moghra tree
10 Cheese

• 3 • (1954, 5)

1 The Owl and the Pussy-Cat, mince and quince
2 Bob Sawyer (*The Pickwick Papers*)
3 The March Hare
4 Jael
5 Sir Walter Scott
6 Mr Holbrook and Miss Matty (*Cranford*)
7 The inn, in *The Deserted Village* (Goldsmith)
8 Tantalus
9 By the rats at Hamelin
10 The Devil

• 4 • (1954, 7)

1 Sir Henry Wotton
2 Holbein
3 Chapuis (*Henry VIII*)
4 Metternich
5 Paulus Jaline (Poland)
6 Portuguese Minister to Edward VII
7 James I for Commons deputation
8 The Papal Envoy
9 Sir Neville Henderson's
10 Her play *The Mousetrap*

• 5 • (1954, 9)

1 Tybalt and Mercutio
2 Thor and Olaf
3 Winkle and Stammer
4 Castlereagh and Canning
5 Deschanel and Clemenceau
6 Macbeth and Siward
7 Duke of Wellington and Earl of Winchelsea
8 Ajax and Hector
9 David and Goliath
10 Don Quixote and windmill

• 6 • (1954, 11)

1 Cassandra's
2 Solomon Eagle

3 The Jabberwock
4 Delenda est Carthago
5 Alexander, St Paul's
6 The peasant's in *Excelsior* (Longfellow)
7 'Plum' Warner – cricketer
8 Jim
9 Meg Merrilies's (Scott, *Guy Mannering*)
10 Fatima (Bluebeard's wife)

• 7 •  (1954, 12)

1 Hiawatha
2 Jonathan
3 From Harold's eye
4 To earth – I know not where
5 The BBC *Archers* thousandth appearance
6 William Tell
7 Ship of the *'Arrow* incident'
8 In England (*Song of the Bow*)
9 Frederick Archer (jockey)
10 House of the Arrow (A E W Mason)

• 8 •  (1954, 15)

1 Viola's (*Twelfth Night*)
2 Falstaff's (*Henry V*)
3 The third dog summoned by the magic tinderbox (H C Andersen)
4 The soldier's (*As You Like It*)
5 Annie Laurie's
6 The winter's wind
7 Julia's
8 The Psalmist's ungodly men
9 The village blacksmith's (Longfellow)
10 William IV's (Pineapple)

• 9 •  (1954, 16)

1 Hatta's (*Through the Looking Glass*)
2 Newgate (Dennis in Gordon Riots)
3 The Conciergerie
4 The Tolbooth
5 Elizabeth I's
6 Anne Boleyn's/Henry VIII's

7 Reading Gaol
8 Philippi (Saint Paul)
9 Château d'If
10 Sing Sing

• 10 •  (1955, 3)

1 Fagin
2 Fatima
3 Little Ease
4 *Mayflower*
5 King James (II)
6 King Alfred
7 Quickly
8 Villa Borghese
9 Gamp
10 Horatius

• 11 •  (1955, 5)

1 Aristophanes' *Clouds*
2 Elijah's servant (*I Kings* 18)
3 Mackerel clouds
4 Cirrus
5 Polonius (*Hamlet*)
6 Jude, of false teachers
7 Zeus
8 'Till the boys come home'
9 'His chariots of wrath' (hymn)
10 Passing Clouds (cigarettes)

• 12 •  (1955, 7)

1 Hiawatha
2 Injun Joe
3 Pocohontas
4 Juarez
5 Tammany Hall
6 Aztecs
7 Pontiac (Gilbert Parker, *When Valmond came to Pontiac*)
8 The Apaches
9 Macaulay
10 Sam Weller (*The Pickwick Papers*)

• 13 •  (1955, 8)

1 Ludlow
2 Eastnor
3 Edinburgh
4 Shandon

5 Aberdovey
6 Dublin
7 Amsterdam
8 Ipswich
9 Manchester
10 London

• 14 •   (1955, 11)

1 *Tit-bits*
2 *Punch*
3 The 'Pink Un'
4 *Comic Cuts* or *Chips*
5 *Ally Sloper*
6 *Life*
7 *Marprelate Tracts*
8 *Figaro*
9 *Vie Parisienne*
10 *Answers*

• 15 •   (1955, 12)

1 'The Mouse-trap' (played in *Hamlet*)
2 Matilda's aunt
3 Mansfield Park
4 *The Mikado* (visit of Japanese Crown Prince in 1906)
5 *Chantecler* (Rostand)
6 *The Merry Wives of Windsor*
7 *Joan of Arc*
8 'Pyramus and Thisbe' in *A Midsummer Night's Dream*
9 *Hamlet* (in *Great Expectations*)
10 Subtitle of *The Critic*

• 16 •   (1955, 13)

1 George V's *Britannia*, sunk after his death
2 Royal Yacht Squadron
3 The barge with Arthur's body
4 The Kaiser
5 The Tsar
6 *Alberta*
7 Cleopatra's
8 'The King ... in Dunfermline' (*Sir Patrick Spens*)
9 *Hohenzollern*
10 *Victoria and Albert*

• 17 •   (1955, 14)

1 The Witch of Endor
2 Jill all alone
3 Harrison Ainsworth's *Lancashire Witches*
4 Vilja (*The Merry Widow*)
5 Madge Wildfire (*The Heart of Midlothian*)
6 Azucena (*Il Trovatore*)
7 The norns (Scandinavia)
8 The brocken (witches' Sabbath)
9 The witch in *Hansel and Gretel*
10 The witches in *Macbeth*

• 18 •   (1955, 16)

1 The reef of Norman's Woe (Longfellow)
2 Battle of the Nile
3 Melrose Abbey (Scott, *The Lay of the Last Minstrel*)
4 Mecheln (Browning)
5 Colchester
6 Frederick Town (Maryland)
7 Spithead
8 Stoke Poges (Gray, *Elegy Written in a Country Churchyard*)
9 Dürnstein (Austria)
10 Niagara Falls

# 1956–1958

• 1 •   (1956, 1)

1 No loss of Calais by Mary
2 No statue of Queen Anne
3 No Lady Jane Grey
4 No marriage of Ferdinand and Isabel resulting in Catherine of Aragon
5 No Armada speech by Elizabeth
6 No Mary II to share the throne with William III
7 Queen Victoria's non-amusement would not have been famous
8 No Mary Queen of Scots to provide target for Knox
9 No Queen Wilhelmina

10 No reason for the Queen of Sheba's visit

• 2 •   (1956, 3)

1 Arthur, son of Igerna
2 Alfred, son of Osburga
3 Perseus, son of Danae
4 Napoleon, son of Letizia
5 William I, son of Arlotta
6 Samuel, son of Hannah
7 Froggy, son of his mother
8 The Yeoman, son of the Motherland, Old England
9 Lord Randal, son of his mother
10 Liberace, son of Momma

• 3 •   (1956, 5)

1 Poker
2 Cribbage
3 Valet
4 Anne of Cleves
5 Solo
6 Nine of Diamonds
7 Bezique
8 Carmen
9 Mrs Wardle (*The Pickwick Papers*)
10 *The Queen of Spades*

• 4 •   (1956, 6)

1 *Kashmiri Song* (Laurence Hope, music by Amy Woodforde-Finden)
2 In the porphyry font
3 *I'll Sing Thee Songs of Araby*
4 *Glorious Devon* (Sir Harold Boulton, music by Edward German)
5 *So, we'll go no more a-roving*
6 Bredon (Housman)
7 On castle walls
8 On a lonely hill (Weatherly, *Jerusalem*)
9 A bicycle made for two
10 The note of a bird

• 5 •   (1956, 7)

1 *Catriona, Kidnapped* (Stevenson)
2 *Barchester Towers, The Warden* (Trollope)

3 *Good Wives, Little Women* (Louisa May Alcott)
4 *II Samuel, I Samuel*
5 *Master Humphrey's Clock, The Pickwick Papers* (Dickens)
6 Any pair of the 39 *William* stories (Richmal Crompton)
7 *Acts, St Luke*
8 Part 2 and Part 1 of *The Pilgrim's Progress* (Bunyan)
9 *The White Company, Sir Nigel* (Conan Doyle)
10 *Twenty Years After, The Three Musketeers* (Dumas)

• 6 •   (1956, 8)

1 St Joseph
2 Ship's carpenter
3 A mouse (small weight used in window structure)
4 The Walrus's partner
5 An old woman's tooth (species of plane)
6 A round-shouldered carpenter
7 Mr Hubble's (*Great Expectations*)
8 Quince (*A Midsummer Night's Dream*)
9 Captain Alfred Carpenter VC (HMS *Vindictive*, raid on Zeebrugge 1918)
10 Hero of *The Golden Vanity*

• 7 •   (1956, 9)

1 John Hasper (*Edwin Drood*)
2 Organ of the Lost Chord
3 The Calvinists
4 The Arsenal at Springfield
5 T E Brown
6 Foundling Hospital
7 Crystal Palace
8 Merbecke
9 Saint Cecilia
10 Mouth organ

• 8 •   (1956, 10)

1 Paul Morphy
2 Caxton

3 Opening game by sacrificing a pawn
4 Budapest Counter-gambit
5 Abraham's
6 'I adjust' (touching a piece without a penalty
7 Moscow
8 Hastings and Bognor Regis
9 Darnley
10 Lily, the White Queen's daughter (*Through the Looking-Glass*)

• 9 •   (1956, 12)

1 A pretty little flower (*Ruddigore*)
2 The arrow, all unbroke (Longfellow)
3 Heart of oak are our ships (David Garrick)
4 The ash and the bonny ivy tree
5 Colonel Careless
6 When it is sported
7 The Reformation Oak (Ket's Rebellion)
8 Herne the Hunter (Windsor)
9 Absolom (*II Samuel* 18)
10 Race named after the Earl of Derby's house at Epsom, where it was instituted

• 10 •   (1956, 13)

1 North-east
2 Euroclydon (*Acts* 27, 14)
3 The wind from the south (Woodforde-Finde, *The Garden of Kama*)
4 Roaring Forties
5 T E Brown
6 Equinox (Longfellow)
7 Mistral
8 Protestant East Wind (which enabled William III to sail)
9 Fremantle Doctor
10 Aeolus

• 11 •   (1956, 14)

1 Taunton
2 Dorchester

3 Ipswich (*The Pickwick Papers*)
4 Winchester
5 Oxford
6 Derby
7 Carlisle (Macaulay)
8 Bodmin (on the Camel)
9 Norwich
10 Salisbury (Sarum use or ritual)

• 12 •   (1956, 15)

1 Veil
2 Nightgown
3 Nightcap
4 Belt
5 Eighteenth-century cape
6 Silk cloak
7 Woman's loose gown
8 Tall head-dress
9 Long, loose coat
10 Doublet

• 13 •   (1957, 2)

1 Skegness
2 Brixham (William III) *or* Hastings (William I)
3 Brighton
4 Lyme Regis
5 Weymouth
6 Ramsgate
7 Bideford
8 Penzance
9 Southend
10 Bournemouth

• 14 •   (1957, 4)

1 Simon Alleyne
2 Dr Primrose
3 Rev. Charles Goldsmith
4 Rev. Patrick Brontë
5 Mr Quiverful
6 Mr Collins
7 Charles Kingsley
8 Wycliffe
9 George Robey
10 Sir Francis Bryan (temp. Henry VIII)

- 15 • (1957, 6)

  1 Tales by Hawthorne
  2 Wood used to build Noah's Ark
  3 Scene of fighting near Ypres in 1917
  4 Malayan wood used in building
  5 Robin Hood
  6 Giant evergreen
  7 Hero of The Bride of Lasmmermoor
  8 Jane Eyre's school
  9 Napoleon's residence on St Helena
  10 Piano makers

- 16 • (1958, 1)

  1 Prince Hal (tried on Henry IV's crown)
  2 The Black Prince, son of Edward III (at Crécy)
  3 Llewellyn, the Last
  4 George, Prince Regent
  5 Frederick, son of George II
  6 George (V), son of Edward VII
  7 James Stuart, the Old Pretender
  8 Edward (V), son of Edward IV
  9 Edward (VII), son of Victoria
  10 (Bonny Prince) Charlie, the Young Pretender (styled as such by Jacobites)

- 17 • (1958, 2)

  1 Anne Boleyn
  2 Luther
  3 Saint John
  4 Daudet
  5 Darcy (*Pride and Prejudice*)
  6 Cicero
  7 R L Stevenson
  8 Horace Walpole
  9 Saint Paul
  10 Sam Weller (*The Pickwick Papers*)

- 18 • (1958, 7)

  1 With the shepherd's star
  2 L'heure du berger (cocktail hour)
  3 Dick the Shepherd (*Love's Labour's Lost*)
  4 Shepherd's tartan (black and white)

  5 *The Shepheardes Calender* (Spenser)
  6 Bo-peep
  7 Silvius, Phebe (*As You Like It*)
  8 Marie Antoinette
  9 Joseph's brethren
  10 Jack Sheppard

# 1959–1960

- 1 • (1959, 1)

  1 Eatanswill (*The Pickwick Papers*)
  2 Dunwich
  3 The Reform Act
  4 Old Sarum (Pitt)
  5 Pocket Breaches (*Our Mutual Friend*)
  6 Mr Nearthewinde
  7 Those claiming votes, as having boiled their own pots for six months
  8 Gladstone
  9 Wilkes
  10 Frederick William of Brandenberg

- 2 • (1959, 2)

  1 Madagascar
  2 Omar Khayam's
  3 The Moonstone
  4 Sea of Fecundity
  5 Diana *or* Cynthia
  6 Jules Verne's *From the Earth to the Moon*
  7 The man in the moon
  8 'This man with lantern, dog and bush of thorns' (*A Midsummer Night's Dream*)
  9 El Dorado (Poe)
  10 Wiltshire peasants raking the moon's reflection out of a pond

- 3 • (1959, 3)

  1 St James's (Charles I)
  2 Prater, Vienna
  3 Phoenix Park, Dublin
  4 Hyde Park (between the Duke of Hamilton and Lord Mohun)

5 Hyde Park (the Serpentine)
6 Royal National Park, New South Wales
7 Finsbury Park
8 Mansfield Park (Jane Austen)
9 Bois de Boulogne, Paris
10 Mungo Park (explorer)

• 4 • (1959, 5)

1 11 am (Armistice, 1918)
2 3.10 am
3 At the mid hour of night (Thomas Moore)
4 One
5 Four and ten (Dean Henry Aldrich)
6 8.44 and 59 seconds pm
7 Midnight (*The Midnight Review*)
8 Seven (Browning, *Pippa Passes*)
9 Three (Shakespeare, *Julius Caesar*)
10 Any time

• 5 • (1959, 6)

1 Hypocausts (Roman heating chambers)
2 'Deep calleth deep at the noise of the waterspouts' (Psalm 42)
3 A pull-through
4 Sir John Harrington (wrote a treatise on plumbing)
5 Cone for enlarging a lead pipe
6 His hand
7 Bauxite
8 With geysers
9 As a block to smooth away solder from a joint
10 His tools

• 6 • (1959, 7)

1 From *tourner* – quick turning of a horse
2 Eglinton Tournament (revived in 1839)
3 Anne Boleyn
4 Ivanhoe
5 Spenser (*The Fairie Queene*)
6 Surrey

7 Tournament where Henri II of France was killed, Paris
8 Tannhäuser's Tournament of Song
9 Field of the Cloth of Gold
10 Red and White Knights fighting for Alice

• 7 • (1959, 8)

1 From the elbow to the tip of the middle finger
2 The Ark
3 Little Ease
4 St Paul's
5 Eiffel Tower
6 Cornhill
7 Goliath's
8 An ell
9 One pound (*The Merchant of Venice*)
10 7 feet of English soil

• 8 • (1959, 9)

1 September Massacre (French Revolution)
2 Bethlehem (the Innocents)
3 Cawnpore (the Indian Mutiny)
4 St Bartholomew
5 Peterloo (Manchester, 1819)
6 Glencoe
7 Piedmont, 1655
8 Sicilian Vespers
9 Wexford *or* Drogheda
10 Withdrawal of bills not discussed in the session

• 9 • (1959, 10)

1 Saint Catherine of Siena
2 Catherine de Medici
3 Catherine Douglas
4 Catherine de Valois (Pepys kissed her mummy in Westminster Abbey)
5 Catherine Morland (*Northanger Abbey*)
6 Catherine Howard (Henry VIII became King of Ireland the week before her execution)

7 Katherine in *The Taming of the Shrew*
8 Catherine I of Russia – Peter the Great's second wife
9 Catherine of Braganza (negotiated Methuen Treaty with Portugal)
10 Saint Catherine of Alexandria (Festival 25 November)

• 10 • (1959, 11)

1 Key West (United State Naval Station)
2 Ciudad Rodrigo (Wellington's 'Key of Spain')
3 Simon Tappertit (*Barnaby Rudge*)
4 H (German of key of B)
5 *Kelly's Key* (crib to Classics)
6 Alice
7 Fatima's Key (*Bluebeard*)
8 The Keys of Heaven
9 Job Trotter (*The Pickwick Papers*)
10 Queen Elizabeth's Keys (Tower of London ceremony)

• 11 • (1959, 12)

1 Knights Hospitallers
2 Florence Nightingale
3 Betsy Prig
4 Alva
5 Nurse Cavell
6 Judith Malmayns (Ainsworth, *Old Saint Paul's*)
7 The nurse in *Romeo and Juliet*
8 Christopher Robin
9 Elizabeth Fry
10 Rose, a nurse of ninety years

• 12 • (1960, 1)

1 No tercentenary stamp
2 Gresham College
3 Wren
4 Flamsteed
5 Newton
6 Banks (Botany Bay)
7 Captain Cook
8 William Herschel
9 Jenner
10 Lord Kelvin (William Thomson)

• 13 • (1960, 6)

1 J H Newman
2 Isaac Watts
3 Charles Wesley
4 John Milton
5 Rudyard Kipling
6 J M Neale
7 William Cowper
8 G K Chesterton
9 J Ellerton
10 John Bunyan

• 14 • (1960, 8)

1 Big Ben
2 Benjamin, son of Jacob
3 Ben Lomond
4 Ben Battle (Hood)
5 Benjamin Disraeli
6 Benelux
7 Benbecula
8 Benjamin West (painting)
9 Ben Arthur
10 Rt Rev Benjamin Pollard (former Bishop of Sodor and Man)

• 15 • (1960, 10)

1 Jacob (*Genesis* 29)
2 Paul (planted) and Apollos (watered) (*I Corinthians* 3)
3 Laodiceans (*Revelation* 3)
4 Mordecai (*Esther* 6)
5 Eliab, David's (*I Samuel* 17)
6 Joash/Jehoash (*II Kings* 11)
7 Belshazzar's (*Daniel* 5)
8 The Galatians (*Galatians* 3)
9 The Cretians (*Titus* 3)
10 Lois's (*II Timothy* 1)

• 16 • (1960, 11)

1 Thrush, Browning in *Home Thoughts from Abroad*
2 Pelican in Psalm 102, 9
3 Cuckoo, Logan in *To the Cuckoo*
4 Nightingale, Keats
5 Cormorant, Shakespeare in *Richard II*, 2

6 Swallows and curlews, Browning in
   *A Grammarian's Funeral*
7 Robin, Scott in *Proud Maisie*
8 Skylark, Shelley
9 The Sparrow killed Cock Robin
   with his bow and arrow, nursery
   rhyme
10 Hamlet, Hawk

• 17 • (1960, 12)

1 Lind
2 Dawson
3 Morgan
4 Newton
5 Hippocrates
6 Darwin
7 Pasteur
8 Lavoisier
9 Appleton
10 Archimedes

• 18 • (1960, 14)

1 The dormouse in *When We Were Very
   Young*
2 The Tailor of Gloucester's
3 Peridarchus (Walter de la Mare)
4 The Crooked Man's (nursery rhyme)
5 Dormouse at the Mad Hatter's tea
   party
6 Decius Mus (Sentium 295 BC)
7 Edward Lear's (*Calico Pie*)
8 Robert Burns's (turned up with a
   plough)
9 A muscle (Latin musculus = little
   mouse)
10 *The Mousetrap* (Agatha Christie) at
   the Ambassadors Theatre

# 1961–1962

• 1 • (1961, 1)

1 Lead us not into temptation (*St Luke*
   11, 4)
2 Now we see through a glass darkly
   (*I Corinthians* 13, 12)

3 Be not wise in your own conceits
   (*Romans* 12, 16)
4 Whom ye slew and hanged on a tree
   (*Acts* 5, 30)
5 Let us not rend it but cast lots for it
   (*St John* 19, 24)
6 Sufficient unto the day is the evil
   thereof (*St Matthew* 6, 34)
7 Having on the breastplate of
   righteousness (*Ephesians* 6, 14)
8 God dwelleth not in temples made
   with hands (*Acts* 17, 24)
9 He hath scattered the proud in the
   imagination of their hearts (*St Luke*
   1, 51)
10 The labourer is worthy of his hire (*St
   Luke* 10, 71)

• 2 • (1961, 3)

1 Cronos (Saturn)
2 Heracles (Hercules)
3 Deucalion
4 Odysseus, Tiresius
5 Prometheus
6 Persephone
7 Midas
8 Epeius
9 Polyneices (*The Seven Against Thebes*)
10 Perseus's (Andromeda)

• 3 • (1961, 5)

1 Oliver Twist
2 Mr Jingle, 570 (*The Pickwick Papers*)
3 David Copperfield
4 Barnaby Rudge
5 Prince Bladud (*The Pickwick Papers*)
6 Little Dorrit
7 Mr Micawber (*David Copperfield*)
8 Wemmick (*Great Expectations*)
9 Jarndyce and Jarndyce (*Bleak House*)
10 Smike's (*Nicholas Nickleby*)

• 4 • (1961, 7)

1 Jack Point (*The Yeomen of the Guard*)
2 Sir Joseph Porter (*HMS Pinafore*)
3 Pooh-Bah (*The Mikado*)
4 Duke of Plaza-Toro (*The Gondoliers*)

5 Rose Maybud (*Ruddigore*)
6 Grosvenor (*Patience*)
7 Princess Ida
8 Private Willis (*Iolanthe*)
9 Major General Stanley (*The Pirates of Penzance*)
10 John Wellington Wells (*The Sorcerer*)

• 5 •   (1961, 8)

1 Robert Graves
2 C Day Lewis
3 Admiral Cunningham
4 Dylan Thomas
5 Peter Scott
6 Howard Spring
7 Sir Thomas Beecham
8 Duff Cooper
9 John Buchan
10 Walter de la Mare

• 6 •   (1961, 11)

1 Cerberus
2 Buggane
3 Roc
4 Sphinx
5 Banshee
6 Chimaera
7 Bandersnatch
8 Centaur
9 Behemoth
10 Manticore

• 7 •   (1961, 12)

1 R L Stevenson
2 Peter Fleming
3 Satan (*Job* 1)
4 George Borrow
5 The Old Superb
6 Wiley Post
7 Puck
8 Celia Fiennes
9 Lelant
10 William Cobbett

• 8 •   (1961, 15)

1 Saint Paul, love of money
2 Cassius (*Julius Caesar*)

3 Father William (Lewis Carroll)
4 Shylock (*The Merchant of Venice*)
5 Mothers of large families (Hilaire Belloc)
6 The Banker in *The Hunting of the Snark* (Lewis Carrroll)
7 Pieman to Simple Simon
8 Mistress Gilpin (Cowper)
9 Dr Johnson
10 The Guard in *Through the Looking Glass* (Lewis Carroll)

• 9 •   (1961, 18)

1 Runcorn – Widnes
2 Duke of Kent
3 Eden (Earl of Avon)
4 Yuri Gagarin and Gherman Titov
5 Duke of Wellington (Goya's portrait)
6 Lord Russell (sit-down strike)
7 Wall in East Berlin
8 Annigoni's portrait of the Queen on Manx notes
9 Lord Snowdon
10 Cocky (Sir Ronald Garvey's parrot) depicted on 4s. Fiji stamp

• 10 •   (1962, 1)

1 *The Book of Common Prayer* was introduced
2 The Royal Navy
3 The Sunday next before Advent
4 A bishop when consecrated
5 a deacon when ordained
6 The Litany
7 The Athanasian Creed
8 Rogation Days
9 The Commination
10 To collect alms for the poor at the Communion service

• 11 •   (1962, 6)

1 Nottinghamshire
2 Cornwall
3 Suffolk
4 Shropshire
5 Dorset

6 Essex
7 Somerset
8 Durham
9 Cornwal
10 Dorset

• 12 • (1962, 8)

1 The Pied Piper's (Browning)
2 Laertes' (*Hamlet*)
3 Colonel Calverley's (*Patience*)
4 Gunga Din's (Kipling)
5 John Gilpin's (Cowper)
6 Malvolio's (*Twelfth Night*)
7 Nanki Poo's (*The Mikado*)
8 Solomon's
9 The Wife of Bath's (Chaucer)
10 Pepys's

• 13 • (1962, 9)

1 Bleriot (aeroplane) *or* Blanchard and Jefferies (balloon)
2 Lord Brabazon
3 Montgolfier brothers
4 Rolls
5 Santos Dumont
6 Kingsford-Smith
7 Stringfellow
8 Wright brothers
9 Kohl and Fitzmaurice
10 Daedalus

• 14 • (1962, 10)

1 Newton's
2 Cicero's
3 Pliny the Elder's
4 Aristotle
5 Francis Bacon
6 Copernicus
7 Huygens
8 Boyle
9 Harvey's
10 Darwin's

• 15 • (1962, 11)

1 Polonius to the Queen, about Hamlet
2 Festus to Paul (*Acts* 26)

3 Dr Johnson
4 Cheshire Cat to Alice
5 Goldsmith, *Elegy on the Death of a Mad Dog*
6 They go out in the mid-day sun
7 Sir Despard Murgatroyd in *Ruddigore*
8 The Bastard in *King John*
9 Kent, Lear (*King Lear*)
10 David among the Philistines

• 16 • (1962, 14)

1 Oak
2 Olive
3 Teak
4 Almug (*I Kings* 10, 12)
5 Elm (Kipling)
6 Cherry (Housman)
7 Juniper (Elijah, in *I Kings* 19)
8 Glastonbury Thorn
9 Yew
10 Birch

• 17 • (1962, 15)

1 Joseph Chamberlain
2 Gandhi
3 Bevin
4 Lloyd-George
5 Macmillan
6 Bevan
7 Neville Chamberlain
8 Goebbels
9 Bethman-Holweg
10 William the Silent

• 18 • (1962, 17)

1 Herrick, daffodils
2 T E Brown, rose
3 Fitzgerald, hyacinth
4 Shelley, violets
5 Elizabeth Browning, lilacs
6 Kipling, begonias
7 Wordsworth, daisy
8 Shakespeare, primrose
9 George Wither, pansy
10 Robert Browning, buttercups

# 1963–1964

## • 1 • (1963, 1)

1 Prometheus
2 Zoroaster
3 Rome, Nero's
4 Moscow, Napoleon's
5 Pepys, London
6 Elijah's
7 Greek fire
8 Beacon on Skiddaw (Macaulay, *The Armada*)
9 air raid on London (10 May 1941)
10 King William's College (while John Ready was Governor of the Isle of Man)

## • 2 • (1963, 2)

1 Malchus (*St John* 23, 10)
2 Samson (*Judges* 16)
3 Ehud's (*Judges* 3, 21)
4 Rehoboam's (*I Kings* 12, 10)
5 Eli's (*I Samuel* 4, 18)
6 Elisha's (*II Kings* 2, 3, 5)
7 a bear and/or lion – killed by David (*I Samuel* 17, 35)
8 Adoni-bezek (*Judges* 1, 6)
9 St James (*James* 3, 8)
10 The Sluggard (*Proverbs* 10, 26)

## • 3 • (1963, 3)

1 Alexander the Great
2 John
3 Louis XIV (Madame de Maintenant)
4 George I (Peter the wild boy)
5 Olaf
6 Anne
7 Nicholas II of Russia
8 Christian IX of Denmark
9 Stephen
10 William IV (to King William's College)

## • 4 • (1963, 6)

1 farthingale
2 doublet
3 baldric
4 tabard
5 chasuble
6 hauberk
7 amico
8 chlamys
9 paludamentum
10 siren suit

## • 5 • (1963, 7)

1 Cork
2 Dingle
3 Londonderry
4 Wexford
5 Ballybunion
6 Cashel
7 Athlone
8 Tara
9 Larne
10 Dublin

## • 6 • (1963, 9)

1 *Song of Quoodle* (Chesterton)
2 *Vicar of Bray*
3 *Cavalier Song* (Browning)
4 *Song of the Shirt* (Hood)
5 *Here's a Health unto His Majesty*
6 *Battle Hymn of the Republic* (Howe)
7 *Song of Honour* (Ralph Hodgson)
8 *Song of the Ungirt Runners* (Sorley)
9 Song of Deborah
10 Song of Solomon

## • 7 • (1963, 11)

1 Medina (622)
2 Gibraltar (711)
3 Tours (732 – defeat by Charles the Hammer)
4 Hattin (1187)
5 Granada (1492)
6 Mohacs (1526)
7 Vienna (1683)
8 Lepanto (1571)

9 Riyadh (1902)

10 Gallipoli (1915)

• 8 • (1963, 13)

1 Crocodile (Lewis Carroll)

2 Donkey (Chesterton)

3 Elephant's child (Kipling)

4 Reynard the Fox (Masefield)

5 Pigs (Orwell, *Animal Farm*)

6 Beaver (Carroll, *The Hunting of the Snark*)

7 Llama (Belloc)

8 Rhinoceros (Kipling)

9 Donkey – Eeyore ( A A Milne)

10 Rats (Browning, *The Pied Piper of Hamelin*)

• 9 • (1963, 14)

1 Village schoolmaster's (Goldsmith)

2 Cawdor's (*Macbeth*)

3 Socrates' (*Apology*)

4 Prince Albert's (Tennyson)

5 Julius Caesar's (Shakespeare)

6 Charles I's (Marvell)

7 Wellington's (Tennyson)

8 Saul's and Jonathan's (*II Samuel* 1)

9 Keats's (Shelley)

10 Spartans at Thermopylae

• 10 • (1964, 3)

1 Seven Wonders of the Ancient World

2 Seven Saxon kingdoms/Saxon Heptarchy

3 Seven Deadly Sins

4 Seven Churches in Asia

5 Seven Sages of Greece

6 Seven Ages of Man (*As You Like It*)

7 The Seven Dwarfs

8 Seven Deacons (*Acts*)

9 Seven Kings of Rome

10 Seven stars of the Plough (Latin *septentriones*)

• 11 • (1964, 4)

1 Samivel

2 Cinna (*Julius Caesar*)

3 The Owl and the Pussycat

4 Strephon (*Iolanthe*)

5 Portia (of the County Palatine and the Neapolitan Prince, *The Merchant of Venice*)

6 Socrates

7 Venice

8 Oedipus

9 Brigham Young (Artemus Ward)

10 Henry VIII (Shakespeare)

• 12 • (1964, 6)

1 The Vagabond (Stevenson)

2 The Snark (Lewis Carroll)

3 The Lord Chancellor (W S Gilbert)

4 Sir Harry Lauder

5 Jackdaw of Rheims

6 Titania

7 Mary Queen (*The Rime of the Ancient Mariner*)

8 Queen Mab (*Romeo and Juliet*)

9 Seven Sleepers of Ephesus

10 Macbeth

• 13 • (1964, 7)

1 successor to Cunarder *Queen Mary*

2 Philippa (wife of Edward III)

3 Caroline (wife of George IV)

4 Elizabeth of Bohemia

5 Elizabeth I (at the Tower)

6 Anne

7 Mary Queen of Scots (according to the King of France)

8 Victoria (Tennyson on the death of The Prince Consort)

9 Margaret (wife of Henry VI)

10 Juliana of the Netherlands

• 14 • (1964, 8)

1 Cambridgeshire

2 Cornwall

3 Somerset

4 Sussex

5 Lincolnshire

6 Surrey

7 Worcestershire

8 Hampshire

9 Kent
10 Staffordshire (Thomas Fuller, *The Worthies of England*, 1672)

• 15 • (1964, 11)

1 Rev. Gilbert White
2 Chatterton
3 Hipparchus
4 Don John of Austria
5 Beau Nash
6 Hobson
7 Pepys
8 Peter the Great
9 I K Brunel
10 Richard Whiting

• 16 • (1964, 12)

1 Farmers
2 Prince of Wales
3 The owl (Keats)
4 white feather
5 an oarsman's
6 little men (William Allingham)
7 The Feathers Inn, Ludlow
8 Job (39, 13)
9 The earliest Cockney who came my way (Kipling – *The River's Tale*)
10 De la Mare, goldfinch

• 17 • (1964, 14)

1 Kirriemuir
2 Jezebel
3 St Paul (*II Corinthians* 11)
4 Eutychus
5 Birdie with a yellow bill (Stevenson)
6 Milton (*Il Penseroso*)
7 Plenty of food in Samaria
8 The Flood
9 Juliet
10 Gloucestershire

• 18 • (1964, 17)

1 Hodgson – singing birds
2 De la Mare – sea birds
3 Hodgson – tigers

4 Kipling – she-bear
5 Browning – horse
6 Barham – sucking pig
7 Fitzgerald – wild ass
8 Marvell – fawn
9 De la Mare – peacocks, tigers
10 Macgillivray – thrush

# 1965–1966

• 1 • (1965, 2)

1 Plague of Athens
2 Black Death
3 Moses and Aaron
4 Lice (the ten plagues of Egypt)
5 Mercutio (*Romeo and Juliet*)
6 Sir Toby Belch (*Twelfth Night*)
7 Calais
8 Great Plague of London, 1665
9 Camus (*La Peste*)
10 Oberammergau passion play

• 2 • (1965, 4)

1 Sir Francis Drake
2 Elizabeth I
3 Cromwell
4 Walpole
5 Pitt the Younger
6 Marshal Masséna
7 Czar Nicholas I
8 Abraham Lincoln
9 Lord Grey
10 Sir Winston Churchill

• 3 • (1965, 6)

1 *Vanity Fair*
2 *The Power and the Glory*
3 *For Whom the Bell Tolls*
4 *Fair Stood the Wind for France*
5 *The Longest Journey*
6 *Brave New World*
7 *Look Homeward, Angel*
8 *Far from the Madding Crowd*
9 *Cakes and Ale*
10 *The Grapes of Wrath*

• 4 •   (1965, 9)

1 Jan Brueghel
2 Peter Brueghel
3 Botticelli
4 Caravaggio
5 El Greco
6 Claude
7 Le Douanier Rousseau
8 Samuel Scott
9 Whistler
10 Oskar Kokoschka

• 5 •   (1965, 11)

1 Thermopylae
2 Caudine Forks
3 Glencoe
4 Brenner
5 Killiecrankie
6 St Gotthard
7 Khyber
8 Truckee
9 Crowsnest
10 Kirkstone

• 6 •   (1965, 12)

1 Phaedra
2 Jael
3 Clodia (Lesbia)
4 Cleopatra
5 Isabella
6 Carmen
7 Kitty O'Shea
8 Manon Lescaut
9 Irene (Galsworthy)
10 Zuleika Dobson

• 7 •   (1965, 13)

1 Hero of Alexandria
2 Hero on packet of Player's cigarettes
3 Leander's
4 Thackeray (*Vanity Fair*)
5 Alexander (*Thaïs*)
6 Raina (Shaw, *Arms and the Man*)
7 Lermontov (*A Hero of Our Time*)
8 Stephen Hero (James Joyce)
9 Judas Maccabaeus
10 Toad of Toad Hall

• 8 •   (1965, 14)

1 Old Tolbooth (Scott)
2 Newgate
3 Millbank
4 Chillon (Byron)
5 Bedford (Bunyan, *The Pilgrim's Progress*)
6 Fleet (Fleet marriages)
7 Black Hole of Calcutta
8 Gatehouse of Westminster (Lovelace, *To Althea*)
9 Marshalsea (*Little Dorrit*)
10 Regina Coeli (Rome)

• 9 •   (1965, 15)

1 Archimedes
2 Zeno
3 Pythagoras
4 Descartes (*cogito, ergo sum*)
5 Galileo
6 Fermat
7 Newton
8 Cardano
9 G H Hardy (*A Mathematician's Apology*)
10 C L Dodgson (Lewis Carroll)

• 10 •   (1966, 3)

1 John Duns Scotus
2 Karl F Gauss
3 Nicholas Chauvin
4 Mausolus
5 Justus von Liebig
6 Tantalus
7 Cardinal Morton
8 William Occam/Ockham
9 Hobson
10 George Boole

• 11 •   (1966, 4)

1 Aristophanes
2 Petronius
3 Horace
4 Aeschylus
5 Vergil
6 Aristotle
7 Juvenal

8 Catullus
9 Ovid
10 Plato

• 12 • (1966, 6)

1 Ben Battle (Thomas Hood, *Faithless Nelly Gray*)
2 The Unknown Citizen JS/07/M/378 (W H Auden)
3 Major-General Stanley (W S Gilbert, *The Pirates of Penzance*)
4 Mark Antony (Shakespeare, *Antony and Cleopatra*)
5 Uncle Toby (Laurence Sterne, *Tristram Shandy*)
6 Captain George Osborne (Thackeray, *Vanity Fair*)
7 Duke of Plaza-Toro (W S Gilbert, *The Gondoliers*)
8 Danny Deever (Rudyard Kipling)
9 Moloch (J Milton, *Paradise Lost* book ii)
10 Denys (C Reade, *The Cloister and the Hearth*)

• 13 • (1966, 11)

1 Alph, the sacred river (Coleridge, *Kubla Khan*)
2 Weser (Browning, *The Pied Piper of Hamelin*)
3 Thames (Spenser, *Epithalamium*)
4 Esk (Scott, *Young Lochinvar*)
5 Tamar (Hawker, *And Shall Trelawney Die?*)
6 Limpopo (Kipling)
7 Yser (Longfellow, *Hohenlinden*)
8 Thames (Wordsworth, *On Westminster Bridge*)
9 Mississippi (negro song)
10 Jordan (negro song)

• 14 • (1966, 12)

1 Sir Thomas More (1535)
2 Judge Jeffreys (Lord Chamberlain, 1689)
3 Spencer Perceval (Prime Minister, 1812)
4 Henry Dundas, Viscount Melville (1806); Thomas Parker, Earl of Macclesfield (1725)
5 Sir Francis Bacon (1626)
6 Abraham Lincoln
7 Henry Brougham (afterwards Lord Chamberlain)
8 Lord Robert Cecil KC, afterwards Viscount Cecil (for Peace)
9 John Singleton Copley, Lord Lyndhurst. (His father, J S C, RA, married the daughter of Richard Clarke, a Boston merchant and consignee of the tea)
10 Judah P Benjamin (Attorney General for Confederate President, Jefferson Davis)

• 15 • (1966, 13)

1 Purcell
2 Cooper
3 Maurice Green
4 Thomas Arne (*Rule Britannia*)
5 Elgar (Powick)
6 Charles Steggall
7 Vaughan Williams
8 Holst (*Savitri*)
9 Delius
10 John Blow

• 16 • (1966, 14)

1 Archer (toxophilite)
2 Sir Nigel Loring or Sir John Hawkswood
3 Gunga Din
4 William, son of Henry I
5 D H Lawrence
6 Richard III's horse
7 Samson Carrasco (*Don Quixote*)
8 Cistercians
9 fictitious bidder at an auction
10 dry-cleaners

• 17 • (1966, 15)

1 1937
2 the weight of a silver penny (24 grains of Troy)

3 Isle of Man, 1839
4 minted at King's Norton
5 1860
6 Puffin Island halfpenny, 1929
7 Scottish coin of base silver of 3 or 5 pence; English halfpenny
8 a hack writer, at so much a line
9 miller's dog or dogfish
10 a low class theatre (slang)

• 18 • (1966, 17)

1 T S Eliot (*East Coker*)
2 Marlowe (*Dr Faustus*)
3 Hilaire Belloc (*Jim*)
4 John Milton (*Samson Agonistes*)
5 Gerard Manley Hopkins (*Thou art indeed just, Lord*)
6 John Donne (*Holy Sonnet* xiv)
7 William Empson (*Legal Fiction*)
8 William Empson (*Just a smack at Auden*)
9 Samuel Johnson
10 Winston Churchill (Mansion House speech, 10 November 1942)

# 1967–1968

• 1 • (1967, 2)

1 Saint Joseph of Arimathea
2 Saint George (at Lydda, near Lod, or Tel Aviv Airport)
3 Saint Fiacre (emblem a spade, cabs first stood near Hotel Fiacre)
4 Saint Francis of Assisi
5 Saint Jerome (church of the Holy Nativity, Bethlehem)
6 Saint Joan of Arc
7 Saint Dunstan (Edgar, 973)
8 Saint Ethelbert (Saint Augustine)
9 Saint Thomas (Didymus)
10 Saint Anthony

• 2 • (1967, 3)

1 Rahere
2 Captain Thomas Coram
3 Benjamin Jesty
4 Thomas Sydenham
5 John Snow
6 John Graunt
7 Paul Berger
8 Paul Langerhans
9 R T H Laennec
10 Thomas Linacre

• 3 • (1967, 7)

1 Knight heads
2 Flemish horse
3 Fancy lines
4 Stealers
5 Cross-trees; cross-sett
6 Sister block
7 Shot, Quarterdeck garlands
8 Truck
9 Guest rope
10 Gammoning, front, side fish

• 4 • (1967, 8)

1 Little Nell (*The Old Curiosity Shop*)
2 Nelly Bly
3 Nelly Moser
4 Nelly Melba
5 Nelly Quickly
6 Nelly Dean (*Wuthering Heights*)
7 Nell Gwyn
8 Nelly Wallace
9 Nelly Lutcher
10 Nelly Bly

• 5 • (1967, 9)

1 Leda
2 Ceres
3 Alemena
4 Juno
5 Danae
6 Latona (Leto)
7 Europa
8 Metis
9 Aegina
10 Callisto

• 6 •   (1967, 10)

1  Helium
2  Argon
3  Krypton
4  Zenon
5  Neon
6  Oxygen
7  Fluorine
8  Hydrogen
9  Chlorine
10  Butane

• 7 •   (1967, 11)

1  E Peate (Oval Test, 1882)
2  Tom Emmett
3  David Denton
4  C B Fry
5  Hedley Verity (1932)
6  A N Hornby
7  A E Fagg (200+ in each innings, 1932)
8  Sir H D G Leveson-Gower
9  R Appleyard (200 wickets in his first season)
10  F T and F G Mann

• 8 •   (1967, 13)

1  Snaefell (2034 feet)
2  Paricutin (Mexico)
3  Scafell Pike (3210 feet)
4  Mauna Kea (Hawaii, 13,796 feet; 33,500 feet from Oceanic base)
5  Olos del Salado (claimed by Chile in 1956 to be 23,293 feet)
6  Barrule (Isle of Man)
7  Ben Venue (Loch Katrine)
8  Black Combe (Cumberland)
9  Sugar Loaf Mountain
10  Mount Rainier (USA)

• 9 •   (1967, 15)

1  Rabelais
2  Corneille
3  Molière
4  Racine
5  Voltaire
6  Balzac
7  Flaubert
8  Victor Hugo
9  Maupassant
10  Camus

• 10 •   (1968, 2)

1  The Derby
2  Eclipse
3  240 yards
4  Fred Archer
5  1889 (Wolverhampton)
6  1 January
7  Harry Wragg
8  Goodwood
9  Gladiateur
10  The Tetrarch

• 11 •   (1968, 3)

1  Pierre Birrabeau
2  Papal tax
3  Peter the Painter
4  The Nurse in *Romeo and Juliet*
5  Peter Pienaar
6  Sherlock Holmes
7  Pedro the Fisherman
8  Tom Sawyer's cat
9  Peter of Pomfret
10  Peter the Great

• 12 •   (1968, 6)

1  Lord Peter Wimsey's
2  Lady Churchill's
3  Jorrocks's
4  Mrs Vardon's
5  the cuckoo's
6  Albert Campion's
7  Queen Victoria's
8  Artemis
9  Richard Coeur de Lion's
10  Don Quixote's

• 13 •   (1968, 7)

1  Nicolai Gogol's
2  Georges Bernanos's
3  *The Times* Diary
4  The Goncourt Brothers; George and Weedon Grossmith

5  John Wesley's
6  Oscar Wilde's
7  Edward VI's
8  Pepys's
9  Anne Frank's
10  Mrs Dale's

• 14 •  (1968, 8)

1  Salic
2  Grimm's
3  Mendel's
4  Poor Law of 1601
5  Martial
6  Order (Pope)
7  Gresham's
8  Boyle's
9  Canon
10  Lynch (Lydford)

• 15 •  (1968, 9)

1  Nausiphanes
2  Epicurus
3  Liebniz
4  Zeno
5  Descartes
6  Diogenes
7  Kant
8  Wittgenstein
9  Hobbes
10  Marx

• 16 •  (1968, 13)

1  Mary I
2  Sarah Josepha Hale ('Mary had a little lamb')
3  Mary Magdalene
4  Mary Ambree
5  Mary Queen of Scots
6  Mary of Gueldres
7  Mary Hobbes, Charles Kingsley
8  Mary II
9  Mary of Modena
10  Mary of France (daughter of Henry VII)

• 17 •  (1968, 15)

1  Peter Ustinov
2  Bing Crosby and Bob Hope
3  The Merry Widow
4  Senoj Nosnibor
5  Carol Day
6  Luiz
7  Bosambo
8  Witherspoon
9  Carlton-Browne (Terry-Thomas)
10  Flavia

• 18 •  (1968, 17)

1  the magnet (W S Gilbert, *Patience*)
2  Jane Austen (*Pride and Prejudice*)
3  Lady Anne (Shakespeare, *Richard III*)
4  James Bond (Fleming, *On Her Majesty's Secret Service*)
5  Othello
6  Winston and Julia (Orwell, *1984*)
7  Miriam and Mr Polly (H G Wells)
8  Alison loved Jimmy Porter (Osborne, *Look Back in Anger*)
9  The Duchess (Webster, *The Duchess of Malfi*)
10  The Wife of Bath (Chaucer)

# 1969–1970

• 1 •  (1969, 1)

1  Suez Canal
2  Lord Acton
3  J S Mill
4  Union and Central Pacific Railways
5  Vatican Council
6  Gandhi
7  Napoleon III
8  Church of Ireland
9  Emily Davies
10  US Secretary of State

• 2 •  (1969, 2)

1  Melancholy (Keats)
2  Elijah

3  Yonder peasant
4  Lucy (Wordsworth)
5  two punctilious envoys: thine and
   mine
6  Deceit (*Romeo and Juliet*)
7  I (Psalm 23)
8  chronic hotel guests (E V Lucas)
9  all people
10 Nawadaha

• 3 •   (1969, 5)

1  *Mary Celeste*
2  *Douglas (Margaret and Jessie)*
3  *Ariel*
4  *Compass Rose*
5  *Manhattan*
6  *Argo*
7  *Revenge*
8  *Golden Hind (Pelican)*
9  *Great Eastern*
10 *La Mouette*

• 4 •   (1969, 6)

1  Margaret of Burgundy
2  Margaret Tudor
3  Margaret, Maid of Norway
4  Margaret, Countess of Snowdon
5  Margaret, Duchess of Newcastle
6  Margaret Rutherford
7  Margaret of Anjou
8  Miss Margaret Hussey
9  Margaret, Queen of Edward I
10 Lady Margaret Beaufort

• 5 •   (1969, 7)

1  June (Emily Dickinson)
2  December
3  February (Howells)
4  May
5  April (T S Eliot)
6  October (John Fletcher)
7  November
8  March
9  September
10 August

• 6 •   (1969, 8)

1  Beau Geste
2  Church of England
3  Noah (G K Chesterton)
4  Cervantes
5  Basilisk
6  Hypochlorite bleach
7  Cheeryble Brothers
8  John Taylor
9  Sandpiper
10 Keats

• 7 •   (1969, 11)

1  Conan Doyle
2  Philosophers' stone
3  Fred Flintstone
4  Touchstone
5  Murdstone
6  National Park, USA
7  Centre of Ka'aba in Mecca
8  balancing rock
9  Wheatstone
10 Ringed Plover

• 8 •   (1969, 12)

1  St Vincent
2  Farewell
3  Finisterre
4  Kennedy
5  Good Hope
6  Cod
7  Jonathan
8  Gris Nez
9  Clear
10 Lopatka

• 9 •   (1969, 14)

1  Dylan Thomas
2  Aunt Jobiska
3  Bustopher Jones
4  Benjamin Britten
5  Rudyard Kipling
6  Thomas Gray
7  The Egyptians
8  Hotspur
9  The Whigs
10 The Robbins Report

• 10 • (1970, 4)

1 Lochinvar
2 Alexander
3 a spiked ball
4 Black Beauty
5 Robert E Lee
6 Roland
7 Fallada
8 Baron Munchausen
9 Four Horsemen of the Apocalypse
10 Pegasus

• 11 • (1970, 5)

1 mountaineering
2 baseball
3 Eton fives
4 wrestling
5 judo
6 skiing
7 sky-diving
8 bowls
9 ice hockey
10 trampolining

• 12 • (1970, 6)

1 Henry VIII
2 Henry Cooper
3 Henry VII
4 Henry King
5 Henry Hall
6 Henry Labouchère
7 Henry Wadsworth Longfellow
8 Henry I
9 Henry Clay
10 Henry III

• 13 • (1970, 7)

1 Potassium ferric ferrocyanide
2 Bismuth nitrate
3 Copper arsenate
4 Lead chromate
5 Lead sulphide
6 Copper phthalocyanine
7 Tin disulphide (stannic sulphide)
8 Dibrom-indigotin
9 Ferric ferricyanide
10 Zinc oxide

• 14 • (1970, 8)

1 Southey of Thomas Telford
2 Henry IV of James I
3 Walpole of Pitt
4 Col. Sapt of Rudolph Rassendyll
5 Sinclair Lewis of the teacher
6 Artemus Ward (Charles Farrar Brown) of Brigham Young
7 Disraeli of Robert Peel
8 Rupert Brooke of Cambridge people
9 Plato of Socrates
10 Sydney Smith of poverty

• 15 • (1970, 10)

1 Château d'If
2 Manhattan
3 Changi
4 Zenda
5 Dartmoor (Princetown)
6 Bastille
7 The Fleet
8 Sing Sing
9 Newgate
10 Alcatraz

• 16 • (1970, 11)

1 Edward I
2 The Thugs
3 Badger
4 Mowgli
5 Ko-Ko
6 Damocles
7 Long John Silver
8 Argumentum (*Argumentum ad baculum*)
9 Jael and Sisera
10 Stalky and Rabbit's Eggs

• 17 • (1970, 12)

1 iron steamship
2 to reach the North Pole
3 Britannia with trident (1d. and 2d.)
4 Poliomyelitis vaccine
5 President of Rhodesia
6 Astronomer Royal
7 aircraft to deck-land
8 battle between ironclads

9 to introduce carnations into England
10 Everest ascent

• 18 • (1970, 13)

1 Calder Hall
2 Dotheboys Hall
3 Lord Hall
4 Rockall
5 Manchester Town Hall
6 Trinity Hall, Cambridge
7 Whitehall
8 King's Hall
9 Edwin Herbert Hall
10 Willis Hall

# 1971

• 1 •

1 Rasputin
2 Isaac Butt
3 Tin
4 Okubo
5 H M Stanley
6 Frankfurt
7 Orville Wright's
8 Test Act
9 Salmon P Chase
10 Griqualand West

• 2 •

1 Iris Murdoch
2 Daphne du Maurier
3 Mary Renault
4 Rumer Godden
5 Jacquetta Hawkes
6 Agatha Christie
7 Nancy Mitford
8 Georgette Heyer
9 Pamela Hansford Johnson
10 Enid Blyton

• 3 •

1 Saygrace
2 Mervyn Noote (Derek Nimmo)

3 Vicar of Bray
4 Father Brown
5 James Bates
6 T E Brown
7 Dean Farrar
8 Cranmer
9 Don Camillo
10 Becket

• 4 •

1 North Africa and Sicily
2 North wind in the Aegean
3 Rocky Mountains
4 Libya
5 Macedonia
6 Sardinia and northern Italy
7 South of France
8 Morocco
9 Southern Spain
10 Egypt

• 5 •

1 Castle Donington
2 Castle Crag (Borrowdale)
3 Cardiff Castle (00 gauge)
4 Barbara Castle
5 Doubting Castle (*The Pilgrim's Progress*)
6 Arundel Castle (Cricket)
7 *Farley Castle*
8 *Hatter's Castle* (Cronin)
9 Castle Douglas
10 *Tantallon Castle*

• 6 •

1 Marshall Jones Brooks
2 Sir Thomas de Cruwe
3 four cubits
4 Virgil
5 the medial and lateral plantar arteries
6 maximum transverse circumference allowed for a parcel
7 L'Equet
8 18
9 General Walker
10 the leadsman

## · 7 ·

1 white and red roses
2 Rose Noble
3 Rosalind
4 rose window (Lincoln Cathedral)
5 *Les Roses*
6 *Der Rosenkavalier*
7 Princess Margaret Rose
8 White Moss rose
9 Queen Alexandra Rose Day
10 a rose is a rose is …

## · 8 ·

1 Stock Exchange dealers
2 energy from the sea
3 Chow
4 oyster
5 Irving Berlin
6 mineral, calcium fluoride; cavern (Derbyshire)
7 Bob Dylan
8 Scottish XI (1928)
9 Army helicopter display team
10 one of the four pursuivants

## · 9 ·

1 Hwang Ti
2 Lucretius
3 Li Shi-chen
4 Andreas Vesalius
5 William Harvey
6 Giovanni Battista Morgagni
7 Edward Jenner
8 Claude Bernard
9 Ignaz Philipp Semmelweiss
10 Joseph Lister

## · 10 ·

1 Longfellow, rabbit
2 Saki (H H Munro), polecat or ferret
3 Manx fairy tale, calf
4 Beatrix Potter, fox
5 Henry Williamson, otter
6 T S Eliot, cat
7 Ernest Thomson Seton, coyote
8 A A Milne, donkey

9 Rudyard Kipling, elephant
10 J M Barrie, dog

## · 11 ·

1 Easter bonnet
2 demob suit
3 handcuffs
4 vest
5 riding coat
6 second-hand clothes
7 Trilby
8 tutu
9 Mae West (lifebelt)
10 waistcoat

## · 12 ·

1 Yorkshiremen
2 men of Lincolnshire (and Wexford)
3 men of South Australia
4 member of US secret society
5 men of Wiltshire
6 men of Perth (Western Australia)
7 natives of Leeds
8 pro-slavery Democrats in USA
9 men of Leicestershire
10 natives of Peel (Isle of Man)

## · 13 ·

1 Great Go
2 Great Tom
3 The Great Cricketer (memorial)
4 The Great Cham
5 The Great Divide
6 The Great War
7 The Great Crested Grebe
8 Great-heart
9 great expectations
10 The Great Commoner

## · 14 ·

1 covey
2 wisp
3 nye
4 fleet
5 trip
6 charm
7 herd

8 murmuration
9 exaltation
10 parliament

• 15 •

1 the owl and the pussy-cat
2 Cushie Butterfield
3 School
4 blackbirds
5 Fifth Day of Christmas
6 Pennsylvania
7 a bachelor gay
8 Willie or Sam
9 Clementine
10 seventy-six trombones

• 16 •

1 A W Pullin
2 William Beldham
3 Alfred Mynn
4 Tom Walker
5 William Lillywhite
6 W G Grace and Richard Newland
7 G O Allen
8 George Osbaldeston
9 J F Cochrane
10 G J V Weigall

• 17 •

1 Charles II
2 Charles Wesley
3 Charles Kingsley
4 Prince Charles (Prince of Wales)
5 Charles I
6 Charles Dupee Blake
7 Charles's Wain
8 Charles Augustus Fortescue
9 Charles Edward (The Young
Pretender)
10 Charles Chaplin

• 18 •

1 D-Day in the Second World War
2 HMS *Belfast*
3 Shah of Persia (Iran)
4 Isle of Man (Common Market)
5 table tennis (US team to China)

6 US 5-megaton bomb on
Amchitka
7 St Kilda in the Outer Hebrides
8 London Bridge
9 astronauts David Scott and James
Irwin
10 Emperor Hirohito

# 1972

• 1 •

1 Ranjitsinhji
2 Yellowstone Park
3 *Alabama* (Confederate ship)
4 Sir Charles Dilke
5 Winslow Homer
6 Ballot Act
7 Joseph Arch
8 *Mary Celeste*
9 Victoria Woodhull
10 H G W Hughes-Games

• 2 •

1 Israel
2 Poland
3 Bulgaria
4 Norway
5 Finland
6 Isle of Man
7 Sweden
8 Iceland
9 Nepal
10 Netherlands

• 3 •

1 egret
2 boiling your eggs in your shoes
3 egg timer
4 an egg without salt
5 egality
6 curate's egg
7 egophony
8 exigence
9 all eggs
10 egotist

• 4 •

1 Wood Warbler
2 Great Grey Shrike
3 Pine Grosbeak
4 Hawfinch
5 Wren
6 Nightjar
7 Snipe
8 Puffin
9 Goldcrest
10 Great Auk

• 5 •

1 Oliver Cromwell
2 Danton
3 George V
4 Charles Stewart Parnell
5 Jonathan Swift
6 Palmerston
7 Bismarck
8 Thomas More
9 Wellington
10 William Pitt (the Younger)

• 6 •

1 Fuserium (killed grass)
2 Emerson Fittipaldi
3 *World Sports*
4 International Weight-lifting
Federation Congress
5 Carwyn James
6 Albert Woods (lost his
watch)
7 Derek Dougan
8 Sir Donald Bradman's son
9 Mark Spitz
10 hot air balloons

• 7 •

1 Beaufighter
2 Blenheim
3 Mosquito
4 Hellcat
5 Lancaster
6 Corsair
7 Dakota
8 Walrus

9 Spitfire
10 Wellington

• 8 •

1 *Tender is the Night*
2 *Strait is the Gate*
3 *Antic Hay*
4 *The First Circle*
5 *The Winter of Our Discontent*
6 *Where Angels Fear to Tread*
7 *There is No Armour*
8 *Richer Than All His Tribe*
9 *Nothing So Strange*
10 *Kind Are Her Answers*

• 9 •

1 *Esmeralda*
2 Great steamers white and gold
3 The Ancient Mariner's
4 The Schooner (T E Brown)
5 The Bellman's (*The Hunting of the
Snark*)
6 Noah's Ark
7 *L'Orient*
8 The *Bolivar*
9 the owl and the pussy-cat's
10 The *Revenge*

• 10 •

1 Professor Lindenbrook
2 Oliver Twist
3 Thoroughly Modern Millie
4 James Bond
5 Ben Hur
6 Richard Hannay
7 Umbopa
8 Bulldog Drummond
9 The Scarlet Pimpernel, Sir Percy
Blakeney
10 David Crawfurd

• 11 •

1 Edward, Earl of Warwick
2 Edward Lear
3 Edward, the Black Prince
4 Edward Bangs
5 Edward Young

6 Edward Heath
7 Edward German
8 Edward VI
9 Edward VII
10 Edward the Martyr

• 12 •

1 Barry Cornwall
2 South Riding
3 Barsetshire
4 *Wessex*
5 Middlesex (Jamaica)
6 Somerset
7 Richard Cumberland
8 Surrey
9 Fife
10 Down

• 13 •

1 Elizabeth Barrett
2 Nick Charles
3 Sexton Blake
4 Bill Sikes
5 Archibald Roylance
6 John Gray
7 Swiss Family Robinson
8 Dick Dastardly
9 Launce
10 The three men in a boat

• 14 •

1 Andrew Ferrara
2 Andrew Mellon
3 Andrew Lang
4 Andrew Gardner
5 Andrew Paterson
6 Andrew Carnegie
7 Andrew Cherry
8 Andrew Cruickshank
9 A merry-andrew
10 Andrew Browne Cunningham

• 15 •

1 President Garfield at Washington Station
2 Becket at Canterbury
3 Admiral Darlan at Algiers

4 Henry IV of Navarre at Paris
5 Archduke and Duchess of Austria at Sarajevo
6 Spencer Perceval at Westminster
7 President McKinley at Buffalo
8 President Kennedy at Dallas
9 Marat in his bath in Paris
10 Rasputin at Petrograd

• 16 •

1 Stoke-upon-Trent
2 Yvonne
3 Dover
4 Omaha
5 Pym
6 St Mary's
7 Stamford
8 Sutlej
9 Lumbar
10 Memory

• 17 •

1 Hungerford at Hock Tide (second Tuesday after Easter)
2 Fenny Stratford on 11 November
3 Helston on 8 May
4 Ashbourne on Shrove Tuesday
5 Tinsley Green on Good Friday
6 Haxey on 6 January
7 Wishford on 29 May
8 Ripon, every evening
9 Honiton on 23 July
10 Marshfield on 26 December

• 18 •

1 *Britannia* (Queen's visit to the Isle of Man)
2 Treasures of Tutankhamen
3 BBC
4 FA Cup
5 Iceland
6 Queen and Duke of Edinburgh's silver wedding service
7 the miners
8 Sir John Betjeman
9 Bobby Fischer
10 Norway

# 1973

**• 1 •**

1 Napoleon II
2 Duke of Sutherland
3 Caruso
4 NW Mounted Police
5 Walter De la Mare
6 Rachmaninov
7 Thomas Young
8 Prince Edward Island
9 Bulwer Lutton
10 Sir John Simon

**• 2 •**

1 Richter; Mercalli
2 Binary
3 Moh (rocks), Brinell (metals)
4 Beaufort
5 fish
6 Whitley
7 Chromatic
8 Libra
9 Burnham
10 Vernier

**• 3 •**

1 Richard (Beau) Nash
2 Richard Burton
3 Richard Sheridan
4 Whittington
5 Richard Lovelace
6 Richard Hooker
7 Richard III
8 Richard Wagner
9 Richard II
10 Richard Nixon

**• 4 •**

1 Ulyanov
2 Buchan
3 Hepburn
4 Ellison
5 Johnson (Swift's pseudonym for Esther);

Devereux (Sidney's pseudonym for Penelope)
6 Bernadotte
7 Breakspeare
8 (Mary Anne) Evans
9 Coggan
10 Manners

**• 5 •**

1 Aphrodite
2 Hephaestus
3 Ariadne
4 Agamemnon
5 Laertes
6 Persephone
7 Perseus
8 Jason
9 Jocasta (Laius was the murdered father)
10 Alcestis

**• 6 •**

1 Twelfth hole at St Andrew's
2 Eighth at Troon
3 Fourteenth at Royal St George's, Sandwich
4 Fourteenth at Royal Portrush
5 Tenth at Carnoustie
6 Seventh at Royal Liverpool, Hoylake
7 Sixteenth at Southport and Ainsdale
8 Tenth (later 7th) at Castletown
9 Fourteenth at Turnberry
10 Sixteenth at Prestwick

**• 7 •**

1 Keats, musk rose
2 Blake, sunflower
3 Beaumont and Fletcher, primrose
4 Arnold, bluebells
5 Burns, daisy
6 Wordsworth, lesser celandine
7 Wordsworth, daisy
8 Lear, bong tree
9 Mark Twain, cauliflower
10 Psalms of David, cedars of Libanus

• 8 •

1 Knot
2 Capercaille (Gaelic: *capull coillie*)
3 Stint
4 Tern
5 Hawk
6 Ruff
7 Nightingale
8 Blackcap
9 Albatross (golf), Magpie
10 Puffin (Lundy)

• 9 •

1 mountains in Rhum
2 sons of Gama in *Princess Ida*
3 part of High Priest's breastplate (*Exodus* 28, 30)
4 afterthought and forethought (Titans in Greek mythology)
5 Shetland Islands
6 characters in *A Midsummer Night's Dream*
7 peninsulas in Skye
8 rivers of Hades
9 originally two naval research ships (mountains of Antarctica)
10 sons of Benjamin (Genesis 46, 21)

• 10 •

1 Cagliostro
2 Anjou (Plantagenet)
3 Tolstoy
4 Arnhem
5 Dracula
6 John McCormack
7 Orloff
8 Zeppelin
9 Almaviva
10 Monte Cristo

• 11 •

1 Chimaera
2 Gorgon (Medusa)
3 Cerberus
4 Sphinx
5 Wyvern
6 Griffin (Gryphon)
7 Satyr (or Pan)
8 Hydra
9 Centaur
10 Siren

• 12 •

1 Carbon dioxide (in mines)
2 Half stout, half champagne
3 Gentleman Usher of the House of Lords
4 Roger Casement's (in evidence against him)
5 Head of the Society of Jesus
6 Sudan
7 George Headley
8 New Zealand international rugby players
9 Richard I in disguise (*Ivanhoe*)
10 'Plague' (epidemic Typhus or Jail Fever) following Oxford Assizes in 1577

• 13 •

1 Aristotle (Alexander)
2 Dante
3 Machiavelli
4 Jean Bodin
5 Sir Thomas More
6 Hobbes
7 Locke
8 Rousseau
9 Burke
10 Plato

• 14 •

1 Brisbane's cricket ground (Woolloongabba)
2 Hambledon
3 Alfred Shaw
4 Kent
5 first secretary of MCC
6 Felix
7 Trent Bridge (Nottingham)
8 team of Australian aborigines in England
9 Viscount Chelsea, presidency of MCC

10 it was where Thomas Lord first opened his ground

• 15 •

1 flag (carried by cavalry)
2 basket filled with earth (for defence work)
3 a positively charged ion
4 type of piano
5 wash basin
6 support for cannon
7 making cotton look like silk
8 solution of cellulose nitrate
9 grinding in a mortar
10 tinkling of bells

• 16 •

1 Limpopo
2 Weser
3 Missouri
4 Styx
5 Cam
6 Parana
7 Dee
8 Plate
9 Erne
10 Barle

• 17 •

1 Saint Paul
2 Samuel Butler
3 Browning
4 Milton
5 Shakespeare (Siward in *Macbeth*)
6 Wolsey
7 Wordsworth
8 Housman
9 Bacon
10 Masefield

• 18 •

1 Dalai Lama
2 Exchequer (VAT)
3 Arab-Israeli War
4 Wedding of Princess Anne and Captain Mark Phillips

5 England rugby team in New Zealand
6 Sydney Opera House
7 Nastase and Taylor for playing at Wimbledon
8 Archibald Cox
9 London Stock Exchange
10 London Bridge

# 1974

• 1 •

1 Disraeli's second ministry
2 Arthur Orton (Tichborne case)
3 Fiji Islands
4 birth of Houdini
5 first Dr Barnardo's Home
6 Alexander McDonald and Thomas Burt
7 birth of Holst
8 birth of Marconi
9 King Coffee
10 Alkali Act

• 2 •

1 Zephyrus
2 Zeugen
3 Zabaglione
4 Zinc
5 Zebedee
6 Zylographer
7 Zest
8 Zoetrope
9 Ziggurat
10 Zolotnik

• 3 •

1 Saône
2 Guadalquivir
3 Rhône
4 Gironde
5 Nahe
6 Marne
7 Danube
8 Douro

9 Mosel(le)
10 Loire

• 4 •

1 Louis Braille
2 John Mercer
3 Evangelista Torricelli
4 Lord Raglan
5 Jules Leotard
6 W L Lewis
7 Étienne de Silhouette
8 Dr T Bowdler
9 Arthur or Benjamin Guinness
10 Charles Pathé

• 5 •

1 Thistle
2 Cormorant
3 Hutton
4 Auk
5 Claymore
6 Josephine
7 Dan
8 Cod
9 Ninian
10 Brent

• 6 •

1 Drake
2 W A Teare
3 Byng
4 E J Smith
5 E C Kennedy
6 Langsdorff
7 Benjamin S Briggs
8 Magellan
9 William Turner
10 Grenville

• 7 •

1 Ambrose
2 Roy Fox
3 Edmundo Ros
4 Eric Winstone
5 Carroll Gibbons
6 Nat Gonella
7 Stanley Black

8 Henry Hall
9 Cyril Stapleton
10 Sid Phillips

• 8 •

1 Nicholas Freeling
2 Edgar Allan Poe
3 Patricia Wentworth
4 Raymond Chandler
5 Collier Young
6 Margery Allingham
7 Len Deighton
8 Michael Innes
9 Arthur Morrison
10 Conan Doyle

• 9 •

1 Duke of Wellington, Queen Victoria
2 Mr Pascoe, Nelson
3 Paul, Timothy
4 Pooh-Bah, Ko-Ko
5 Benjamin Franklin, young tradesman
6 gallant young airman, mechanics
7 Norman Baron, his son
8 Bob Sawyer, Mr Pickwick
9 George Dewey, Charles Gridley
10 Old Father William, young man

• 10 •

1 Anna Magdalena Wilcken
2 Henry VIII
3 Poppaea Sabina
4 Helena Gorska
5 Nelson
6 Darnley
7 Madison
8 Mary Wollstonecraft
9 John Millais
10 Count Rumford

• 11 •

1 Sir Wilfred Lucas-Dockery
2 Lorenzo Medici
3 Dr Akonanga
4 Miss Aimée Thanatogenos

5 Everard Spruce
6 Mr and Mrs Prettyman-Partridge
7 Mr Sniggs
8 Sir Ralph Brompton
9 Apthorpe
10 Miss Florence Selina Fagan

• 12 •

1 Veronese
2 El Greco
3 Raphael
4 Caravaggio
5 Giorgione
6 Botticelli
7 Tintoretto
8 Titian
9 Correggio
10 Sir Peter Lely

• 13 • First postage stamps of:

1 Brazil
2 British Guiana
3 New South Wales
4 Trinidad
5 India
6 Geneva Canton
7 Basle Canton
8 Uruguay
9 Hawaii
10 Gambia

• 14 •

1 Lewis Carroll, Wordsworth
2 Swinburne, Tennyson
3 Max Beerbohm, Kipling
4 Samuel Hoffenstein,
   A E Housman
5 Henry Reed, T S Eliot
6 A E Housman, Greek tragedy
7 J C Squire, G K Chesterton
8 James Clerk-Maxwell, Burns
9 H D Traill, D G Rossetti
10 Swinburne, Swinburne

• 15 •

1 William II ( Rufus)
2 William Wilberforce

3 William Brown (Richmal
   Crompton's)
4 William I (The Conqueror)
5 William IV
6 William the Breton
7 William Wordsworth
8 William the Silent
9 Kaiser William II
10 William Makepeace Thackeray

• 16 •

1 Thomas Edison
2 Sam Clemens (Mark Twain)
3 William Gilbert
4 Patrick Brontë
5 Charles Dodgson (Lewis Carroll)
6 Henry Longfellow
7 William Thackeray
8 Jerome K Jerome
9 Julian Huxley
10 Richard Sheridan

• 17 •

1 *Pride and Prejudice*, Jane Austen
2 *Kim*, Rudyard Kipling
3 *The Manxman*, Hall Caine
4 *Cold Comfort Farm*, Stella Gibbons
5 *Gulliver's Travels*, Jonathan Swift
6 *The Good Soldier*, Ford Madox Ford
7 *Ulysses*, James Joyce
8 *A Tale of Two Cities*, Charles
   Dickens
9 *Jude the Obscure*, Thomas Hardy
10 *Moby Dick*, Herman Melville

• 18 •

1 *Mona Lisa*
2 Lockheed SR-71 Blackbird
3 Sam Goldwyn
4 Edward Heath
5 Arthur Haley's book (paperback
   edition)
6 Ford and Rockefeller
7 Linda Goldwill
8 Charles Lindbergh
9 Prince Charles
10 The Brownies

# 1975

## • 1 •

1 Captain Webb
2 Artisans' Dwellings and Public Health Acts
3 Gerard Manley Hopkins'
4 First performance of *Trial By Jury*
5 Albert Schweitzer born
6 Sold Suez Canal shares
7 Charles Kingsley
8 Sir Stafford Northcote
9 Gallium
10 John Buchan (Lord Tweedsmuir)

## • 2 •

1 Executioner in *The Mikado*
2 Wild sugar cane
3 A toy
4 Fermented breadfruit
5 Resort in Mozambique
6 A quadruped from Malagasy (Madagascar)
7 A tree or its perfume
8 West African spirit or charm
9 South American canoe
10 Town in New Zealand

## • 3 •

1 Balloon
2 Telephone
3 Atomic bomb
4 Wireless telegraphy
5 Tunnelling shield
6 Phonograph
7 Diesel engine
8 Photography
9 Dynamite
10 Cinematograph

## • 4 •

1 Bedloe Island
2 Isle of Ely
3 Islay
4 Treasure Island
5 Inchcolm
6 Gull Island
7 Rhodes
8 Roanoke Island
9 Hoy
10 Long Island

## • 5 •

1 Aeschylus
2 Duncan
3 Cock Robin
4 Dennis
5 Mrs De Ropp
6 Sisera
7 Socrates
8 Nedda
9 English cricket
10 President McKinley

## • 6 •

1 Compton Mackenzie
2 Jack Kerouac
3 Ludovic Kennedy
4 Henry James
5 Charles Brackett and Billy Wilder
6 Richard Rodgers
7 Marcel Proust
8 Bob Dylan
9 Damon Runyon
10 Nell Dunn

## • 7 •

1 Kensitas cigarettes
2 Johnny Walker whisky
3 Woolworths
4 Bovril
5 Lyle's Golden Syrup
6 Wall's ice cream
7 Beecham's pills
8 Palmolive soap
9 Lifebuoy soap
10 Horlicks

## • 8 •

1 New College, Oxford
2 Newborough (near Beaumaris)
3 Newmarket

4 New Riverhead
5 New Goa
6 Newhaven
7 *New Moon*
8 New Sarum
9 New-style calendar
10 New France

• 9 •

1 Citizen Kane
2 Sir Alec Rose
3 Camrose Trophy
4 American servicemen
5 Rose Macaulay
6 Gertrude Stein
7 Rose of Sharon
8 Texas
9 Rose Noble
10 Fokine

• 10 •

1 Admiral Thomas Smith
2 Admiral the Hon. Edward Boscawen
3 Rear Admiral Hyde Parker
4 Admiral Edward Vernon
5 Admiral the Hon. William Cornwallis
6 Admiral of the Fleet Richard Earl Howe
7 Vice Admiral Cuthbert Lord Collingwood
8 Vice Admiral the Hon. John Byron
9 Admiral of the Fleet James Lord Gambier
10 Admiral Sir William Young

• 11 •

1 Fire
2 Connaught
3 Zephyrus
4 Iodine
5 Music
6 Exhaust
7 Melancholy
8 Hyperbola

9 Ferio
10 Calisto

• 12 •

1 Normandy, France
2 Lombardy, Italy
3 Vaud, Switzerland
4 Sardinia, Italy
5 Alsace, France
6 Worcester/Somerset, England
7 Akershus, Norway
8 Thessaly, Greece
9 Limburg, Belgium
10 Dorset, England

• 13 •

1 Dallas
2 Pasadena
3 Indiana
4 Promontory Point, Utah
5 Lake Placid/North Elba NY
6 Baltimore
7 Maryland
8 Georgia
9 Boston
10 Chicago

• 14 •

1 Peter the Wild Boy
2 Patrick (Peter) Lord Robertson
3 Peter I, the Great
4 Peter Cheyney
5 Peter des Roches
6 Blue Peter
7 Peter the Hermit
8 Peter Piper
9 Peter Abelard
10 Peter Pan

• 15 •

1 Black Rod
2 Black pudding
3 Blackwood
4 Black Monday
5 The Black Hole
6 Black-damp
7 Blackjack

8 A black hole
9 Blackball
10 The Moddhey Doo (Black Dog)

**• 16 •**

1 The stout woman, *The History of Mr Polly*
2 Mistress Quickly, *Henry IV*
3 Mrs Hawkins, *Treasure Island*
4 Stingo, *She Stoops to Conquer*
5 Mrs Weller, *The Pickwick Papers*
6 Barliman Butterbur, *The Fellowship of the Ring*
7 Mary Robbins, *The Girl of the Golden West*
8 Roy Alciatore, *Dinner at Antoine's*
9 Benoit, *La Bohème*
10 John Willet, *Barnaby Rudge*

**• 17 •**

1 Friend of Humanity, *The Knife Grinder*
2 Uncle Abishai, *Captains Courageous*
3 J, *Three Men in a Boat*
4 Macbeth, *Macbeth*
5 Robert de Baudricourt, *Saint Joan*
6 The Cardinal, *The Jackdaw of Rheims*
7 Old Finn, *Huckleberry Finn*
8 Grandfather, *The Night the Ghost Got In*
9 Mr Collopy, *The Hard Life*
10 Rabelais, *Pantagruel*

**• 18 •**

1 Sir Garfield (Gary) Sobers
2 L'Escargot
3 BBC weather map
4 Beachcomber (J B Morton)
5 Billie-Jean King
6 General Gowon
7 Wales (v. Japan 82–6)
8 Houses of Parliament (German China)
9 Frederic March died
10 K Murphy in Channel swim

# 1976–1977

**• 1 •**   (1976, 3)

1 *The Man of La Mancha*
2 *Carousel*
3 *Hello, Dolly!*
4 *Kismet*
5 *The New Moon*
6 *High Society*
7 *Kiss Me, Kate*
8 *Chitty Chitty Bang Bang*
9 *Show Boat*
10 *Oklahoma*

**• 2 •**   (1976, 4)

1 Marx
2 Montgolfier
3 William and John Hunter
4 Warner
5 George and Weedon Goldsmith
6 Mills
7 Jacob and Johann Bernoulli
8 Grimm
9 Wright
10 Mike and Leon Spinks

**• 3 •**   (1976, 5)

1 Sam Langford
2 John C Heenan
3 Joe Louis
4 Tom Hickman
5 James J Corbett
6 James Braddock
7 William Thompson
8 Henry Armstrong
9 Henry Pearce
10 Jimmy Wilde

**• 4 •**   (1976, 6)

1 Ivor Novello, Hamlet
2 Thomas Hardy, Amiens
3 Julian Slade, Cleopatra
4 H E Bates, Shakespeare
5 Cole Porter, Petruchio
6 Somerset Maugham, Sir Toby Belch

7 John Van Druten, The Bastard
8 Duff Cooper, Henry V
9 Noel Coward, Shelley
10 Francis Chichester, John Masefield

• 5 •   (1976, 7)

1 Avignon
2 Tacoma Narrows
3 Sighs
4 Menai
5 Pons Asinorum
6 Clifton Suspension Bridge
7 Contact Bridge
8 Maidenhead
9 Westminster
10 Tallahatchie

• 6 •   (1976, 10)

1 John Walter (*The Times*)
2 Walter Tyrrel (or Tirel)
3 Rt Hon. Walter Long
4 Walter Mitty
5 Walter of Evesham; Walter
   Odington
6 Walter De la Mare
7 Lucy Walter
8 Hubert Walter
9 Walter the Penniless
10 Walter Raleigh

• 7 •   (1976, 12)

1 Southern Cross
2 Charing Cross
3 Cross Fell
4 Crossbow
5 Red Cross
6 Victoria Cross
7 Cross-head
8 Gaut's Cross
9 Crossover
10 Crossword

• 8 •   (1976, 13)

1 Oregon
2 Texas
3 Louisiana
4 Massachusetts

5 Illinois
6 Kentucky
7 Tennessee
8 Arizona
9 West Virginia
10 Utah

• 9 •   (1976, 15)

1 Mr Mell
2 Mr Prendergast
3 An old crab
4 Dr Skinner
5 Mr King
6 Holofernes
7 Mr Squeers
8 Mr Pugh
9 Dr Thorneycroft Huxtable
10 Dr Smart-Allick

• 10 •   (1976, 16)

1 Salerno
2 Reggio
3 Avranches
4 Rangoon
5 Gilbert Islands
6 Sicily
7 Okinawa
8 Rimini
9 Anzio
10 Taranto

• 11 •   (1977, 3)

1 G B Shaw
2 Duke of Wellington
3 John Addison
4 G B Shaw
5 John Milton
6 Kathy (*The Student Prince*)
7 Gustave Flaubert
8 Mark Twain
9 John Ruskin
10 Henry Brougham

• 12 •   (1977, 5)

1 Quadriceps
2 Quality Street
3 Quignon

4 Quasr
5 Quintessence
6 Quelch
7 Quern
8 Quasimodo
9 Quadrivium
10 Quotidian

• 13 • (1977, 6)

1 Fish Benjie
2 Ben Jonson
3 Benjamin Disraeli
4 Benjamin Bunny
5 Big Ben
6 Ben Gunn
7 Benjamin, son of Jacob
8 Ben Backstay
9 Ben Travers
10 Benjamin Britten

• 14 • (1977, 7)

1 Samuel Plimsoll
2 George Westinghouse
3 J E Lundström
4 Percy Shaw
5 Lionel Lukin
6 Benjamin Franklin
7 R T H Laënnec
8 King Camp Gillette
9 Humphry Davy
10 Leslie Hore Belisha

• 15 • (1977, 9)

1 Philip IV of France
2 Philip II of Macedon
3 Philip II of Spain
4 Philip, Duke of Edinburgh
5 Philip V of Spain
6 Philip V of Macedon
7 Philip the Arabian
8 Sir Philip Sidney
9 Philip the Good of Burgundy
10 Philip, Duke of Orleans

• 16 • (1977, 10)

1 *The Old Curiosity Shop*
2 The Old Vic

3 Old Maid
4 Old Parr
5 Old Sarum
6 The Old Pretender
7 The Old 97
8 Old Mother Riley
9 Sir John Oldcastle
10 The Old Grey Mare

• 17 • (1977, 13)

1 of Oyo, Nigeria
2 of Calicut, India
3 King of Malaya
4 High King of Ireland
5 Wife of Doge – Venice, Genoa
6 Annual magistrate of Carthage
7 Count Palatine, of Rhine
8 of Chitral, Pakistan
9 of Ethiopia
10 Zambezi area (16th century)

• 18 • (1977, 15)

1 The Pooters
2 Mrs Ogmore-Pritchard
3 Thaddeus and Bartholomew
  Sholto
4 Jim Hawkins
5 Leopold Bloom
6 John Wellington Wells
7 David Copperfield
8 Theobald Pontifex
9 Charles Augustus Fortescue
10 The Earl of Littlehampton

# 1978

• 1 •

1 Vincent Joachim Pecci
2 British prisons
3 General Mezentseff
4 Martinez de Campos
5 John Dixon
6 Humbert/Umberto I
7 James McNeill Whistler
8 Major Cavagnari

9  Alfonso XII
10  Terence V Powderly

• 2 •

1  Poland and Russia
2  Pennsylvania and Maryland (North and South USA)
3  India and Pakistan
4  Those above and below 40% educational ability
5  France and Spain
6  Oman and Yemen
7  British and French armies
8  Finland and Russia
9  North and South Cyprus
10  India and China

• 3 •

1  Private Bamforth
2  Corporal Nym
3  Sergeant Troy
4  Regimental Sergeant Major Raskin
5  Lieutenant Cassio
6  Captain Drummond
7  Major O'Dowd
8  Colonel Jack
9  Brigadier Gerard
10  General Tilney

• 4 •

1  Mercedes
2  Wolseley
3  Stanley
4  Peerless, Pierce-Arrow and Packard
5  Jeeps
6  Trojan
7  Silver Ghost and Phantom I (Rolls Royce)
8  Morris Minor
9  Bentley
10  Hon. Charles Stewart Rolls

• 5 •

1  Tannenberg
2  Bosworth

3  Zela
4  Kolin
5  New Orleans
6  Kosovo
7  Jutland
8  Salamanca
9  Stalingrad
10  Talikota

• 6 •

1  Waterloo and City
2  The Great Western
3  Lancashire and Yorkshire
4  London and North-eastern Railway
5  London Chatham and Dover
6  Manchester, Sheffield and Lincolnshire
7  Oxford, Worcester and Wolverhampton
8  Midland and Great Northern
9  Somerset and Dorset Joint Railway
10  South-eastern and Chatham

• 7 •

1  *Flying Dutchman*
2  Flying trapeze
3  *Flying Scotsman*
4  'Flying Home'
5  Flying Childers
6  Flying shuttle
7  Flying Flea
8  Flying Finn (Paavo Nurmi)
9  Flying Fortress
10  Flying Arrow

• 8 •

1  lawn tennis court
2  building brick
3  Beaufort Scale
4  Mikado-type locomotive or McArthur
5  cricket wicket
6  railway ticket
7  cricket ball
8  railway standard gauge
9  A1 size paper
10  discus

## • 9 •

1 Kenneth Grahame, *The Reluctant Dragon*
2 Charles Dickens, *Martin Chuzzlewit*
3 E Nesbit, *The Magic World*
4 J B S Haldane, *My Friend Mr Leakey*
5 Naomi Mitchison, *Graeme and the Dragon*
6 C S Lewis, *Narnia* books
7 St John the Divine, *The Revelation*
8 J R R Tolkien, *The Hobbit*
9 Grace Cox-Ife, *The Sentimental Dragon*
10 Oliver Postgate, *Ivor the Engine*

## • 10 •

1 *Straight Shootiong*
2 *She Wore a Yellow Ribbon*
3 *Stagecoach*
4 *Three Godfathers*
5 *The Searchers*
6 *The Quiet Man*
7 *Two Rode Together*
8 *They Were Expendable*
9 *The Man Who Shot Liberty Valance*
10 *Donovan's Reef*

## • 11 •

1 Walter and John Huston
2 Auguste and Jacques Piccard
3 Sir William and Sir John Herschel
4 George and Robert Stephenson
5 Sir Marc and Isambard Brunel
6 John and John Quincy Adams
7 Sir Malcolm and Donald Campbell
8 Nicholas and Sir James Douglass
9 Sir William and Sir Lawrence Bragg
10 Philip and Edmund Gosse

## • 12 •

1 Eratosthenes
2 de Moivre
3 Todhunter
4 Anaxagoras
5 Kronecker
6 Kepler
7 Klein
8 T H Huxley
9 Arthur Caley or Silvester
10 Bernoulli

## • 13 •

1 Ağustos
2 Dudek
3 E Merkure
4 Joulukuu
5 Szaz
6 Halv fjerdsinstyve
7 Agosto
8 Dezasete
9 West
10 Cetvrti

## • 14 •

1 Royal Air Force
2 United States of America
3 London Zoo
4 City of Lancaster
5 The Orkneys
6 Metro Goldwyn Mayer
7 The Dambusters (617 Squadron)
8 The Royal Engineers or Royal Artillery
9 California
10 *The New York Times*

## • 15 •

1 Junot
2 Suchet
3 Victor
4 Soult
5 Bessières
6 Lannes
7 Marmont
8 Oudinot
9 MacDonald
10 Mortier

## • 16 •

1 Erewhon
2 Ruritania

3  Ishmaelia
4  Aeaea
5  Laputa
6  Utopia
7  Avalon
8  Niflheim
9  Oz
10  Freedonia

• 17 •

1  crows
2  starlings
3  turkeys
4  shelducks
5  larks
6  ravens
7  magpies
8  goldfinches
9  snipe
10  eagles

• 18 •

1  The Flying Scotsman (Inter-City 125)
2  Orion (oil rig)
3  English £1 note – Queen's head on new £1 note
4  Argentina (World Cup and Miss World)
5  Bendalis Adema (Irish bull)
6  Times Crossword 30 November
7  Mickey Mouse
8  BBC
9  Wales XV (Triple Crown thrice)
10  Prince Charles

# 1979–1980

• 1 •  (1979, 2)

1  *The Critic*, R B Sheridan
2  *Frank Mildmay*, Captain Marryat
3  *Symphonie Fantastique*, Berlioz
4  *Pride and Prejudice*, Jane Austen
5  *Oliver Twist*, Charles Dickens
6  *All for Love*, Dryden

7  *Sybil*, Benjamin Disraeli
8  *The Beggars' Opera*, Gay
9  *The Devil's Disciple*, Shaw
10  *Isabella*, Keats

• 2 •  (1979, 3)

1  Peter II of Russia
2  Peter the Hermit
3  Lord Peter Wimsey
4  Peter III of Russia
5  Peter Piper
6  Peter I of Cyprus
7  Peter the Great
8  Bell in York Minster
9  Peter the Painter
10  Peter IV of Portugal and I of Brazil

• 3 •  (1979, 5)

1  Balaam's ass
2  Chaucer's Reeve's horse
3  a bear (*The Winter's Tale*)
4  Thomas Gray's cat
5  an albatross (*The Ancient Mariner*)
6  a nightingale (Keats)
7  Thomas Campbell's poor dog, Tray
8  a jackdaw
9  R L Stevenson's donkey, Modestine
10  a seagull (Chekhov)

• 4 •  (1979, 11)

1  June, Eliza Doolittle
2  June, Blaydon
3  January, Carousel
4  May, in the park
5  December, Keats
6  May, Gray
7  July, 'Don Juan'
8  August, Auden
9  March, cargoes
10  June, Lowell

• 5 •  (1979, 13)

1  Uncle Tom, H B Stowe
2  Harold Skimpole, Charles Dickens
3  Robinson Crusoe, Daniel Defoe
4  Jekyll and Hyde, R L Stevenson

5 Juliana Bordereau, Henry James
6 Marie Roget, Poe
7 Emma Bovary, Gustave Flaubert
8 Marguerite Gautier, Alexandre Dumas
9 Sherlock Holmes, Conan Doyle
10 Clyde Griffiths, Theodore Dreiser

• 6 •   (1979, 14)

1 Two sticks and an apple
2 Sep no Iun Ap triginta dato; reliquis magis uno
3 Cackle cackle, Mother Goose
4 Hana, mana, mona, mike
5 Who kill'd John Keats?
6 The King sent his lady on the first Yule day
7 Hushie ba, birdie beeton
8 A soldier, a sailor, a tinker and a tailor
9 Ich wollte gern über die Magdeburger Brücke
10 I, William of the Wastle

• 7 •   (1979, 15)

1 *Strangers on a Train*
2 *Blackmail*
3 *Young and Innocent*
4 *Lifeboat*
5 *Family Plot*
6 *North by North West*
7 *The Birds*
8 *Dial M for Murder*
9 *Rebecca*
10 Sir Alfred Hitchcock

• 8 •   (1979, 16)

1 Labouchère
2 Hamlet
3 Gerald Ford
4 Kipling
5 Rev. Dr E Norman
6 Valéry
7 Nietzsche
8 Donne
9 Voltaire
10 Conan Doyle

• 9 •   (1979, 17)

1 DH6
2 Sopwith triplane
3 Graham-White Lizzie
4 Humphreys monoplane
5 Maurice Farman
6 RE8
7 Curtiss JN-4
8 Short Tractor-Pusher monoplane
9 AD Scout
10 Short S57/T4

• 10 •   (1980, 2)

1 Whitestone
2 Whitehall
3 White Rose
4 white collar
5 The White Ship
6 white elephant
7 whitebait
8 The White Knight
9 white dwarves
10 The White Tower

• 11 •   (1980, 4)

1 Burke and Hare
2 Laurel and Hardy
3 Alcock and Brown
4 Faber and Faber
5 Beaumont and Fletcher
6 Romulus and Remus
7 Boulton and Watt
8 Galton and Simpson
9 Panhard and Levassor
10 Chang and Eng

• 12 •   (1980, 6)

1 *The Idiot*, Dostoevsky
2 *The Warden*, Trollope
3 *The Sorcerer*, Gilbert and Sullivan
4 *The Manxman*, Hall Caine
5 *The Philanderer*, Shaw
6 *The Trumpet-Major*, Hardy
7 *The Egoist*, Meredith
8 *The Specialist*, Charles Sale
9 *The Alchemist*, Jonson
10 *The Caretaker*, Pinter

• 13 • (1980, 7)

1 Cat and Mouse Act
2 Cat Stane
3 Cat's eye
4 catcall
5 cat's whisker
6 Dick Whittington's cat
7 cats' concert
8 cat's brains
9 Cat and Fiddle (near Buxton)
10 catacomb

• 14 • (1980, 9)

1 Frederick Barbarossa
2 Alexius V of Byzantium
3 Gustav III of Sweden
4 Inca Atahualpa
5 Nero
6 Charles VIII of France
7 Henry of Champagne, King of Jerusalem
8 James II of Scotland
9 Pyrrhus of Epirus
10 William Rufus

• 15 • (1980, 10)

1 Indonesia
2 Venezuela
3 Qatar
4 Abu Dhabi
5 Libya
6 Algeria
7 Iraq
8 Nigeria
9 Gabon
10 Dubai

• 16 • (1980, 13)

1 William Hamilton
2 Michael Collins
2 Francis Bacon
4 Samuel Butler
5 Ted Ray
6 Ted Heath
7 Jack Dempsey
8 William Morris
9 Tom Jones
10 William Wallace

• 17 • (1980, 14)

1 The Lone Ranger
2 Two Gentlemen of Verona
3 The Three Musketeers
4 The Four Just Men
5 The Five Guildsmen
6 The Six Burghers of Calais
7 The Seven Sleepers
8 The eight who survived the flood (*I Peter*, 3:20)
9 The Nine Worthies
10 The Council of Ten

• 18 • (1980, 16)

1 Blue John stone
2 Dear John
3 Long John Silver
4 a demi-john
5 John R R Tolkien
6 Prince (later King) John
7 John O'Groats
8 Little John
9 Pope John XX
10 John Barleycorn

# A Bespoke Quiz

1   what sheds light over the Skerries?

2   who began by addressing the 'Lover of God'?

3   who started his account in Chilworth on 22 September ?

4   what started in the house of the royal baker off Eastcheap?

5   which character began by admitting to a ruling passion for roving?

6   whose tale started with him sitting astride a gun opposite the Wonder House?

7   what started with my sister-in-law questioning my ambition?

8   what started on 3 March and would continue for 46 hours?

9   who succeeded and preceded like-named Premiers?

10  when is there a remembrance of green?


• 2 •   *Who or what:*

1   was the Beal?

2   is Carraig Dá Bhiola?

3   was Kalle in England?

4   was shot dead by Crooked Nose?

5   was hanged by accident off Bermondsey?

6   addressed sleepy head from the window sill?

7   enabled a verdict of guilty without trial?

8   was code-named Gerald?

9   were the Naked Men?

10  is a Goosander?

• 3 •  *Who depicted:*

1    a marital couple with a griffon?
2    a naked lady with a white poodle?
3    Sforza's mistress with a mustelid pet?
4    a bear with a naked lady, with a man firing a gun?
5    a supine young woman enjoying a vulpine embrace?
6    a teenager clad in herringbone upper hose with a white greyhound?
7    a donkey masquerading as an attentive physician?
8    a two-year-old girl with a King Charles Spaniel?
9    a lonely Jew next to a cow and a fiddle?
10   a lady with *Sciurus* and *Sturnus*?


• 4 •

1    what did Santiago find in the dolphin's maw?
2    who failed to turn up for his murder at Henry's lunch-room?
3    what tale ended tragically with the death of a baby and his mother in Lausanne?
4    who wrapped Bocanegra's ear in a handkerchief and left it in the drawer of the bed-table in the hotel?
5    who had the status of protector of a Widow and earned eighty-six shillings a month betraying anyone betrayable?
6    what was Fisi ...... hermaphroditic, self-eating devourer of the dead, ...... potential biter-off of your face at night while you slept......?
7    who killed and mutilated the bodies of three of his countrymen in the Palace Hotel to conceal their national identity?
8    what went in pairs, on bicycles, and moved absolutely silently on the pavements?
9    where did Olz drown his sorrows after burying his long-dead wife?
10   who were not Othello and Desdemona, thank God?

**• 5 •** *Where:*

1 was *Le Pharaon's* first mate incarcerated?

2 was the Cardinal assassinated on Christmas Eve?

3 did a ransom of 100,000 marks secure the Lionheart's release?

4 was Orkney overtaken with insanity during his prolonged incarceration?

5 was the King assassinated and where did his younger twin son later commit murder?

6 did Claude's grand-daughter face the headsman wearing an auburn wig and red underwear?

7 was the noblewoman, credited with exsanguination of 650 girls, immured?

8 did the schizophrenic King initiate the murder of three noble kinsmen?

9 did the regicide Dowager live for almost 28 years?

10 did the eponymous traitor face the firing squad?


**• 6 •** *Of the multi-talented successors of Hippocrates:*

1 who should have been XX?

2 who was likened to *Odobenus*?

3 who was absolved of apostasy by Paul III?

4 who described his dual activities as his lawful wife and his mistress?

5 who became the lover of the Princess of Wales's daughter and was beheaded and then quartered?

6 whose epic travels took in an open-cast copper mine and an Amazonian colony for Hansen's sufferers?

7 whose first success was inspired by working on the district near his medical school?

8 whose cadaver was incorrectly described as leprous?

9 who was killed to save 100,000?

10 who had whom caught for 110?

### • 7 •

1   where is Mimosa?
2   'Buy one, get one free'?
3   who was tutored by Whitford?
4   what could be found under a bicoloured rag?
5   what commemorates the fourth halting of the eviscerated Royal cadaver?
6   who, with two others, committed perjury in a successful libel suit against *The Spectator*?
7   where might the rider be assured of ubiquitous music?
8   what is on the way to the Duns?
9   what is nominally psittacine?
10  what shares with Lyth?

### • 8 •

1   what is Petra?
2   who died from laburnum poisoning?
3   who wrote of Aunt Dot and her camel?
4   who had a hundred lines of *Marmion* flung at her?
5   who ate all the left-over fingers and ears from the hospital?
6   which spy's execution resulted from her brother's false testimony?
7   where are there wasp-like wings in the green yards?
8   what quickens a weak memory and the senses?
9   who was Mary with truth in her eyes?
10  what test can identify RF?

## • 9 • *Where:*

1   can one climb 111 ft in 75 seconds?

2   shall I ne'er be lonely, asleep with these or those?

3   is the town named after a saintly Northumbrian King?

4   did the vanquished son of Henrietta hide in a priest's hole?

5   was the collapsed Norman structure replaced with a rotunda two years later?

6   did the youngster from Styche Hall climb the church tower and sit astride a gargoyle?

7   did Isabella's son-in-law succumb to the sweating sickness?

8   was the Priory partly restored by an acclaimed nudist?

9   did the windborne crest of light stream in crimson?

10   was Darby able to facilitate the river crossing?

## • 10 •

1   what is Stinking Tommy?

2   where is the seat of haemopoiesis?

3   what, according to Joyce, does Ireland eat?

4   as what did David liken himself alone atop a house?

5   which Master engaged a noted astronomer from the other place to design a library?

6   where did the guard fall between two carriages and lose both legs, with fatal consequences?

7   where did cagebirds cut the mustard (at least sometimes)?

8   who used the Goat and Bagpipes as their HQ?

9   who began with Mediterranean Avenue?

10   what is the outlook from Newark?

## • 11 •

1    what circles Iveragh?

2    who hunted with Bellman and others?

3    who described himself as a soldier to the last day?

4    what recounted lutrine frolics by the Sound of Sleat?

5    by what English name do we know a bird labelled *collared* by Linnaeus?

6    what structure was suggested by a German Professor at the University of Ghent?

7    where may seven circuits raise the Devil with a bowl of gruel?

8    where did the Grand Duchy stage its F1 Grand Prix?

9    what reveals abnormal copper metabolism?

10    what shed new light on animal ways?


## • 12 • *Who:*

1    was Flash Harry?

2    was the stupid boy's Uncle Arthur?

3    strictly speaking, seemed very promising but was a drop-out?

4    questioned whether a warming-pan was a mere cover for hidden fire?

5    told of the Christian beauty twice set adrift due to the plotting of her mothers-in-law?

6    assured the visitor that Major Major never saw anyone in his office while he was in his office?

7    took over from Seegrave (a mass of human infirmity), but was later dismissed?

8    was played first by James Coburn and then by Richard Burton?

9    was twice Master of the Mother Lodge?

10    was RA15042699?

## • 13 •

1    who adopted the pseudonym Melos?

2    who called himself, in his imagination, Eusebius?

3    who succeeded Casimir, Jules, Prosper, Alfred et al?

4    whose gluttony was caricatured with the caption *The Charming Brute*?

5    who arrogantly compared the music of Brahms to that of a Jewish czardas player?

6    which renowned gourmet and wit remarked 'I have just received a Stilton and a cantata from Cipriani Potter. The cheese was very good'?

7    whose Great work was not performed until eleven years after his death?

8    whose skeleton was confirmed as his by His 145 years after his death?

9    who was once described as 'Mephistopheles in a cassock'?

10    who, with Giuseppina, owned a Maltese Spaniel?

## • 14 •

1    who painted Bardot?

2    what were named Los Martires?

3    who reminisced with a display of flags?

4    where are the matchstick men pre-eminent?

5    what is the response to the sentry's second enquiry at 2153?

6    who attacked the German submarine pens and adopted the name of the sea port for his title?

7    what half of Jones's dead servant did he request?

8    who found Slender's servant in his closet?

9    what does the cloaked Shadow keep?

10    what was the Wolfsspitz?

### • 15 •

1    who studies leptosporangiates?

2    who brought salad in a string bag?

3    which ten-year-old was supervised by the eunuch Pothinus?

4    what has associations with Johann Friedrich Horner and Henry Pancoast?

5    which class includes virtually all hexapods which have, or once had, wings?

6    aboard which 'beastly motor-biscuit-box' did the egg-collector offer Dick a guinea?

7    who was both brother and husband of the lioness-headed goddess of war?

8    what cadaveric poison took the blame prior to Salmonella et al?

9    what leaves Alva, bitter, rich and fruity?

10    what travels mainly via Wharton?

### • 16 •

1    what is a tiny dingle?

2    what did Eliza say about her aunt's alcoholic tolerance?

3    being of the bovine ilk, with what ends is the cow credited?

4    following the King's death threat, what did Perdita resolve to do?

5    what nutritious investment is, according to Churchill, superior to all others?

6    what contain substances, scientifically proved, which are absolutely necessary for the well-being of a brain-worker?

7    whereunto would Lightfoot, Whitefoot and Jetty no longer be called?

8    what diabolical name is given to the toxic euphorbial juice?

9    what might boys be sent to the shop to buy on 1st April?

10    what Monarch takes an occasional transatlantic flight?

## • 17 •

1   which sometime curate of St Clement's would eventually earn a scarlet biretta?

2   what name was adopted by a Roman Catholic on becoming the second British Buddhist monk?

3   which believer in Sol Invictus had a vision of the inscription 'Εν Τούτω Νίκα' and embraced Christianity?

4   which Rugbeian Jew responded to a vision of Christ saying 'Follow me!' and eventually became leader of a Midland diocese?

5   who, following paternal conflict with the Bevis Marks Synagogue underwent Anglican baptism at the age of twelve, but was later known as 'The Jew' and heckled with cries of 'Shylock'?

6   who always believed himself to be a Protestant (although his mother had him secretly baptised as a Roman Catholic at the age of four) and only formally converted shortly before his execution?

7   which 'evil-doer' developed anopia following a heavenly illumination, but was restored by the hands of a disciple and was promptly baptised?

8   which Lieutenant, having escaped the death penalty 'on account of her sex', converted to Roman Catholicism?

9   which Methodist lawyer of Manx parentage converted to Islam and founded Britain's first Mosque?

10   which Baptist, claiming singular lepidopteran and apian skills, converted to Islam?

## • 18 •

1   what ended with the words *Hot dog!*?

2   for what does Mora provide the finish?

3   what ended with an axial surrender on 2 February?

4   what reveals the demise of another Raleigh 300 years later?

5   who, when interrupted, would state that having begun, he would complete the interrogation?

6   whose end came in Rome, although he had maintained that it should have happened in Siorrachd Inbhir Nis 42 years earlier?

7   what ended with the Castle's beacon calling everyone within twenty miles to rejoice?

8   what ended with a reference to a lifetime daily allowance?

9   who ended with 0 and a reduction to 99.94?

10   what, according to Hector, crowns all?

# *Win £1000–worth of books!*

The bespoke set of questions (see p. 317) has been compiled especially for this book by Pat Cullen, and just to tantalise quiz aficionados, the answers are not given here…

Answers will be published online at www.liverpooluniversitypress.co.uk and on Twitter (https://twitter.com/LivUniPress) on 31 July 2013 and will also be available on request from the publisher from that date onwards.

To enter a competition for a prize of *£1000–worth* of Liverpool University Press books, send in the answers by **15 July 2013** to:
LUP World's Most Difficult Quiz
Liverpool University Press
4 Cambridge St
Liverpool
L69 7ZU

or email entries to lup@liv.ac.uk with the subject line 'World's Most Difficult Quiz'.
Entries should include full contact details (name, address, phone number and email address).

All the correct sets of answers will be placed into a prize draw and a winner picked out on 31 July 2013. The lucky (and erudite) victor will be given £1000-worth of Liverpool University Press books of his or her choice.

For any enquiries about the competition, or to request a set of answers, please contact the publisher at:
Liverpool University Press
4 Cambridge Street
Liverpool
L69 7ZU, UK
Tel: +44 (0)151 795 2149
Email: lup@liv.ac.uk
Twitter: https://twitter.com/LivUniPress
Web: www.liverpooluniversitypress.co.uk

# *Good luck!*